The West Indies and the Spanish Main

Anthony Trollope

Introduction by Fred D'Aguair

CARROLL & GRAF PUBLISHERS, INC.
NEW YORK

Introduction copyright © 1999 by Fred D'Aguiar

First Carroll & Graf edition 1999

Carroll & Graf Publishers, Inc.
19 West 21 Street
New York, NY 10010-6805

Library of Congress Cataloging-in-Publication Data is available.
ISBN: 0-7867-0638-4

Manufactured in the United States of America

The West Indies and the Spanish Main

INTRODUCTION

READING Anthony Trollope's *The West Indies and the Spanish Main* (first published in London in 1860) is like flying at 35,000 feet and then hearing from the captain that there is a massive engine failure. From being in relative comfort one moment, post decent three-course meal, complete with wine and brandy (we are talking business class here, courtesy of a frequent-flier air miles upgrade) one is flung into shallow-breathing, emergency mode. Suddenly all the things taken for granted—family, friends, enemies—disappear from the immediate vicinity of the near future. All that matters is this bright attention to surrounding details, to the things about me that would still be mine were I to be stripped naked: my memory, imagination, the fact that I have loved, am a father, write, read, dreamed, tried an oyster, drew the line at frog's legs and alligator, stood before the Taj Mahal. In other words, an essential humanity kicks in at this point and jettisons all the frills of pretense and style, all the trappings of an assumed social and opinionated self. In effect, the gloves are off and this is an out and out rumble with one's notions of civility and decorum.

Anthony Trollope challenges everything I assume about civility and decorum. He writes beautifully weighted and frequently witty sentences, qualifying as an English stylist of exceptional talent, and yet he exhibits all the symptoms of a mind produced during the reign of Queen Victoria. His writing style certainly transcends his time, but what he has to say is woefully and perhaps rightfully stuck in the imaginative enclosures of the day. He is at his best when confronted with nature and at his weakest as an intellectual animal in cultures and among people other than the majority who graced his "sceptred isle." People like me, that is, black folks, come off badly under Trollope's gaze. And yet, the Caribbean itself, as a geographical space, has never been serenaded in quite such lyrical and memorable terms. This contradiction between Trollope's obvious veneration of nature and his ostensible talent for denigrating the inhabitants of this veritable paradise defines both Trollope and his times.

As a Victorian he embraced the notions of Charles Darwin's (1809-1882) natural selection theory governing the evolution of species, an argument used by late-Victorians for conveniently locating civilization in the West (with them) and barbarism among the far-flung regions ripe for colonization and, by extension, open to the improving influence of the Victorians' civilizing zeal. After Darwin, the second pillar of Victorian thought might well be Jeremy Bentham (1748-1832) whose theory of "utility"—which, roughly summarized, argued for rewards and punishments, that is, a penal code, based on a morality grounded in principles of pleasure and pain that would benefit the greatest number—left an awful lot of people out of the loop of its munificence, but seduced the likes of Anthony Trollope because of its unignorable rationalist position. Samuel Taylor Coleridge (1772-1834), pillar number three, a poet and philosopher, deployed rationalist principles of knowledge gained by deduction to enquire into government and social beliefs which inspired badly needed reform. Coleridge along with other Romantic poets spearheaded a theory of the sublime, of man dwarfed by grand old nature and therefore liable to improve as a species if only he pays humble homage at nature's altar.

Enter Anthony Trollope. Like all good writing of the imagination, there are frailties, subtle fractures, endearing vulnerabilities running all the way through this readable, maddening, and ultimately triumphant book. There would have to be, I suppose, to earn my legitimizing stamp. Throughout *The West Indies and the Spanish Main* Trollope appears to be battling two demons simultaneously: an attraction to the region and a revulsion of the people. But even this is too simplistic a rendition of the contradiction within Trollope. On many occasions his attraction spills over from the place to the people and his scorn frequently spreads to include the climate. Therefore an imaginative inclusiveness about the people resonates much more powerfully than all the scorn and invective poured onto their broad shoulders and elaborate white cotton petticoats. He watches his subjects so closely that, after he says what a Victorian of his upper-class and conservative standing is destined to say, the libertarian gene in him trumps the recalcitrant gene and he manages to concede, somewhat grudgingly, that the sophistication of blacks is equal to that of any comparable English -man's or -woman's. What gets in the way of Trollope's parity of vision seems to be a technological superiority that bolsters one people in his eyes over a less technologically endowed "other." He confuses civilization with a dodgy, slippery lineage stretching back to Greece and Rome. The mask of slavery in a region recently emancipated (1833) blinds Trollope to the fact of black people's equality before God and nature.

Trollope is not to blame for marring his gifts with gross racial prejudice. As readers with the gift of hindsight we are lucky to be blessed with a complex sense of irony necessary for tackling any text from recent antiquity, not least Trollope's. Not to have this book available for discussions—about the formation of race theory, the nature of the travelogue, Victorian justifications for colonial expansion, models of biographical narration, cultural theory, and displacement, the destabilizing influence of the "other," the need for a demonized "other" in order to bolster notions of the rightful, benevolent dominance over them by a host race—would be a travesty. All these schools of thought point to Anthony Trollope's seminal text.

Trollope shapes the context for contemporary discussions about race, culture, and place. Hopefully, reading him improves our understanding of recurring problems between ethnic groups sharing the same geography and, if lucky, even promulgates solutions for their amelioration. In other words, Trollope's text brings with it a necessary, albeit heavy, freight.

Back to that emergency landing with Trollope as the malfunctioning craft in which I find myself trapped. Everything good about life becomes crystal clear during that emergency. All the things taken for granted transform into priceless, diamond absolutes. Trollope's judgments poured on my skin run off like water. I see and hear his long galloping sentences building clause by clause, balanced like a house of cards or a roomful of upright dominoes waiting for the first one to be pushed over. I empty the frame of his sentences, keeping their cadence, and slip in my own content. It is within this frailty that Trollope invites a contemporary reader into his world. His complex style is an invitation to the reader to delight in a coveted space. Fortunately, the medium is *not* the message. The latter is malleable, negotiable, ultimately easily substituted by what one holds dear.

—Fred D'Aguiar,
University of Miami
February 1999

CONTENTS.

CHAP.		PAGE
I. INTRODUCTORY	. . . . .	5
II. JAMAICA—TOWN	. . . .	15
III. JAMAICA—COUNTRY	. . . .	28
IV. JAMAICA—BLACK MEN	. . . .	55
V. JAMAICA—COLOURED MEN	. .	72
VI. JAMAICA—WHITE MEN	. . .	87
VII. JAMAICA—SUGAR	. . . .	98
VIII. JAMAICA—EMPEROR SOULOUQUE	. .	109
IX. JAMAICA—GOVERNMENT	. . . .	114
X. CUBA	. . . . . .	125
XI. THE PASSAGE OF THE WINDWARD ISLANDS	.	149
XII. BRITISH GUIANA	.	161
XIII. BARBADOS	. . .	192
XIV. TRINIDAD	. . . .	206
XV. ST. THOMAS	. . . . .	223
XVI. NEW GRANADA, AND THE ISTHMUS OF PANAMÁ		230

CONTENTS.

CHAP.		PAGE
XVII.	CENTRAL AMERICA. PANAMÁ TO SAN JOSÉ	243
XVIII.	CENTRAL AMERICA. COSTA RICA—SAN JOSÉ	258
XIX.	CENTRAL AMERICA. COSTA RICA—MOUNT IRAZU	275
XX.	CENTRAL AMERICA. SAN JOSÉ TO GREYTOWN	298
XXI.	CENTRAL AMERICA. RAILWAYS, CANALS, AND TRANSIT	316
XXII.	THE BERMUDAS	345
XXIII.	CONCLUSION	365

The West Indies and the Spanish Main

WEST INDIES AND SPANISH MAIN.

CHAPTER I.

INTRODUCTORY.

I AM beginning to write this book on board the brig ———, trading between Kingston, in Jamaica, and Cien Fuegos, on the southern coast of Cuba. At the present moment there is not a puff of wind, neither land breeze nor sea breeze; the sails are flapping idly against the masts; there is not motion enough to give us the command of the rudder; the tropical sun is shining through upon my head into the miserable hole which they have deluded me into thinking was a cabin. The marine people—the captain and his satellites—are bound to provide me; and all that they have provided is yams, salt pork, biscuit, and bad coffee. I should be starved but for the small ham—would that it had been a large one—which I thoughtfully purchased in Kingston; and had not a kind medical friend, as he grasped me by the hand at Port Royal, stuffed a box of sardines into my pocket. He suggested two boxes. Would that I had taken them!

It is now the 25th January, 1859, and if I do not reach Cien Fuegos by the 28th, all this misery will have been in vain. I might as well in such case have gone to St. Thomas, and spared myself these experiences of the merchant navy. Let it be understood by all men that in these latitudes the respectable, comfortable, well-to-do route from every place to every other place is viâ the little Danish island of St. Thomas. From Demerara to the Isthmus of Panama, you go by St. Thomas. From Panama to Jamaica and Honduras, you go by St. Thomas. From Honduras and Jamaica to Cuba and Mexico, you go by St. Thomas. From Cuba to the Bahamas, you go by St. Thomas—or did when this was written. The Royal Mail Steam Packet Company dispense all their branches from that favoured spot.

But I was ambitious of a quicker transit and a less beaten path, and here I am lying under the lee of the land, in a dirty, hot, motionless tub, expiating my folly. We shall never make Cien Fuegos by the 28th, and then it will be eight days more before I can reach the Havana. May God forgive me all my evil thoughts!

Motionless, I said; I wish she were. Progressless should have been my word. She rolls about in a nauseous manner, disturbing the two sardines which I have economically eaten, till I begin to fear that my friend's generosity will become altogether futile. To which result greatly tends the stench left behind it by the cargo of salt fish with which the brig was freighted when she left St. John, New Brunswick, for these parts. ' We brought but a very small quantity,' the skipper says. If so, that very small quantity was stowed above and below the very bunk which has been given up to me as a sleeping-place. Ugh!

' We are very poor,' said the blue-nosed skipper, when he got me on board. 'Well; poverty is no disgrace,' said I, as one does when cheering a poor man. 'We are very poor indeed; I cannot even offer you a cigar.' My cigar-case was immediately out of my pocket. After all, cigars are but as coals going to Newcastle when one intends to be in Cuba in four days.

'We are very poor indeed, sir,' said the blue-nosed skipper again when I brought out my solitary bottle of brandy—for I must acknowledge to a bottle of brandy as well as to the small ham. 'We have not a drop of spirits of any kind on board.' Then I altered my mind, and began to feel that poverty was a disgrace. What business had this man to lure me into his stinking boat, telling me that he would take me to Cien Fuegos, and feed me on the way, when he had not a mouthful to eat, or a drop to drink, and could not raise a puff of wind to fill his sails? 'Sir,' said I, 'brandy is dangerous in these latitudes, unless it be taken medicinally; as for myself, I take no other kind of physic.' I think that poverty on shipboard is a disgrace, and should not be encouraged. Should I ever be on shore again, my views may become more charitable.

Oh, for the good ship 'Atrato,' which I used to abuse with such objurgations because the steward did not come at my very first call; because the claret was only half iced; because we were forced to close our little whist at 11 P.M., the serjeant-at-arms at that hour inexorably extinguishing all the lights! How rancorous were our tongues! 'This comes of monopoly,' said a stern and eloquent neighbour at the dinner-table, holding up to sight a somewhat withered apple. 'And dis,' said a grinning Frenchman from Martinique with a curse, exhibiting a rotten walnut—'dis, dis! They give me dis for my moneys—for my thirty-five pounds!' And glancing round with angry eye, he dropped the walnut on to his plate.

Apples! and walnuts!! What would I give for the 'Atrato' now; for my berth, then thought so small; for its awning; for a bottle of its soda water; for one cut from one of all its legs of mutton; for two hours of its steam movement! And yet it is only now that I am learning to forgive that withered apple and that ill-iced claret.

Having said so much about my present position, I shall be glad to be allowed to say a few words about my present person. There now exists an opportunity for doing so, as I have before me the Spanish passport, for which I paid sixteen shillings in Kingston the day before I left it. It is signed simply Pedro Badan. But it is headed Don Pedro Badan Calderon de la Barca, which sounds to me very much as though I were to call myself Mr. Anthony Trollope Ben Jonson. To this will be answered that such might have been my name. But then I should not have signed myself Anthony Trollope. The gentleman, however, has doubtless been right according to his Spanish lights; and the name sounds very grand, especially as there is added to it two lines declaring how that Don Pedro Badan is a Caballero. He was as dignified a personage as a Spanish Don should be, and seemed somewhat particular about the sixteen shillings, as Spanish and other Dons generally are.

He has informed me as to my 'Talla,' that it is Alta. I rather like the old man on the whole. Never before this have I obtained in a passport any more dignified description of my body than robust. I certainly like the word 'Alta.' Then my eyes are azure. This he did not find out by the unassisted guidance of personal inspection. 'Ojos, blue,' he suggested to me, trying to look through my spectacles. Not understanding 'Ojos,' I said 'Yes.' My 'cejas' are 'castañas,' and so is my cabello also. Castañas must be chestnut surely,—cejas may mean eyebrows—cabello is certainly hair. Now any but a Spaniard would have declared that as to hair, I was bald; and as to eyebrows, nothing in particular. My colour is sano. There is great comfort in that. I like the word sano. 'Mens sana in corpore sano.' What has a man to wish for but that? I thank thee once more, Don Pedro Badan Calderon de la Barca.

But then comes the mystery. If I have any personal vanity, it is wrapped up in my beard. It is a fine, manly article of dandyism, that wears well in all climates, and does not cost much, even when new. Well, what has the Don said of my beard?

It is poblada. I would give five shillings for the loan of a Spanish dictionary at this moment. Poblada! Well, my first effort, if ever I do reach Cuba, shall be made with reference to that word.

Oh; we are getting into the trade-winds, are we? Let Æolus be thanked at last. I should be glad to get into a monsoon or a simoom at the present moment, if there be monsoons and simooms in these parts. Yes; it comes rippling down upon us with a sweet, cool, airy breeze; the sails flap rather more loudly, as though they had some life in them, and then fill themselves with a grateful motion. Our three or four sailors rise from the deck where they have been snoring, and begin to stretch themselves. 'You may put her about,' says the skipper; for be it known that for some hours past her head has been lying back towards Port Royal. 'We shall make fine track now, sir,' he says, turning to me. 'And be at Cien Fuegos on the 28th?' I demanded. 'Perhaps, sir; perhaps. We've lost twenty-four hours, sir, doing nothing, you know.'

Oh, wretched man that I am! the conveyance from Cien Fuegos to the Havana is but once a week.

The sails are still flopping against the yard. It is now noon on the 29th of January, and neither captain, mate, crew, nor the one solitary passenger have the least idea when the good brig —— will reach the port of Cien Fuegos; not even whether she will reach it at all. Since that time we have had wind enough in all conscience—lovely breezes as the mate called them. But we have oversailed our mark; and by how much no man on board this vessel can tell. Neither the captain nor the mate were ever in Cien Fuegos before; and I begin to doubt whether they ever will be there. No one knows where we are. An old stove has, it seems, been stowed away right under the compass, giving a false bias to the needle, so that our only guide guides us wrong. There is not a telescope on board. I very much doubt the skipper's power of taking an observation, though he certainly goes through the form of holding a machine like a brazen spider up to his eye about midday. My brandy and cigars are done; and altogether we are none of us jolly.

Flap, flap, flap! roll, roll, roll! The time passes in this way very tediously. And then there has come upon us all a feeling not expressed, though seen in the face of all, of utter want of confidence in our master. There is none of the excitement of danger, for the land is within a mile of us; none of the exhaustion of work, for there is nothing to do. Of pork and biscuits and water there is, I believe, plenty. There is nothing tragic to be made out of it. But comic misery wears one quite as deeply as that of a sterner sort.

It is hardly credible that men should be sent about a job for which they are so little capable, and as to which want of experience must be so expensive! Here we are, beating up the coast of Cuba against the prevailing wind, knowing nothing of the points which should guide us, and looking out for a harbour without a sea-glass to assist our eyes. When we reach port, be it Cien Fuegos or any other, the first thing we must do will be to ask the name of it! It is incredible to myself that I should have found my way into such circumstances.

I have been unable not to recount my present immediate

troubles, they press with such weight upon my spirits; but I have yet to commence my journeyings at their beginning. Hitherto I have but told under what circumstances I began the actual work of writing.

On the 17th of November, 1858, I left the port of Southampton in the good ship 'Atrato.' My purposed business, O cherished reader! was not that of writing these pages for thy delectation; but the accomplishment of certain affairs of State, of import grave or trifling as the case may be, with which neither thou nor I shall have further concern in these pages. So much it may be well that I should say, in order that my apparently purposeless wanderings may be understood to have had some method in them.

And in the good ship 'Atrato' I reached that emporium of travellers, St. Thomas, on the 2nd of December. We had awfully bad weather, of course, and the ship did wonders. When men write their travels, the weather has always been bad, and the ship has always done wonders. We thought ourselves very uncomfortable—I, for one, now know better—and abused the company, and the captain, and the purser, and the purveyor, and the stewards, every day at breakfast and dinner; not always with the eloquence of the Frenchman and his walnut, but very frequently with quite equal energy. But at the end of our journey we were all smiles, and so was the captain. He was tender to the ladies and cordial to the gentlemen; and we, each in our kind, reciprocated his attention. On the whole, O my readers! if you are going to the West Indies, you may do worse than go in the 'Atrato.' But do not think too much of your withered apples.

I landed at St. Thomas, where we lay for some hours; and as I put my foot on the tropical soil for the first time, a lady handed me a rose, saying, 'That's for love, dear.' I took it, and said that it should be for love. She was beautifully, nay, elegantly dressed. Her broad-brimmed hat was as graceful as are those of Ryde or Brighton. The well-starched skirts of her muslin dress gave to her upright figure that look of easy compressible bulk, which, let 'Punch' do what it will, has become so sightly to our eyes. Pink gloves were on her hands. 'That's for love, dear.' Yes, it shall be for love; for thee and thine, if I can find that thou deservest it. What was it to me that she was as black as my boot, or that she had come to look after the ship's washing?

I shall probably have a word or two to say about St. Thomas; but not now. It is a Niggery-Hispano-Dano-Yankee-Doodle place; in which, perhaps, the Yankee-Doodle element, declaring itself in nasal twang and sherry cobblers, seems to be of the strongest flavour; as undoubtedly will be the case in many of these parts as years go on revolving. That nasal twang will sound as the Bocca Romana in coming fashionable western circles; those sherry cobblers will be the Falernian drink of a people masters of half the world. I dined at the hotel, but should have got a better dinner on board the 'Atrato,' in spite of the withered apples.

From St. Thomas we went to Kingston, Jamaica, in the 'Derwent.' We were now separated from the large host of Spaniards who had come with us, going to Peru, the Spanish Main, Mexico, Cuba, or Porto Rico; and, to tell the truth, we were not broken-hearted on the occasion. Spaniards are bad fellow-travellers; the Spaniard, at least, of the Western hemisphere. They seize the meats upon the table somewhat greedily; their ablutions are not plentiful; and their timidity makes them cumbersome. That they are very lions when facing an enemy on terra firma, I do not doubt. History, I believe, tells so much for them. But half a gale of wind lays them prostrate, at all hours except feeding-time.

We had no Spaniards in the 'Derwent,' but a happy jovial little crew of Englishmen and Englishwomen—or of English subjects rather, for the majority of them belonged to Jamaica. The bad weather was at an end, and all our nautical troubles nearly over; so we ate and drank and smoked and danced, and swore mutual friendship, till the officer of the Board of Health visited us as we rounded the point at Port Royal, and again ruffled our tempers by delaying us for some thirty minutes under a broiling sun.

Kingston harbour is a large lagune, formed by a long narrow bank of sand which runs out into the sea, commencing some three or four miles above the town of Kingston, and continuing parallel with the coast on which Kingston is built till it reaches a point some five or six miles below Kingston. This sandbank is called 'The Palisades,' and the point or end of it is Port Royal. This is the seat of naval supremacy for Jamaica, and, as far as England is concerned, for the surrounding islands and territories. And here lies our flag-ship; and here we maintain a commodore, a dock-yard, a naval hospital, a pile of invalided anchors, and all the usual adjuncts of such an establishment. Some years ago—I am not good at dates, but say seventy, if you will—Port Royal was destroyed by an earthquake.

Those who are geographically inclined should be made to understand that the communication between Port Royal and Kingston, as, indeed, between Port Royal and any other part of the island, is by water. It is, I believe, on record that hardy Subs, and hardier Mids, have ridden along the Palisades, and not died from sun-stroke in the effort. But the chances are much against them. The ordinary ingress and egress is by water. The ferry-boats usually take about an hour, and the charge is a shilling. The writer of these pages, however, has been two hours and a quarter in the transit.

CHAPTER II.

JAMAICA—TOWN.

WERE it arranged by Fate that my future residence should be in Jamaica, I should certainly prefer the life of a country mouse. The town mice, in my mind, have but a bad time of it. Of all towns that I ever saw, Kingston is perhaps, on the whole, the least alluring, and is the more absolutely without any point of attraction for the stranger than any other.

It is built down close to the sea—or rather, on the lagune which forms the harbour, has a southern aspect, and is hot even in winter. I have seen the thermometer considerably above eighty in the shade in December, and the mornings are peculiarly hot, so that there is no time at which exercise can be taken with comfort. At about 10 A.M., a sea-breeze springs up, which makes it somewhat cooler than it is two hours earlier—that is, cooler in the houses. The sea-breeze, however, is not of a nature to soften the heat of the sun, or to make it even safe to walk far at that hour. Then, in the evening, there is no twilight, and when the sun is down it is dark. The stranger will not find it agreeable to walk much about Kingston in the dark.

Indeed, the residents in the town, and in the neighbourhood of the town, never walk. Men, even young men, whose homes are some mile or half-mile distant from their offices, ride or drive to their work as systematically as a man who lives at Watford takes the railway.

Kingston, on a map—for there is a map even of Kingston—looks admirably well. The streets all run in parallels. There is a fine large square, plenty of public buildings, and almost a plethora of places of worship. Everything is named with propriety, and there could be no nicer town anywhere. But this word of promise to the ear is strangely broken when the performance is brought to the test. More than half the streets are not filled with houses. Those which are so filled, and those which are not, have an equally rugged, disreputable, and bankrupt appearance. The houses are mostly of wood, and are unpainted, disjointed, and going to ruin. Those which are built with brick, not unfrequently appear as though the mortar had been diligently picked out from the interstices.

But the disgrace of Jamaica is the causeway of the streets themselves. There never was so odious a place in which to move. There is no pathway or trottoir to the streets, though there is very generally some such—I cannot call it accommodation—before each individual house. But as these are all broken from each other by steps up and down, as they are of different levels, and sometimes terminate abruptly without any steps, they cannot be used by the public. One is driven, therefore, into the middle of the street. But the street is neither paved, nor macadamized, nor prepared for traffic in any way. In dry weather it is a bed of sand, and in wet weather it is a watercourse. Down the middle of this the unfortunate pedestrian has to wade, with a tropical sun on his head; and this he must do in a town which, from its position, is hotter than almost any other in the West Indies. It is no wonder that there should be but little walking.

But the stranger does not find himself naturally in pos-

session of a horse and carriage. He may have a saddle-
horse for eight shillings; but that is expensive as well as
dilatory if he merely wishes to call at the post-office, or
buy a pair of gloves. There are articles which they call
omnibuses, and which ply cheap enough, and carry men
to any part of the town for sixpence; that is, they will
do so if you can find them. They do not run from any
given point to any other, but meander about through the
slush and sand, and are as difficult to catch as the musquitoes.

The city of Havana, in Cuba, is lighted at night by
oil-lamps. The little town of Cien Fuegos, in the same
island, is lighted by gas. But Kingston is not lighted
at all!

We all know that Jamaica is not thriving as once it
throve, and that one can hardly expect to find there all
the energy of a prosperous people. But still I think
that something might be done to redeem this town from
its utter disgrace. Kingston itself is not without wealth.
If what one hears on such subjects contains any indica-
tions towards the truth, those in trade there are still
doing well. There is a mayor, and there are aldermen.
All the paraphernalia for carrying on municipal improvements are ready. If the inhabitants have about themselves any pride in their locality, let them, in the name
of common decency, prepare some sort of causeway in
the streets; with some drainage arrangement, by which
rain may run off into the sea without lingering for hours
in every corner of the town. Nothing could be easier,
for there is a fall towards the shore through the whole
place. As it is now, Kingston is a disgrace to the country that owns it.

One is peculiarly struck also by the ugliness of the
buildings—those buildings, that is, which partake in any
degree of a public character—the churches and places

of worship, the public offices, and such like. We have no right, perhaps, to expect good taste so far away from any school in which good taste is taught; and it may, perhaps, be said by some that we have sins enough of our own at home to induce us to be silent on this head. But it is singular that any man who could put bricks and stones and timber together should put them together in such hideous forms as those which are to be seen here.

I never met a wider and a kinder hospitality than I did in Jamaica, but I neither ate nor drank in any house in Kingston except my hotel, nor, as far as I can remember, did I enter any house except in the way of business. And yet I was there—necessarily there, unfortunately—for some considerable time. The fact is, that hardly any Europeans, or even white Creoles, live in the town. They have country seats, pens as they call them, at some little distance. They hate the town, and it is no wonder they should do so.

That which tends in part to the desolation of Kingston—or rather, to put the proposition in a juster form, which prevents Kingston from enjoying those advantages which would naturally attach to the metropolis of the island—is this: the seat of government is not there, but at Spanish Town. Then our naval establishment is at Port Royal.

When a city is in itself thriving, populous, and of great commercial importance, it may be very well to make it wholly independent of the government. New York, probably, might be no whit improved were the National Congress to be held there; nor Amsterdam, perhaps, if the Hague were abandoned; but it would be a great thing for Kingston if Spanish Town were deserted.

The Governor lives at the latter place, as do also those satellites or moons who revolve round the larger luminary—the secretaries, namely, and executive officers. These in Jamaica are now so reduced in size that they could not perhaps do much for any city; but they would do a little, and to Kingston any little would be acceptable. Then the Legislative Council and the House of Assembly sit at Spanish Town, and the members—at any rate of the latter body—are obliged to live there during some three months of the year, not generally in very comfortable lodgings.

Respectable residents in the island, who would pay some attention to the Governor if he lived at the principal town, find it impossible to undergo the nuisance of visiting Spanish Town, and in this way go neither to the one nor the other, unless when passing through Kingston on their biennial or triennial visits to the old country.

And those visits to Spanish Town are indeed a nuisance. In saying this, I reflect in no way on the Governor or the Governor's people. Were Gabriel Governor of Jamaica with only five thousand pounds a year, and had he a dozen angels with him as secretaries and aides-de-camp, mortal men would not go to them at Spanish Town after they had once seen of what feathers their wings were made.

It is like the city of the dead. There are long streets there in which no human inhabitant is ever seen. In others a silent old negro woman may be sitting at an open door, or a child playing, solitary, in the dust. The Governor's house—King's House as it is called—stands on one side of a square; opposite is the house of the Assembly; on the left, as you come out from the Governor's, are the executive offices and house of the Council, and on the right some other public buildings. The place would have some pretension about it did it not seem to be stricken with an eternal death. All the walls are of a dismal dirty yellow, and a stranger cannot but think that the colour is owing to the dreadfully prevailing disease of the country. In this square there are no sounds; men and women never frequent it; nothing enters it but sunbeams—and such sunbeams! The glare from those walls seems to forbid that men and women should come there.

The parched, dusty, deserted streets are all hot and perfectly without shade. The crafty Italians have built their streets so narrow that the sun can hardly enter them, except when he is in the mid heaven; but there has been no such craft at Spanish Town. The houses are very low, and when there is any sun in the heavens it can enter those streets; and in those heavens there is always a burning, broiling sun.

But the place is not wholly deserted. There is there the most frightfully hideous race of pigs that ever made a man ashamed to own himself a bacon-eating biped. I have never done much in pigs myself, but I believe that pigly grace consists in plumpness and comparative short-ness—in shortness, above all, of the face and nose. The Spanish Town pigs are never plump. They are the very ghosts of swine, consisting entirely of bones and bristles. Their backs are long, their ribs are long, their legs are long, but, above all, their heads and noses are hideously long. These brutes prowl about in the sun, and glare at the unfrequent strangers with their starved eyes, as though doubting themselves whether, by some little exertion, they might not become beasts of prey.

The necessity which exists for white men going to Spanish Town to see the Governor results, I do not doubt, in some deaths every year. I will describe the first time I was thus punished. Spanish Town is thirteen miles from Kingston, and the journey is accomplished by railway in somewhat under an hour. The trains run about every four hours. On my arrival a public vehicle took me from the station up to King's House, and everything seemed to be very convenient. The streets, certainly, were rather dead, and the place hot; but I was under cover, and the desolation did not seem to affect me. When I was landed on the steps of the government-house, the first idea of my coming sorrows flitted across my mind. ' Where shall I call for you?' said the driver; ' the train goes at a quarter-past four.' It was then one : and where was he to call for me? and what was I to do with myself for three hours? ' Here,' I said; ' on these steps.' What other place could I name? I knew no other place in Spanish Town.

The Governor was all that was obliging—as Governors now-a-days always are—and made an appointment for me to come again on the following day, to see some one or say something, who or which could not be seen or said on that occasion. Thus some twenty minutes were exhausted, and there remained two hours and fifty minutes more upon my hands.

How I wished that the big man's big men had not been so rapidly courteous—that they had kept me waiting for some hour or so, to teach me that I was among big people, as used to be done in the good old times! In such event, I should at any rate have had a seat, though a hard one, and shelter from the sun. But not a moment's grace had been afforded me. At the end of twenty minutes I found myself again standing on those glaring steps.

What should I do? Where should I go? Looking all around me, I did not see as much life as would serve to open a door if I asked for shelter? I stood upon those desolate steps till the perspiration ran down my face with the labour of standing. Where was I to go? What was I to do? ' Inhospitalem Caucasum !' I exclaimed, as I slowly made my way down into the square.

When an Englishman has nothing to do, and a certain

time to wait, his one resource is to walk about. A Frenchman sits down and lights a cigar, an Italian goes to sleep, a German meditates, an American invents some new position for his limbs as far as possible asunder from that intended for them by nature, but an Englishman always takes a walk. I had nothing to do. Even under the full fury of the sun, walking is better than standing still. I would take a walk.

I moved slowly round the square, and by the time that I had reached an opposite corner all my clothes were wet through. On I went, however, down one dead street and up another. I saw no one but the pigs, and almost envied them their fleshlessness. I turned another corner and I came upon the square again. That seemed to me to be the lowest depth of all that fiery Pandemonium, and with a quickened step I passed through but a corner of it. But the sun blazed even fiercer and fiercer. Should I go back and ask for a seat, if it were but on a bench in the government scullery, among the female negroes?

Something I must do, or there would soon be an end of me. There must be some inn in the place, if I could only find it. I was not absolutely in the midst of the Great Sahara. There were houses on each side of me, though they were all closed. I looked at my watch, and found that ten minutes had passed by since I had been on my legs. I thought I had wandered for an hour.

And now I saw an old woman—the first human creature I had seen since I left the light of the Governor's face; the shade I should say, meaning to speak of it in the most complimentary terms. 'Madam,' said I, ' is there an inn here; and if so, where may it be?'—'Inn!' repeated the ancient negress, looking at me in a startled way. 'Me know noting, massa;' and so she passed on. Inns in Jamaica are called lodging-houses, or else taverns ; but I did not find this out till afterwards.

And then I saw a man walking quickly with a basket across the street, some way in advance of me. If I did not run I should miss him; so I did run; and I hallooed also. I shall never forget the exertion. 'Is there a public-house,' I exclaimed, feverishly, 'in this ———— place?' I forget the exact word which should fill up the blank, but I think it was ' blessed.'

' Pubberlic-house, massa, in dis d—m place,' said the grinning negro, repeating my words after me, only that I know *he* used the offensive phrase which I have designated. ' Pubberlic-house! what dat?' and then he adjusted his basket on his head, and proceeded to walk on.

By this time I was half blind, and my head reeled through the effects of the sun. But I could not allow myself to perish there, in the middle of Spanish Town, without an effort. It behoved me as a man to do something to save my life. So I stopped the fellow, and at last succeeded in making him understand that I would give him sixpence if he would conduct me to some house of public entertainment.

' Oh, de Vellington tavern,' said he; and taking me to a corner three yards from where we stood, he showed me the sign-board. ' And now de two quatties,' he said. I knew nothing of quatties then, but I gave him the sixpence, and in a few minutes I found myself within the ' Wellington.'

It was a miserable hole, but it did afford me shelter. Indeed, it would not have been so miserable had I known at first, as I did some few minutes before I left, that there was a better room up stairs. But the people of the house could not suppose but what every one knew the ' Wellington;' and thought, doubtless, that I preferred remaining below in the dirt.

I was over two hours in this place, and even that was not pleasant. When I went up into the fashionable room above, I found there, among others, a negro of exceeding blackness. I do not know that I ever saw skin so purely black. He was talking eagerly with his friends, and after a while I heard him say, in a voice of considerable dignity, ' I shall bring forward a motion on de subject in de house to-morrow.' So that I had not fallen into bad society.

But even under these circumstances two hours spent in a tavern without a book, without any necessity for eating or drinking, is not pleasant; and I trust that when I next visit Jamaica I may find the seat of government moved to Kingston. The Governor would do Kingston some good; and it is on the cards that Kingston might return the compliment.

The inns in Kingston rejoice in the grand name of halls. Not that you ask which is the best hall, or inquire at what hall your friend is staying; but such is the title given to the individual house. One is the Date-tree Hall, another Blundle Hall, a third Barkly Hall, and so on. I took up my abode at Blundle Hall, and found that the land-lady in whose custody I had placed myself was a sister of good Mrs. Seacole. ' My sister wanted to go to India,' said my landlady, ' with the army, you know. But Queen Victoria would not let her; her life was too pre-cious.' So that Mrs. Seacole is a prophet, even in her own country.

Much cannot be said for the West Indian hotels in general. By far the best that I met was at Cien Fuegos, in Cuba. This one, kept by Mrs. Seacole's sister, was not worse, if not much better, than the average. It was clean, and reasonable as to its charges. I used to wish that the patriotic lady who kept it could be induced to aban-don the idea that beefsteaks and onions, and bread and cheese and beer composed the only diet proper for an Englishman. But it is to be remarked all through the island that the people are fond of English dishes, and that they despise, or affect to despise, their own productions. They will give you ox-tail soup when turtle would be much cheaper. Roast beef and beefsteaks are found at almost every meal. An immense deal of beer is consumed. When yams, avocado pears, the mountain cabbage, plaintains, and twenty other delicious vegetables may be had for the gathering, people will insist on eating bad English potatoes; and the desire for English pickles is quite a passion. This is one phase of that love for England which is so predominant a characteristic of the white inhabitants of the West Indies.

At the inns, as at the private houses, the household servants are almost always black. The manners of these people are to a stranger very strange. They are not absolutely uncivil, except on occasions; but they have an easy, free, patronizing air. If you find fault with them, they insist on having the last word, and are generally successful. They do not appear to be greedy of money; rarely ask for it, and express but little thankfulness when they get it. At home, in England, one is apt to think that an extra shilling will go a long way with boots and chambermaid, and produce hotter water, more copious towels, and quicker attendance than is ordinary. But in the West Indies a similar result does not follow in a similar degree. And in the West Indies it is absolutely necessary that these people should be treated with dignity; and it is not always very easy to reach the proper point of dignity. They like familiarity, but are singularly averse to ridicule; and though they wish to be on good terms with you, they do not choose that these shall be reached without the proper degree of antecedent ceremony.

'Halloo, old fellow! how about that bath?' I said one morning to a lad who had been commissioned to see a bath filled for me. He was cleaning boots at the time, and went on with his employment, sedulously, as though he had not heard a word. But he was over sedulous, and I saw that he heard me.

'I say, how about that bath?' I continued. But he did not move a muscle.

'Put down those boots, sir,' I said, going up to him; 'and go and do as I bid you.'

'Who you call fellor? You speak to a gen'lman gen'lmanly, and den he fill de bath.'

'James,' said I, 'might I trouble you to leave those boots, and see the bath filled for me?' and I bowed to him.

''Es, sir,' he answered, returning my bow; 'go at once.' And so he did, perfectly satisfied. Had he imagined, however, that I was quizzing him, in all probability he would not have gone at all.

There will be those who will say that I had received a good lesson; and perhaps I had. But it would be rather cumbersome if we were forced to treat our juvenile servants at home in this manner—or even those who are not juvenile.

I must say this for the servants, that I never knew them to steal anything, or heard of their doing so from any one else. If any one deserves to be robbed, I deserve it; for I leave my keys and my money everywhere, and seldom find time to lock my portmanteau. But my carelessness was not punished in Jamaica. And this I think is the character of the people as regards absolute personal property—personal property that has been housed and garnered—that has, as it were, been made the possessor's very own. There can be no more diligent thieves than they are in appropriating to themselves the fruits of the earth while they are still on the trees. They will not understand that this is stealing. Nor can much be said for their honesty in dealing. There is a great difference between cheating and stealing in the minds of many men, whether they be black or white.

There are good shops in Kingston, and I believe that men in trade are making money there. I cannot tell on what principle prices range themselves as compared with those in England. Some things are considerably cheaper than with us, and some much, very much dearer. A pair of excellent duck trousers, if I may be excused for alluding to them, cost me eighteen shillings when made to order. Whereas, a pair of evening white gloves could not be had under four-and-sixpence. That, at least, was the price charged, though I am bound to own that the shop-boy considerately returned me sixpence, discount for ready money.

The men in the shops are generally of the coloured race, and they are also extremely free and easy in their manners. From them this is more disagreeable than from the negroes. 'Four-and-sixpence for white gloves!' I said; 'is not that high?'—'Not at all, sir; by no means. We consider it rather cheap. But in Kingston, sir, you must not think about little economies.' And he leered at me in a very nauseous manner as he tied his parcel. However, I ought to forgive him, for did he not return to me sixpence discount, unasked?

There are various places of worship in Kingston, and the negroes are fond of attending them. But they love best that class of religion which allows them to hear the most of their own voices. They are therefore fond of being Baptists; and fonder of the Wesleyans than of the Church of England. Many also are Roman Catholics. Their singing-classes are constantly to be heard as one walks through the streets. No religion is worth anything to them which does not offer the allurement of some excitement.

Very little excitement is to be found in the Church-of-

England Kingston parish church. The church itself, with its rickety pews, and creaking doors, and wretched seats made purposely so as to render genuflexion impossible, and the sleepy, droning, somnolent service are exactly what was so common in England twenty years since; but which are common no longer, thanks to certain much-abused clerical gentlemen. Not but that it may still be found in England if diligently sought for.

But I must not finish my notice on the town of Kingston without a word of allusion to my enemies, the musquitoes. Let no European attempt to sleep there at any time of the year without musquito-curtains. If he do, it will only be an attempt; which will probably end in fever and madness before morning.

Nor will musquito-curtains suffice unless they are brushed out with no ordinary care, and then tucked in; and unless, also, the would-be-sleeper, after having cunningly crept into his bed at the smallest available aperture, carefully pins up that aperture. Your Kingston musquito is the craftiest of insects, and the most deadly.

CHAPTER III.

JAMAICA—COUNTRY.

I HAVE spoken in disparaging terms of the chief town in Jamaica, but I can atone for this by speaking in very high terms of the country. In that island one would certainly prefer the life of the country mouse. There is scenery in Jamaica which almost equals that of Switzerland and the Tyrol; and there is also, which is more essential, a temperature among the mountains in which a European can live comfortably.

I travelled over the greater part of the island, and was very much pleased with it. The drawbacks on such a tour are the expensiveness of locomotion, the want of hotels, and the badness of the roads. As to cost, the tourist always consoles himself by reflecting that he is going to take the expensive journey once, and once only. The badness of the roads forms an additional excitement; and the want of hotels is cured, as it probably has been caused, by the hospitality of the gentry.

And they are very hospitable—and hospitable, too, under adverse circumstances. In olden times, when nobody anywhere was so rich as a Jamaica planter, it was not surprising that he should be always glad to see his own friends and his friends' friends, and their friends. Such visits dissipated the ennui of his own life, and the expense was not appreciable—or, at any rate, not undesirable. An open house was his usual rule of life. But matters are much altered with him now. If he be a planter of the olden days, he will have passed through fire and water in his endeavours to maintain his position. If, as is more frequently the case, he be a man of new date on his estate, he will probably have established himself with a small capital; and he also will have to struggle. But, nevertheless, the hospitality is maintained, perhaps not on the olden scale, yet on a scale that by no means requires to be enlarged.

'It is rather hard on us,' said a young planter to me, with whom I was on terms of sufficient intimacy to discuss such matters—'We send word to the people at home that we are very poor. They won't quite believe us, so they send out somebody to see. The somebody comes, a pleasant-mannered fellow, and we kill our little fatted calf for him. Probably it is only a ewe lamb. We bring out our bottle or two of the best, that has been put by for a gala day, and so we make his heart glad. He goes home, and what does he say of us? "These Jamaica planters are princes—the best fellows living; I liked them amazingly: but as for their poverty, don't believe a word of it. They swim in claret, and usually bathe in champagne." Now that is hard, seeing that our common fare is salt fish and rum and water.' I advised him in future to receive such inquirers with his ordinary fare only. 'Yes,' said he, 'and then we should get it on the other cheek. We should be abused for our stinginess. No Jamaica man could stand that.'

It is of course known that the sugar-cane is the chief production of Jamaica; but one may travel for days in the island and only see a cane-piece here and there. By far the greater portion of the island is covered with wild wood and jungle—what is there called bush. Through this, on an occasional favourable spot, and very frequently

on the road-sides, one sees the gardens or provision-grounds
of the negroes. These are spots of land cultivated by
them, for which they either pay rent, or on which, as
is quite as common, they have squatted without payment of
any rent.

These provision-grounds are very picturesque. They
are not filled, as a peasant's garden in England or in
Ireland is filled, with potatoes and cabbages, or other
vegetables similarly uninteresting in their growth; but
contain cocoa-trees, breadfruit-trees, oranges, mangoes,
limes, plantains, jack-fruit, sour-sop, avocado pears, and
a score of others, all of which are luxuriant trees, some of
considerable size, and all of them of great beauty. The
breadfruit-tree and the mango are especially lovely, and
I know nothing prettier than a grove of oranges in
Jamaica. In addition to this, they always have the
yam, which is with the negro somewhat as the potato is
with the Irishman; only that the Irishman has nothing
else, whereas the negro generally has either fish or meat,
and has also a score of other fruits besides the yam.

The yam, too, is picturesque in its growth. As with
the potato, the root alone is eaten, but the upper part is
fostered and cared for as a creeper, so that the ground
may be unencumbered by its thick tendrils. Support is
provided for it as for grapes or peas. Then one sees also
in these provision-grounds patches of coffee and arrowroot,
and occasionally also patches of sugar-cane.

A man wishing to see the main features of the whole
island, and proceeding from Kingston as his head-quarters,
must take two distinct tours, one to the east and the other
to the west. The former may be best done on horseback,
as the roads are, one may say, non-existent for a considerable portion of the way, and sometimes almost worse than
non-existent in other places.

One of the most remarkable characteristics of Jamaica

is the copiousness of its rivers. It is said that its original name Xaymaca, signifies a country of streams; and it certainly is not undeserved. This copiousness, though it adds to the beauty, as no doubt it does also to its salubrity and fertility, adds something too to the difficulty of locomotion. Bridges have not been built, or, sad to say, have been allowed to go to destruction. One hears that this river or that river is 'down,' whereby it is signified that the waters are swollen; and some of the rivers when so down are certainly not easy of passage. Such impediments are more frequent in the east than elsewhere, and on this account travelling on horseback is the safest as well as the most expeditious means of transit. I found four horses to be necessary—one for the groom, one for my clothes, and two for myself. A lighter weight might have done with three.

An Englishman feels some bashfulness in riding up to a stranger's door with such a cortége, and bearing as an introduction a message from somebody else to say that you are to be entertained. But I always found that such a message was a sufficient passport. 'It is our way,' one gentleman said to me, in answer to my apology. 'When four or five come in for dinner after ten o'clock at night, we do think it hard, seeing that meat won't keep in this country.'

Hotels, as an institution, are, on the whole, a comfortable arrangement. One prefers, perhaps, ordering one's dinner to asking for it; and many men delight in the wide capability of finding fault which an inn affords. But they are very hostile to the spirit of hospitality. The time will soon come when the backwoodsman will have his tariff for public accommodation, and an Arab will charge you a fixed price for his pipe and cup of coffee in the desert. But that era has not yet been reached in Jamaica.

Crossing the same river four-and-twenty times is tedious; especially if this be done in heavy rain, when the road is a narrow track through thickly-wooded ravines, and when an open umbrella is absolutely necessary. But so often had we to cross the Waag-water in our route from Kingston to the northern shore.

It was here that I first saw the full effect of tropical vegetation, and I shall never forget it. Perhaps the most graceful of all the woodland productions is the bamboo. It grows either in clusters, like clumps of trees in an English park, or, as is more usual when found in its indigenous state, in long rows by the riversides. The trunk of the bamboo is a huge hollow cane, bearing no leaves except at its head. One such cane alone would be uninteresting enough. But their great height, the peculiarly graceful curve of their growth, and the excessive thickness of the drooping foliage of hundreds of them clustered together produce an effect which nothing can surpass.

The cotton-tree is almost as beautiful when standing alone. The trunk of this tree grows to a magnificent height, and with magnificent proportions : it is frequently straight; and those which are most beautiful throw out no branches till they have reached a height greater than that of an ordinary tree with us. Nature, in order to sustain so large a mass, supplies it with huge spurs at the foot, which act as buttresses for its support, connecting the roots immediately with the trunk as much as twenty feet above the ground. I measured more than one, which, including the buttresses, were over thirty feet in circumference. Then from its head the branches break forth in most luxuriant profusion, covering an enormous extent of ground with their shade.

But the most striking peculiarity of these trees consists in the parasite plants by which they are enveloped, and which hang from their branches down to the ground with tendrils of wonderful strength. These parasites are of various kinds, the fig being the most obdurate with its embraces. It frequently may be seen that the original tree has departed wholly from sight, and I should imagine almost wholly from existence; and then the very name is changed, and the cotton-tree is called a fig-tree. In others the process of destruction may be observed, and the interior trunk may be seen to be stayed in its growth and stunted in its measure by the creepers which surround it. This pernicious embrace the natives describe as 'The Scotchman hugging the Creole.' The metaphor is sufficiently satirical upon our northern friends, who are supposed not to have thriven badly in their visits to the Western islands.

But it often happens that the tree has reached its full growth before the parasites have fallen on it, and then, in place of being strangled, it is adorned. Every branch is covered with a wondrous growth—with plants of a thousand colours and a thousand sorts. Some droop with long and graceful tendrils from the boughs, and so touch the ground; while others hang in a ball of leaves and flowers, which swing for years, apparently without changing their position.

The growth of these parasite plants must be slow, though it is so very rich. A gentleman with whom I was staying, and in whose grounds I saw by far the most lovely tree of this description that met my sight, assured me that he had watched it closely for more than twenty years, and that he could trace no difference in the size or arrangement of the parasite plants by which it was surrounded.

We went across the island to a little village called Annotta Bay, traversing the Waag-water twenty-four times, as I have said; and from thence through the

D

parishes of Metcalf and St. George, to Port Antonio.
'Fuit ilium et ingens gloria.' This may certainly be
said of Port Antonio and the adjacent district. It was
once a military station, and the empty barracks, standing so beautifully over the sea, on an extreme point of
land, are now waiting till time shall reduce them to
ruin. The place is utterly desolate, though not yet
broken up in its desolation, as such buildings quickly
become when left wholly untenanted. A rusty cannon
or two still stand at the embrasures, watching the entrance
to the fort; and among the grass we found a few metal
balls, the last remains of the last ordnance supplies.

But Port Antonio was once a goodly town, and the
country round it, the parish of Portland, is as fertile as
any in the island. But now there is hardly a sugar estate
in the whole parish. It is given up to the growth of
yams, cocoas, and plantains. It has become a provision-
ground for negroes, and the palmy days of the town are
of course gone.

Nevertheless, there was a decent little inn at Port
Antonio, which will always be memorable to me on account of the love sorrows of a young maiden whom I
chanced to meet there. The meeting was in this wise:—

I was sitting in the parlour of the inn, after dinner,
when a young lady walked in, dressed altogether in white.
And she was well dressed, and not without the ordinary
decoration of crinoline and ribbons. She was of the
coloured race; and her jet black, crisp, yet wavy hair
was brushed back in a becoming fashion. Whence she
came or who she was I did not know, and never learnt.
That she was familiar in the house I presumed from her
moving the books and little ornaments on the table, and
arranging the cups and shells upon a shelf. 'Heigh-ho!'
she ejaculated, when I had watched her for about a
minute.

I hardly knew how to accost her, for I object to the word Miss, as standing alone; and yet it was necessary that I should accost her. 'Ah, well: heigh-ho!' she repeated. It was easy to perceive that she had a grief to tell.

'Lady,' said I—I felt that the address was somewhat stilted, but in the lack of any introduction I knew not how else to begin—'Lady, I fear that you are in sorrow?'

'Sorrow enough!' said she. 'I'se in de deepest sorrow. Heigh-ho me! Well, de world will end some day,' and turning her face full upon me, she crossed her hands. I was seated on a sofa, and she came and sat beside me, crossing her hands upon her lap, and looking away to the opposite wall. I am not a very young man; and my friends have told me that I show strongly that steady married appearance of a paterfamilias which is so apt to lend assurance to maiden timidity.

'It will end some day for us all,' I replied. 'But with you, it has hardly yet had its beginning.'

' 'Tis a very bad world, and sooner over de better. To be treated so's enough to break any girl's heart; it is! My heart's clean broke, I know dat.' And as she put both her long, thin dark hands to her side, I saw that she had not forgotten her rings.

'It is love then that ails you?'

'No!' She said this very sharply, turning full round upon me, and fixing her large black eyes upon mine. 'No; I don't love him one bit; not now, and never again. No; not if he were down dere begging.' And she stamped her little foot upon the ground as though she had an imaginary neck beneath her heel.

'But you did love him?'

'Yes.' She spoke very softly now, and shook her head gently. 'I did love him—oh, so much! He was so handsome, so nice! I shall never see such a man again: such eyes; such a mouth! and then his nose! He was a Jew, you know.'

I had not known it before, and received the information perhaps with some little start of surprise.

'Served me right; didn't it? And I'se a Baptist, you know. They'd have read me out, I know dat. But I didn't seem to mind it den.' And then she gently struck one hand with the other, as she smiled sweetly in my face. The trick is customary with the coloured women in the West Indies when they have entered upon a nice, familiar, pleasant bit of chat. At this period I felt myself to be sufficiently intimate with her to ask her name.

'Josephine; dat's my name. D'you like dat name?'

'It's as pretty as its owner—nearly.'

'Pretty! no; I'se not pretty. If I was pretty, he'd not have left me so. He used to call me Feeny.'

'What! the Jew did.' I thought it might be well to detract from the merit of the lost admirer. 'A girl like you should have a Christian lover.'

'Dat's what dey all says.'

'Of course they do: you ought to be glad it's over.'

'I ain't tho'; not a bit; tho' I do hate him so. Oh, I hate him; I hate him! I hate him worse dan poison.' And again her little foot went to work. I must confess that it was a pretty foot; and as for her waist, I never saw one better turned, or more deftly clothed. Her little foot went to work upon the floor, and then clenching her small right hand, she held it up before my face as though to show me that she knew how to menace.

I took her hand in mine and told her that those fingers had not been made for threats. 'You are a Christian,' said I, 'and should forgive.'

'I'se a Baptist,' she replied; 'and in course I does forgive him: I does forgive him; but—! He'll be

wretched in this life, I know; and she—she'll be wretch-
eder; and when he dies—oh-h-h-h!'

In that prolonged expression there was a curse as deep
as any that Ernulphus ever gave. Alas! such is the
forgiveness of too many a Christian!

'As for me, I wouldn't demean myself to touch de
hem of her garment! Poor fellow! What a life he'll
have; for she's a virgo with a vengeance.' This at the
moment astonished me; but from the whole tenor of the
lady's speech I was at once convinced that no satirical
allusion was intended. In the hurry of her fluttering
thoughts she had merely omitted the letter 'a.' It was
her rival's temper, not her virtue, that she doubted.

'The Jew is going to be married then?'

'He told her so; but p'raps he'll jilt her too, you
know.' It was easy to see that the idea was not an unpleasant one.

'And then he'll come back to you?'

'Yes, yes; and I'll spit at him;' and in the fury of
her mind she absolutely did perform the operation. 'I
wish he would; I'd sit so, and listen to him;' and she
crossed her hands and assumed an air of dignified quies-
cence which well became her. 'I'd listen every word he
say; just so. Every word till he done; and I'd smile'—
and she did smile—'and den when he offer me his hand'
—and she put out her own—'I'd spit at him, and leave
him so.' And rising majestically from her seat she stalked
out of the room.

As she fully closed the door behind her, I thought that
the interview was over, and that I should see no more of
my fair friend; but in this I was mistaken. The door
was soon reopened, and she again seated herself on the
sofa beside me.

'Your heart would permit of your doing that?' said I;
'and he with such a beautiful nose?'

'Yes; it would. I'd 'spise myself to take him now, if he was ever so beautiful. But I'se sure of this, I'll never love no oder man—never again. He did dance so genteelly.'

'A Baptist dance!' I exclaimed.

'Well; it wasn't de ting, was it? And I knew I'd be read out. Oh, but it was so nice! I'll never have no more dancing now. I've just taken up with a class now, you know, since he's gone.'

'Taken up with a class?'

'Yes; I teaches the nigger children; and I has a card for the minister. I got four dollars last week, and you must give me something.'

Now I hate Baptists—as she did her lover—like poison; and even under such pressure as this I could not bring myself to aid in their support.

'You very stingy man! Caspar Isaacs'—he was her lost lover—'gave me a dollar.'

'But perhaps you gave him a kiss.'

'Perhaps I did,' said she. 'But you may, be quite sure of this, quite; I'll never give him anoder,' and she again slapped one hand upon the other, and compressed her lips, and gently shook her head as she made this declaration. 'I'll never give him anoder kiss—dat's sure as fate.'

I had nothing further to say, and began to feel that I ought not to detain the lady longer. We sat together, however, silent for a while, and then she arose and spoke to me standing. 'I'se in a reg'lar difficulty now, however; and it's just about that I am come to ask you.'

'Well, Josephine, anything that I can do to help you—'

''Tain't much; I only want your advice. I'se going to Kingston, you see.'

'Ah, you'll find another lover there.'

'It's not for dat den, for I don't want none ; but I'se going anyways, 'cause I live dere.'

'Oh, you live at Kingston ?'

'Course I does. And I'se no ways to go but just in de droger '—the West Indian coasting vessels are so called.

'Don't you like going in the droger?' I asked.

'Oh, yes ; I likes it well enough.'

'Are you sea-sick ?'

'Oh, no.'

'Then what's the harm of the droger?'

'Why, you see '—and she turned away her face and looked towards the window—' why you see, Isaacs is the captain of her, and 'twill be so odd like.'

'You could not possibly have a better opportunity for recovering all that you have lost.'

'You tink so ?'

'Certainly.'

'Den you know noting about it. I will never recover noting of him, never. Bah ! But I tell you what I'll do. I'll pay him my pound for my passage ; and den it'll be a purely 'mercial transaction.'

On this point I agreed with her, and then she offered me her hand with the view of bidding me farewell. 'Good-bye, Josephine,' I said ; 'perhaps you would be happier with a Christian husband.'

'P'raps I would ; p'raps better with none at all. But I don't tink I'll ever be happy no more. 'Tis so dull : good-bye.' Were I a girl, I doubt whether I also would not sooner dance with a Jew than pray with a Baptist.

'Good-bye, Josephine.' I pressed her hand, and so she went, and I neither saw nor heard more of her.

There was not about my Josephine all the pathos of Maria ; nor can I tell my story as Sterne told his. But Josephine in her sorrow was I think more true to human nature than Maria. It may perhaps be possible that

Sterne embellished his facts. I, at any rate, have not
done that.

I had another adventure at Port Antonio. About two
o'clock in the morning there was an earthquake, and we
were all nearly shaken out of our beds. Some one rushed
into my room, declaring that not a stone would be left
standing of Port Royal. There were two distinct blows,
separated by some seconds, and a loud noise was heard.
I cannot say that I was frightened, as I had not time to
realize the fact of the earthquake before it was all over.
No harm was done, I believe, anywhere, beyond the dis-
severance of a little plaster from the walls.

The largest expanse of unbroken cane-fields in Jamaica
is at the extreme south-east, in the parish of St. George's
in the East. Here I saw a plain of about four thousand
acres under canes. It looked to be prosperous; but I
was told by the planter with whom I was staying that
the land had lately been deluged with water; that the
canes were covered with mud; and that the crops would
be very short. Poor Jamaica! It seems as though all
the elements are in league against her.

I was not sorry to return to Kingston from this trip, for
I was tired of the saddle. In Jamaica everybody rides,
but nobody seems to get much beyond a walk. Now to
me there is no pace on horseback so wearying as an unbroken walk. I did goad my horse into trotting, but it
was clear that the animal was not used to it.

Shortly afterwards I went to the west. The distances
here were longer, but the journey was made on wheels,
and was not so fatiguing. Moreover, I stayed some little
time with a friend in one of the distant parishes of the
island. The scenery during the whole expedition was
very grand. The road goes through Spanish Town, and
then divides itself, one road going westward by the

northern coast, and the other by that to the south. I went by the former, and began my journey by the bog or bogue walk, a road through a magnificent ravine, and then over Mount Diabolo. The Devil assumes to himself all the finest scenery in all countries. Of a delicious mountain tarn he makes his punch-bowl; he loves to leap from crag to crag over the wildest ravines; he builds picturesque bridges in most impassable sites; and makes roads over mountains at gradients not to be attempted by the wildest engineer. The road over Mount Diabolo is very fine, and the view back to Kingston very grand.

From thence I went down into the parish of St. Anns, on the northern side. They all speak of St. Anns as being the most fertile district in the island. The inhabitants are addicted to grazing rather than sugarmaking, and thrive in that pursuit very well. But all Jamaica is suited for a grazing-ground, and all the West Indies should be the market for their cattle.

On the northern coast there are two towns, Falmouth and Montego Bay, both of which are, at any rate in appearance, more prosperous than Kingston. I cannot say that the streets are alive with trade; but they do not appear to be so neglected, desolate, and wretched as the metropolis or the seat of government. They have jails and hospitals, mayors and magistrates, and are, except in atmosphere, very like small country towns in England.

The two furthermost parishes of Jamaica are Hanover and Westmoreland, and I stayed for a short time with a gentleman who lives on the borders of the two. I certainly was never in a more lovely country. He was a sugar planter; but the canes and sugar, which, after all, are ugly and by no means savoury appurtenances, were located somewhere out of sight. As far as I myself might know, from what I saw, my host's ordinary occupations were exactly those of a country gentleman in England.

He fished and shot, and looked after his estate, and acted as a magistrate ; and over and above this, was somewhat particular about his dinner, and the ornamentation of the land immediately round his house. I do not know that Fate can give a man a pleasanter life. If, however, he did at unseen moments inspect his cane-holes, and employ himself among the sugar hogsheads and rum puncheons, it must be acknowledged that he had a serious drawback on his happiness.

Country life in Jamaica certainly has its attractions. The day is generally begun at six o'clock, when a cup of coffee is brought in by a sable minister. I believe it is customary to take this in bed, or rather on the bed ; for in Jamaica one's connection with one's bed does not amount to getting into it. One gets within the mosquito net, and then plunges about with a loose sheet, which is sometimes on and sometimes off. With the cup of coffee comes a small modicum of dry toast.

After that the toilet progresses, not at a rapid pace. A tub of cold water and dilettante dressing will do something more than kill an hour, so that it is half-past seven or eight before one leaves one's room. When one first arrives in the West Indies, one hears much of early morning exercise, especially for ladies ; and for ladies, early morning exercise is the only exercise possible. But it appeared to me that I heard more of it than I saw. And even as regards early travelling, the eager promise was generally broken. An assumed start at five A.M. usually meant seven ; and one at six, half-past eight. This, however, is the time of day at which the sugar grower is presumed to look at his canes, and the grazier to inspect his kine. At this hour—eight o'clock, that is—the men ride, and *sometimes* also the ladies. And when the latter ceremony does take place, there is no pleasanter hour in all the four-and-twenty.

At ten or half-past ten the nation sits down to break-fast; not to a meal, my dear Mrs. Jones, consisting of tea and bread and butter, with two eggs for the master of the family and one for the mistress; but a stout, solid ban-quet, consisting of fish, beefsteaks—a breakfast is not a breakfast in the West Indies without beefsteaks and onions, nor is a dinner so to be called without bread and cheese and beer—potatoes, yams, plaintains, eggs, and half a dozen 'tinned' productions, namely, meats sent from England in tin cases. Though they have every delicacy which the world can give them of native pro-duction, all these are as nothing, unless they also have something from England. Then there are tea and choco-late upon the table, and on the sideboard beer and wine, rum and brandy. 'Tis so that they breakfast at rural quarters in Jamaica.

Then comes the day. Ladies may not subject their fair skin to the outrages of a tropical sun, and therefore, unless on very special occasions, they do not go out between breakfast and dinner. That they occupy them-selves well during the while, charity feels convinced. Sarcasm, however, says that they do not sin from over energy. For my own part I do not care a doit for sar-casm. When their lords reappear, they are always found smiling, well-dressed, and pretty; and then after dinner they have but one sin—there is but one drawback—they will go to bed at nine o'clock.

But by the men during the day it did not seem to me that the sun was much regarded, or that it need be much regarded. One cannot and certainly should not walk much; and no one does walk. A horse is there as a matter of course, and one walks upon that; not a great beast sixteen hands high, requiring all manner of levers between its jaws, capricoling and prancing about, and giving a man a deal of work merely to keep his seat and look stately; but a canny little quiet brute, fed chiefly on grass, patient of the sun, and not inclined to be troublesome. With such legs under him, and at a distance of some twenty miles from the coast, a man may get about in Jamaica pretty nearly as well as he can in England.

I saw various grazing farms—pens they are here called —while I was in this part of the country; and I could not but fancy that grazing should in Jamaica be the natural and most beneficial pursuit of the proprietor, as on the other side of the Atlantic it certainly is in Ireland. I never saw grass to equal the guinea grass in some of the parishes; and at Knockalva I looked at Hereford cattle which I have rarely, if ever, seen beaten at any agricultural show in England. At present the island does not altogether supply itself with meat; but it might do so, and supply, moreover, nearly the whole of the remaining West Indies. Proprietors of land say that the sea transit is too costly. Of course it is at present; the trade not yet existing; for indeed at present there is no means of such transit. But screw steamers now always appear quickly enough wherever freight offers itself; and if the cattle were there, they would soon find their way down to the Windward Islands.

But I am running away from my day. The inspection of a pen or two, perhaps occasionally of the sugar works when they are about, soon wears through the hours, and at five preparations commence for the six o'clock dinner. The dressing again is a dilettante process, even for the least dandified of mankind. It is astonishing how much men think, and must think, of their clothes when within the tropics. Dressing is necessarily done slowly, or else one gets heated quicker than one has cooled down. And then one's clothes always want airing, and the supply of clean linen is necessarily copious, or, at any rate, should be so. Let no man think that he can dress for dinner in ten minutes because he is accustomed to do so in England. He cannot brush his hair, or pull on his boots, or fasten his buttons at the same pace he does at home. He dries his face very leisurely, and sits down gravely to rest before he draws on his black pantaloons.

Dressing for dinner, however, is *de rigueur* in the West Indies. If a black coat, &c., could be laid aside anywhere as barbaric, and light loose clothing adopted, this should be done here. The soldiers, at least the privates, are already dressed as Zouaves; and children and negroes are hardly dressed at all. But the visitor, victim of tropical fashionable society, must appear in black clothing, because black clothing is the thing in England. 'The Governor won't see you in that coat,' was said to me once on my way to Spanish Town, ' even on a morning.' The Governor did see me, and as far as I could observe did not know whether or no I had on any coat. Such, however, is the feeling of the place. But we shall never get to dinner.

This again is a matter of considerable importance, as, indeed, where is it not? While in England we are all writing letters to the ' Times,' to ascertain how closely we can copy the vices of Apicius on eight hundred pounds a year, and complaining because in our perverse stupidity we cannot pamper our palates with sufficient variety, it is not open to us to say a word against the luxuries of a West Indian table. We have reached the days when a man not only eats his best, but complains bitterly and publicly because he cannot eat better ; when we sigh out loud because no Horace will teach us where the sweetest cabbage grows ; how best to souse our living poultry, so that their fibres when cooked may not offend our teeth. These lessons of Horace are accounted among his Satires. But what of that ? That which was satire to Augustine

Rome shall be simple homely teaching to the subject of
Victoria with his thousand a year.

But the cook in the Jamaica country house is a person
of importance, and I am inclined to think that the lady
whom I have accused of idleness does during those vacant
interlunar hours occasionally peer into her kitchen. The
results at any rate are good—sufficiently so to break the
hearts of some of our miserable eight-hundred-a-year men
at home.

After dinner no wine is taken—none, at least, beyond
one glass with the ladies, and, if you choose it, one after
they are gone. Before dinner, as I should have mentioned
before, a glass of bitters is as much *de rigueur* as the black
coat. I know how this will disgust many a kindly friend
in dear good old thickly-prejudiced native England. ‘Yes,
ma’am, bitters! No; not gin and bitters, such as the cab-
men take at the gin-palaces; not gin and bitters at all,
unless you specially request it; but sherry and bitters;
and a very pretty habit it is for a warm country.’ If you
don’t drink your wine after dinner, why not take it before?
I have no doubt that it is the more wholesome habit of
the two.

Not that I recommend, even in the warmest climate, a
second bitter, or a third. There are spots in the West
Indies where men take third bitters, and long bitters,—in
which the bitter time begins when the soda water and
brandy time ends—in which the latter commences when
the breakfast beer-bottles disappear. There are such places,
but they must not be named by me in characters plainly
legible. To kiss and tell is very criminal, as the whole
world knows. But while on the subject of bitters, I must
say this : Let no man ever allow himself to take a long
bitter such as men make at ———. It is beyond the power
of man to stop at one. A long bitter duly swizzled is your
true West Indian syren.

And then men and women saunter out on the verandah,
or perhaps, if it be starlight or moonlight, into the garden.
Oh, what stars they are, those in that western tropical
world! How beautiful a woman looks by their light, how
sweet the air smells, how gloriously legible are the con-
stellations of the heavens! And then one sips a cup of
coffee, and there is a little chat, the lightest of the light,
and a little music, light enough also, and at nine one retires to one's light slumbers. It is a pleasant life for a
short time, though the flavour of the *dolce far niente* is
somewhat too prevalent for Saxon energies fresh from
Europe.

Such are the ordinary evenings of society ; but there
are occasions when no complaint can be made of lack of
energy. The soul of a Jamaica lady revels in a dance.
Dancing is popular in England—is popular almost everywhere; but in Jamaica it is the elixir of life, the Medea's
caldron, which makes old people young, the cup of
Circe, which neither man nor woman can withstand.
Look at that lady who has been content to sit still and
look beautiful for the last two hours; let but the sound of
a polka meet her ears, and she will awake to life as lively,
to motion as energetic, as that of a Scotch sportsman on
the 12th of August. It is singular how the most listless girl, who seems to trail through her long days almost
without moving her limbs, will continue to waltz and
polk and rush up and down a gallopade from ten till five;
and then think the hours all too short!

And it is not the girls only, and the boys—begging
their pardon—who rave for dancing. Steady matrons
of five-and-forty are just as anxious, and grave senators,
whose years are past naming. See that gentleman with
the bald head and grizzled beard, how sedulously he is
making up his card! 'Madam, the fourth polka,' he
says to the stout lady in the turban and the yellow slip,

who could not move yesterday because of her rheumatism. 'I'm full up to the fifth,' she replies, looking at the MS. hanging from her side; 'but shall be so happy for the sixth, or perhaps the second schottische.' And then, after a little grave conference, the matter is settled between them.

'I hope you dance quick dances,' a lady said to me. 'Quick!' I replied in my ignorance; 'has not one to go by the music in Jamaica?' 'Oh, you goose! don't you know what quick dances are? I never dance anything but quick dances; quadrilles are so deadly dull.' I could not but be amused at this new theory as to the quick and the dead—new at least to me, though, alas! I found myself tabooed from all the joys of the night by this invidious distinction.

In the West Indies, polkas and the like are quick dances; quadrilles and their counterparts are simply dead. A lady shows you no compliment by giving you her hand for the latter; in that you have merely to amuse her by conversation. Flirting, as any practitioner knows, is spoilt by much talking. Many words make the amusement either absurd or serious, and either alternative is to be avoided.

And thus I soon became used to quick dances and long drinks—that is, in my vocabulary. 'Will you have a long drink or a short one?' It sounds odd, but is very expressive. A long drink is taken from a tumbler, a short one from a wine-glass. The whole extent of the choice thus becomes intelligible.

Many things are necessary, and many changes must be made before Jamaica can again enjoy all her former prosperity. I do not know whether the total abolition of the growth of sugar be not one of them. But this I do know, that whatever be their produce, they must have roads on which to carry it before they can grow rich.

The roads through the greater part of the island are very bad indeed; and those along the southern coast, through the parishes of St. Elizabeth, Manchester, and Clarendon, are by no means among the best. I returned to Kingston by this route, and shall never forget some of my difficulties. On the whole, the south-western portion of the island is by no means equal to the northern.

I took a third expedition up to Newcastle, where are placed the barracks for our white troops, to the Blue Mountain Peak, and to various gentlemen's houses in these localities. For grandeur of scenery this is the finest part of the island. The mountains are far too abrupt, and the land too much broken for those lovely park-like landscapes of which the parishes of Westmoreland and Hanover are full, and of which Shuttlestone, the property of Lord Howard de Walden, is perhaps the most beautiful specimen. But nothing can be grander, either in colour or grouping, than the ravines of the Blue Mountain ranges of hills. Perhaps the finest view in the island is from Raymond Lodge, a house high up among the mountains, in which—so local rumour says—' Tom Cringle's Log' was written.

To reach these regions a man must be an equestrian— as must also a woman. No lady lives there so old but what she is to be seen on horseback, nor any child so young. Babies are carried up there on pillows, and whole families on ponies. 'Tis here that bishops and generals love to dwell, that their daughters may have rosy cheeks, and their sons stalwart limbs. And they are right. Children that are brought up among these mountains, though they live but twelve or eighteen miles from their young friends down at Kingston, cannot be taken as belonging to the same race. I can imagine no more healthy climate than the mountains round Newcastle.

I shall not soon forget my ride to Newcastle. Two

ladies accompanied me and my excellent friend who was pioneering me through the country; and they were kind enough to show us the way over all the break-neck passes in the country. To them and to their horses, these were like easy highroads; but to me, ——! It was manifestly a disappointment to them that my heart did not faint visibly within me.

I have hunted in Carmarthenshire, and a man who has done that ought to be able to ride anywhere; but in riding over some of these razorback crags, my heart, though it did not faint visibly, did almost do so invisibly. However, we got safely to Newcastle, and our fair friends returned over the same route with no other escort than that of a black groom. In spite of the crags the ride was not unpleasant.

One would almost enlist as a full private in one of her Majesty's regiments of the line if one were sure of being quartered for ever at Newcastle—at Newcastle, Jamaica, I mean. Other Newcastles of which I wot have by no means equal attraction. This place also is accessible only by foot or on horseback; and is therefore singularly situated for a barrack. But yet it consists now of a goodly village, in which live colonels, and majors, and chaplains, and surgeons, and purveyors, all in a state of bliss—as it were in a second Eden. It is a military paradise, in which war is spoken of, and dinners and dancing abound. If good air and fine scenery be dear to the heart of the British soldier, he ought to be happy at Newcastle. Nevertheless, I prefer the views from Raymond Lodge to any that Newcastle can afford.

And now I have a mournful story to tell. Did any man ever know of any good befalling him from going up a mountain; always excepting Albert Smith, who, we are told, has realized half a million by going up Mont Blanc? If a man can go up his mountains in Piccadilly, it may be all very well; in so doing he perhaps may see the sun rise, and be able to watch nature in her wildest vagaries. But as for the true ascent—the nasty, damp, dirty, slippery, boot-destroying, shin-breaking, veritable mountain! Let me recommend my friends to let it alone, unless they have a gift for making half a million in Piccadilly. I have tried many a mountain in a small way, and never found one to answer. I hereby protest that I will never try another.

However, I did go up the Blue Mountain Peak, which ascends—so I was told—to the respectable height of 8,000 feet above the sea level. To enable me to do this, I provided myself with a companion, and he provided me with five negroes, a supply of beef, bread, and water, some wine and brandy, and what appeared to me to be about ten gallons of rum; for we were to spend the night on the Blue Mountain Peak, in order that the rising sun might be rightly worshipped.

For some considerable distance we rode, till we came indeed to the highest inhabited house in the island. This is the property of a coffee-planter who lives there, and who divides his time and energies between the growth of coffee and the entertainment of visitors to the mountain. So hospitable an old gentleman, or one so droll in speech, or singular in his mode of living, I shall probably never meet again. His tales as to the fate of other travellers made me tremble for what might some day be told of my own adventures. He feeds you gallantly, sends you on your way with a God-speed, and then hands you down to derision with the wickedest mockery. He is the gibing spirit of the mountain, and I would at any rate recommend no ladies to trust themselves to his courtesies.

Here we entered and called for the best of everything— beer, brandy, coffee, ringtailed doves, salt fish, fat fowls, English potatoes, hot pickles, and Worcester sauce.

'What, C——, no Worcester sauce! Gammon; make
the fellow go and look for it.' 'Tis thus hospitality is
claimed in Jamaica; and in process of time the Worcester
sauce was forthcoming. It must be remembered that
every article of food has to be carried up to this place on
mules' backs, over the tops of mountains for twenty or
thirty miles.

When we had breakfasted and drunk and smoked, and
promised our host that he should have the pleasure of
feeding us again on the morrow, we proceeded on our
way. The five negroes each had loads on their heads and
cutlasses in their hands. We ourselves travelled without
other burdens than our own big sticks.

I have nothing remarkable to tell of the ascent. We
soon got into a cloud, and never got out of it. But that
is a matter of course. We were soon wet through up to
our middles, but that is a matter of course also. We
came to various dreadful passages, which broke our toes
and our nails and our hats, the worst of which was called
Jacob's ladder—also a matter of course. Every now and
then we regaled the negroes with rum, and the more rum
we gave them the more they wanted. And every now
and then we regaled ourselves with brandy and water, and
the oftener we regaled ourselves the more we required to
be regaled. All which things are matters of course. And
so we arrived at the Blue Mountain Peak.

Our first two objects were to construct a hut and collect
wood for firing. As for any enjoyment from the position,
that, for that evening, was quite out of the question. We
were wet through and through, and could hardly see
twenty yards before us on any side. So we set the men
to work to produce such mitigation of our evil position as
was possible.

We did build a hut, and we did make a fire; and we
did administer more rum to the negroes, without which

they refused to work at all. When a black man knows that you want him he is apt to become very impudent, especially when backed by rum ; and at such times they altogether forget, or at any rate disregard, the punishment that may follow in the shape of curtailed gratuities.

Slowly and mournfully we dried ourselves at the fire ; or rather did not dry ourselves, but scorched our clothes and burnt our boots in a vain endeavour to do so. It is a singular fact, but one which experience has fully taught me, that when a man is thoroughly wet he may burn his trousers off his legs and his shoes off his feet, and yet they will not be dry—nor will he. Mournfully we turned ourselves before the fire—slowly, like badly-roasted joints of meat ; and the result was exactly that : we were badly roasted—roasted and raw at the same time.

And then we crept into our hut, and made one of these wretched repasts in which the collops of food slip down and get sat upon ; in which the salt is blown away and the bread saturated in beer ; in which one gnaws one's food as Adam probably did, but as men need not do now, far removed as they are from Adam's discomforts. A man may cheerfully go without his dinner and feed like a beast when he gains anything by it ; but when he gains nothing, and has his boots scorched off his feet into the bargain, it is hard then for him to be cheerful. I was bound to be jolly, as my companion had come there merely for my sake ; but how it came to pass that he did not become sulky, that was the miracle. As it was, I knew full well that he wished me—safe in England.

Having looked to our fire and smoked a sad cigar, we put ourselves to bed in our hut. The operation consisted in huddling on all the clothes we had. But even with this the cold prevented us from sleeping. The chill damp air penetrated through two shirts, two coats, two pairs of trousers. It was impossible to believe that we were in the tropics.

And then the men got drunk and refused to cut more firewood, and disputes began which lasted all night; and all was cold, damp, comfortless, wretched, and endless. And so the morning came.

That it was morning our watches told us, and also a dull dawning of muddy light through the constant mist; but as for sunrise —— ! The sun may rise for those who get up decently from their beds in the plains below, but there is no sunrising on Helvellyn, or Righi, or the Blue Mountain Peak. Nothing rises there; but mists and clouds are for ever falling.

And then we packed up our wretched traps, and again descended. While coming up some quips and cranks had passed between us and our sable followers; but now all was silent as grim death. We were thinking of our sore hands and bruised feet; were mindful of the dirt which clogged us, and the damp which enveloped us; were mindful also a little of our spoilt raiment, and ill-requited labours. Our wit did not flow freely as we descended.

A second breakfast with the man of the mountain, and a glorious bath in a huge tank somewhat restored us, and as we regained our horses the miseries of our expedition were over. My friend fervently and loudly declared that no spirit of hospitality, no courtesy to a stranger, no human eloquence should again tempt him to ascend the Blue Mountains; and I cordially advised him to keep his resolution. I made no vows aloud, but I may here protest that any such vows were unnecessary.

I afterwards visited another seat, Flamstead, which, as regards scenery, has rival claims to those of Raymond Lodge. The views from Flamstead were certainly very beautiful; but on the whole I preferred my first love.

CHAPTER IV.

JAMAICA—BLACK MEN.

To an Englishman who has never lived in a slave country, or in a country in which slavery once prevailed, the negro population is of course the most striking feature of the West Indies. But the eye soon becomes accustomed to the black skin and the thick lip, and the ear to the broken patois which is the nearest approach to English which the ordinary negro ever makes. When one has been a week among them, the novelty is all gone. It is only by an exercise of memory and intellect that one is enabled to think of them as a strange race.

But how strange is the race of Creole negroes—of negroes, that is, born out of Africa! They have no country of their own, yet have they not hitherto any country of their adoption; for, whether as slaves in Cuba, or as free labourers in the British isles, they are in each case a servile people in a foreign land. They have no language of their own, nor have they as yet any language of their adoption; for they speak their broken English as uneducated foreigners always speak a foreign language. They have no idea of country, and no pride of race; for even among themselves, the word 'nigger' conveys their worst term of reproach. They have no religion of their own, and can hardly as yet be said to have, as a people, a religion by adoption; and yet there is no race which has more strongly developed its own physical aptitudes and inaptitudes, its own habits, its own tastes, and its own faults.

The West Indian negro knows nothing of Africa except that it is a term of reproach. If African immigrants are put to work on the same estate with him, he will not eat with them, or drink with them, or walk with them. He will hardly work beside them, and regards himself as a creature immeasurably the superior of the new comer. But yet he has made no approach to the civilization of his white fellow-creature, whom he imitates as a monkey does a man.

Physically he is capable of the hardest bodily work, and that probably with less bodily pain than men of any other race; but he is idle, unambitious as to worldly position, sensual, and content with little. Intellectually, he is apparently capable of but little sustained effort; but, singularly enough, here he is ambitious. He burns to be regarded as a scholar, puzzles himself with fine words, addicts himself to religion for the sake of appearance, and delights in aping the little graces of civilization. He despises himself thoroughly, and would probably be content to starve for a month if he could appear as a white man for a day; but yet he delights in signs of respect paid to him, black man as he is, and is always thinking of his own dignity. If you want to win his heart for an hour, call him a gentleman; but if you want to reduce him to a despairing obedience, tell him that he is a filthy nigger, assure him that his father and mother had tails like monkeys, and forbid him to think that he can have a soul like a white man. Among the West Indies one may frequently see either course adopted towards them by their unreasoning ascendant masters.

I do not think that education has as yet done much for the black man in the Western world. He can always

observe, and often read; but he can seldom reason. I
do not mean to assert that he is absolutely without mental
power, as a calf is. He does draw conclusions, but he
carries them only a short way. I think that he seldom
understands the purpose of industry, the object of truth,
or the results of honesty. He is not always idle, perhaps
not always false, certainly not always a thief; but his
motives are the fear of immediate punishment, or hopes of
immediate reward. He fears that and hopes that only.
Certain virtues he copies, because they are the virtues of
a white man. The white man is the god present to his
eye, and he believes in him—believes in him with a
qualified faith, and imitates him with a qualified con-
stancy.

And thus I am led to say, and I say it with sorrow
enough, that I distrust the negro's religion. What I
mean is this: that in my opinion they rarely take in
and digest the great and simple doctrines of Christianity,
that they should love and fear the Lord their God, and
love their neighbours as themselves.

Those who differ from me—and the number will
comprise the whole clergy of these western realms, and
very many beside the clergy—will ask, among other
questions, whether these simple doctrines are obeyed in
England much better than they are in Jamaica. I
would reply that I am not speaking of obedience. The
opinion which I venture to give is, that the very first
meaning of the terms does not often reach the negro's
mind, not even the minds of those among them who are
enthusiastically religious. To them religious exercises
are in themselves the good thing desirable. They sing
their psalms, and believe, probably, that good will result;
but they do not connect their psalms with the practice of
any virtue. They say their prayers; but, having said
them, have no idea that they should therefore forgive

offences. They hear the commandments and delight in
the responses; but those commandments are not in their
hearts connected with abstinence from adultery or calumny.
They delight to go to church or meeting; they are energetic in singing psalms; they are constant in the responses;
and, which is saying much more for them, they are
wonderfully expert at Scripture texts; but—and I say it
with grief of heart, and with much trembling also at the
reproaches which I shall have to endure—I doubt whether
religion does often reach their minds.

As I greatly fear being misunderstood on this subject,
I must explain that I by no means think that religious
teaching has been inoperative for good among the negroes.
Were I to express such an opinion I should be putting
them on the same footing with the slaves in Cuba, who
are left wholly without such teaching, and who, in consequence, are much nearer the brute creation than their
more fortunate brethren. To have learnt the precepts
of Christianity—even though they be not learnt faithfully—softens the heart and expels its ferocity. That
theft is esteemed a sin; that men and women should live
together under certain laws; that blood should not be shed
in anger; that an oath should be true; that there is one
God the Father who made us, and one Redeemer who
would willingly save us—these doctrines the negro in a
general way has learnt, and in them he has a sort of belief.
He has so far progressed that by them he judges of the
conduct of others. What he lacks is a connecting link
between these doctrines and himself—an appreciation
of the fact that these doctrines are intended for his own
guidance.

But, though he himself wants the link, circumstances
have in some measure produced it. As he judges others,
so he fears the judgment of others; and in this manner
Christianity has prevailed with him.

In many respects the negro's phase of humanity differs much from that which is common to us, and which has been produced by our admixture of blood and our present extent of civilization. They are more passionate than the white men, but rarely vindictive, as we are. The smallest injury excites their eager wrath, but no injury produces sustained hatred. In the same way, they are seldom grateful, though often very thankful. They are covetous of notice as is a child or a dog; but they have little idea of earning continual respect. They best love him who is most unlike themselves, and they despise the coloured man who approaches them in breed. When they have once recognized a man as their master, they will be faithful to him; but the more they fear that master, the more they will respect him. They have no care for to-morrow, but they delight in being gaudy for to-day. Their crimes are those of momentary impulse, as are also their virtues. They fear death; but if they can lie in the sun without pain for the hour they will hardly drag themselves to the hospital, though their disease be mortal. They love their offspring, but in their rage will ill use them fearfully. They are proud of them when they are praised, but will sell their daughter's virtue for a dollar. They are greedy of food, but generally indifferent as to its quality. They rejoice in finery, and have in many cases begun to understand the benefit of comparative cleanliness; but they are rarely tidy. A little makes them happy, and nothing makes them permanently wretched. On the whole, they laugh and sing and sleep through life; and if life were all, they would not have so bad a time of it.

These, I think, are the qualities of the negro. Many of them are in their way good; but are they not such as we have generally seen in the lower spheres of life? Much of this is strongly opposed to the idea of the

Creole negro which has lately become prevalent in
England. He has been praised for his piety, and especially praised for his consistent gratitude to his benefactors
and faithful adherence to his master's interests.

On such subjects our greatest difficulty is perhaps that
of avoiding an opinion formed by exceptional cases. That
there are and have been pious negroes I do not doubt.
That many are strongly tinctured with the language and
outward bearing of piety I am well aware. I know that
they love the Bible—love it as the Roman Catholic girl
loves the doll of a Madonna which she dresses with muslin
and ribbons. In a certain sense this is piety, and such
piety they often possess.

And I do not deny their family attachments; but it
is the attachment of a dog. We have all had dogs whom
we have well used, and have prided ourselves on their
fidelity. We have seen them to be wretched when they
lose us for a moment, and have smiled at their joy when
they again discover us. We have noted their patience as
they wait for food from the hand they know will feed
them. We have seen with delight how their love for us
glistens in their eyes. We trust them with our children
as the safest playmates, and teach them in mocking sport
the tricks of humanity. In return for this the dear brutes
give us all their hearts, but it is not given in gratitude;
and they abstain with all their power from injury and
offence, but they do not abstain from judgment. Let his
master ill use his dog ever so cruelly, yet the animal has
no anger against him when the pain is over. Let a
stranger save him from such ill usage, and he has no
thankfulness after the moment. Affection and fidelity
are things of custom with him.

I know how deep will be the indignation I shall draw
upon my head by this picture of a fellow-creature and a
fellow-Christian. Man's philanthropy would wish to look

on all men as walking in a quick path towards the perfection of civilization. And men are not happy in their good efforts unless they themselves can see their effects. They are not content to fight for the well-being of a race, and to think that the victory shall not come till the victors shall for centuries have been mingled with the dust. The friend of the negro, when he puts his shoulder to the wheel, and tries to rescue his black brother from the degradation of an inferior species, hopes to see his client rise up at once with all the glories of civilization round his head. 'There; behold my work; how good it is!' That is the reward to which he looks. But what if the work be not as yet good? What if it be God's pleasure that more time be required before the work be good—good in our finite sense of the word—in our sense, which requires the show of an immediate effect?

After all, what we should desire first, and chiefly—is it not the truth? It will avail nothing to humanity to call a man a civilized Christian if the name be not deserved. Philanthropy will gain little but self-flattery and gratification of its vanity by applying to those whom it would serve a euphemistic but false nomenclature. God, for his own purposes—purposes which are already becoming more and more intelligible to his creatures—has created men of inferior and superior race. Individually, the state of an Esquimaux is grievous to an educated mind: but the educated man, taking the world collectively, knows that it is good that the Esquimaux should be, should have been made such as he is; knows also, that that state admits of improvement; but should know also that such cannot be done by the stroke of a wand—by a speech in Exeter Hall—by the mere sounds of Gospel truth, beautiful as those sounds are.

We are always in such a hurry; although, as regards

the progress of races, history so plainly tells us how vain such hurry is! At thirty, a man devotes himself to pro-selytizing a people ; and if the people be not proselytized when he has reached forty, he retires in disgust. In early life we have aspirations for the freedom of an ill-used nation; but in middle life we abandon our protégé to tyranny and the infernal gods. The process has been too long. The nation should have risen free, at once, upon the instant. It is hard for man to work without hope of seeing that for which he labours.

But to return to our sable friends. The first desire of a man in a state of civilization is for property. Greed and covetousness are no doubt vices; but they are the vices which have grown from cognate virtues. Without a desire for property, man could make no progress. But the negro has no such desire ; no desire strong enough to induce him to labour for that which he wants. In order that he may eat to-day and be clothed to-morrow, he will work a little ; as for anything beyond that, he is content to lie in the sun.

Emancipation and the last change in the sugar duties have made land only too plentiful in Jamaica, and enor-mous tracts have been thrown out of cultivation as un-profitable. And it is also only too fertile. The negro, consequently, has had unbounded facility of squatting, and has availed himself of it freely. To recede from civilization and become again savage—as savage as the laws of the community will permit—has been to his taste. I believe that he would altogether retrograde if left to himself.

I shall now be asked, having said so much, whether I think that emancipation was wrong. By no means. I think that emancipation was clearly right; but I think that we expected far too great and far too quick a result from emancipation.

These people are a servile race, fitted by nature for the hardest physical work, and apparently at present fitted for little else. Some thirty years since they were in a state when such work was their lot; but their tasks were exacted from them in a condition of bondage abhorrent to the feelings of the age, and opposed to the religion which we practised. For us, thinking as we did, slavery was a sin. From that sin we have cleansed ourselves. But the mere fact of doing so has not freed us from our difficulties. Nor was it to be expected that it should. The discontinuance of a sin is always the commencement of a struggle.

Few, probably, will think that Providence has permitted so great an exodus as that which has taken place from Africa to the West without having wise results in view. We may fairly believe that it has been a part of the Creator's scheme for the population and cultivation of the earth; a part of that scheme which sent Asiatic hordes into Europe, and formed, by the admixture of nations, that race to which it is our pride to belong. But that admixture of blood has taken tens of centuries. Why should we think that Providence should work more rapidly now in these latter ages?

No Englishman, no Anglo-Saxon, could be what he now is but for that portion of wild and savage energy which has come to him from his Vandal forefathers. May it not then be fair to suppose that a time shall come when a race will inhabit those lovely islands, fitted by nature for their burning sun, in whose blood shall be mixed some portion of northern energy, and which shall owe its physical powers to African progenitors,—a race that shall be no more ashamed of the name of negro than we are of the name of Saxon?

But, in the mean time, what are we to do with our friend, lying as he now is at his ease under the cotton-tree, and declining to work after ten o'clock in the morning? 'No, tankee, massa, me tired now; me no want more money.' Or perhaps it is, 'No; workee no more; money no 'nuff; workee no pay.' These are the answers which the suppliant planter receives when at ten o'clock he begs his negro neighbours to go a second time into the cane-fields and earn a second shilling, or implores them to work for him more than four days a week, or solicits them at Christmas-time to put up with a short ten days' holiday. His canes are ripe, and his mill should be about; or else they are foul with weeds, and the hogsheads will be very short if they be not cleansed. He is anxious enough, for all his world depends upon it. But what does the negro care? 'No; me no more workee now.'

The busher (overseer; elide the o and change v into b, and the word will gradually explain itself)—The busher, who remembers slavery and former happy days, d—s him for a lazy nigger, and threatens him with coming starvation, and perhaps with returning monkeydom. 'No, massa; no starve now; God send plenty yam. No more monkey now, massa.' The black man is not in the least angry, though the busher is. And as for the canes, they remain covered with dirt, and the return of the estate is but one hundred and thirty hogsheads instead of one hundred and ninety. Let the English farmer think of that; and in realizing the full story, he must imagine that the plenteous food alluded to has been grown on his own ground, and probably planted at his own expense. The busher was wrong to curse the man, and wrong to threaten him with the monkey's tail; but it must be admitted that the position is trying to the temper.

And who can blame the black man? He is free to work, or free to let it alone. He can live without work and roll in the sun, and suck oranges and eat bread-fruit;

ay, and ride a horse perhaps, and wear a white waistcoat and plaited shirt on Sundays. Why should he care for the busher? I will not dig cane-holes for half a crown a day; and why should I expect him to do so? I can live without it; so can he.

But, nevertheless, it would be very well if we could so contrive that he should not live without work. It is clearly not Nature's intention that he should be exempted from the general lot of Adam's children. We would not have our friend a slave; but we would fain force him to give the world a fair day's work for his fair day's provender, if we knew how to do so without making him a slave. The fact I take it is, that there are too many good things in Jamaica for the number who have to enjoy them. If the competitors were more in number, more trouble would be necessary in their acquirement.

And now, just at this moment, philanthropy is again busy in England protecting the Jamaica negro. He is a man and a brother, and shall we not regard him? Certainly, my philanthropic friend, let us regard him well. He *is* a man; and, if you will, a brother; but he is the very idlest brother with which a hardworking workman was ever cursed, intent only on getting his mess of pottage without giving anything in return. His petitions about the labour market, my excellently-soft-hearted friend, and his desire to be protected from undue competition are——Oh, my friend, I cannot tell you how utterly they are—gammon. He is now eating his yam without work, and in that privilege he is anxious to be maintained. And you, are you willing to assist him in his views?

The negro slave was ill treated—ill treated, at any rate, in that he was a slave; and therefore, by that reaction which prevails in all human matters, it is now thought necessary to wrap him up in cotton and put him under

F

a glass case. The wind must not blow on him too roughly, and the rose-leaves on which he sleeps should not be ruffled. He has been a slave; therefore now let him be a Sybarite. His father did an ample share of work; therefore let the son be made free from his portion in the primeval curse. The friends of the negro, if they do not actually use such arguments, endeavour to carry out such a theory.

But one feels that the joke has almost been carried too far when one is told that it is necessary to protect the labour market in Jamaica, and save the negro from the dangers of competition. No immigration of labourers into that happy country should be allowed, lest the rate of wages be lowered, and the unfortunate labourer be made more dependent on his master! But if the unfortunate labourers could be made to work, say four days a week, and on an average eight hours a day, would not that in itself be an advantage? In our happy England, men are not slaves; but the competition of the labour market forces upon them long days of continual labour. In our own country, ten hours of toil, repeated six days a week, for the majority of us will barely produce the necessaries of life. It is quite right that we should love the negroes; but I cannot understand that we ought to love them better than ourselves.

But with the most sensible of those who are now endeavouring to prevent immigration into Jamaica the argument has been, not the protection of the Jamaica negro, but the probability of ill usage to the immigrating African. In the first place, it is impossible not to observe the absurdity of acting on petitions from the negroes of Jamaica on such a pretence as this. Does any one truly imagine that the black men in Jamaica are so anxious for the welfare of their cousins in Africa, that they feel themselves bound to come forward and express their anxiety to the English Houses of Parliament? Of course nobody believes it. Of course it is perfectly understood that those petitions are got up by far other persons, and with by far other views; and that not one negro in fifty of those who sign them understands anything whatever about the matter, or has any wish or any solicitude on such a subject.

Lord Brougham mentions it as a matter of congratulation, that so large a proportion of the signatures should be written by the subscribers themselves—that there should be so few marksmen; but is it a matter of congratulation that this power of signing their names should be used for so false a purpose?

And then comes the question as to these immigrants themselves. Though it is not natural to suppose that their future fellow-labourers in Jamaica should be very anxious about them, such anxiety on the part of others is natural. In the first place, it is for the government to look to them; and then, lest the government should neglect its duty it is for such men as Lord Brougham to look to the government. That Lord Brougham should to the last be anxious for the welfare of the African is what all men would expect and all desire; but we would not wish to confide even to him the power of absolutely consummating the ruin of the Jamaica planter. Is it the fact that labourers immigrating to the West Indies have been ill treated, whether they be Portuguese from Madeira, Coolies from India, Africans from the Western Coast, or Chinese? In Jamaica, unfortunately, their number is as yet but scanty, but in British Guiana they are numerous. I think I may venture to say that no labourers in any country are so cared for, so closely protected, so certainly saved from the usual wants and sorrows incident to the labouring classes. And this is equally so in Jamaica as far as the system has gone. What would

be the usage of the African introduced by voluntary con-
tribution may be seen in the usage of him who has been
brought into the country from captured slave-ships.
Their clothing, their food, their house accommodation,
their hospital treatment, their amount of work and obligatory period of working with one master—all these
matters are under government surveillance; and the
planter who has allotted to him the privilege of employ-
ing such labour becomes almost as much subject to government inspection as though his estate were government
property.

It is said that an obligatory period of labour amounts
to slavery, even though the contract shall have been entered into by the labourer of his own free will. I will
not take on myself to deny this, as I might find it difficult to define the term slavery; but if this be so, English
apprentices are slaves, and so are indentured clerks; so
are hired agricultural servants in many parts of England
and Wales; and so, certainly, are all our soldiers and sailors.

But in the ordinary acceptation of the word slavery,
that acceptation which comes home to us all, whether we
can define it or no, men subject to such contracts are not
slaves.

There is much that is prepossessing in the ordinary
good humour of the negro; and much also that is picturesque in his tastes. I soon learned to think the women
pretty, in spite of their twisted locks of wool; and to like
the ring of their laughter, though it is not exactly silver-
sounding. They are very rarely surly when spoken to;
and their replies, though they seldom are absolutely witty,
contain, either in the sound or in the sense, something
that amounts to drollery. The unpractised ear has great
difficulty in understanding them, and I have sometimes
thought that this indistinctness has created the fun which

I have seemed to relish. The tone and look are humorous ; and the words, which are hardly heard, and are not understood, get credit for humour also.

Nothing about them is more astonishing than the dress of the women. It is impossible to deny to them considerable taste and great power of adaptation. In England, among our housemaids and even haymakers, crinoline, false flowers, long waists, and flowing sleeves have become common ; but they do not wear their finery as though they were at home in it. There is generally with them, when in their Sunday best, something of the hog in armour. With the negro woman there is nothing of this. In the first place she is never shame-faced. Then she has very frequently a good figure, and having it, she knows how to make the best of it. She has a natural skill in dress, and will be seen with a boddice fitted to her as though it had been made and laced in Paris.

Their costumes on fête days and Sundays are perfectly marvellous. They are by no means contented with coloured calicoes ; but shine in muslin and light silks at heaven only knows how much a yard. They wear their dresses of an enormous fulness. One may see of a Sunday evening three ladies occupying a whole street by the breadth of their garments, who on the preceding day were scrubbing pots and carrying weights about the town on their heads. And they will walk in full-dress too as though they had been used to go in such attire from their youth up. They rejoice most in white—in white muslin with coloured sashes ; in light-brown boots, pink gloves, parasols, and broad-brimmed straw hats with deep veils and glittering bugles. The hat and the veil, however, are mistakes. If the negro woman thoroughly understood effect, she would wear no head-dress but the coloured handkerchief, which is hers by right of national custom.

Some of their efforts after dignity of costume are inef-

fably ludicrous. One Sunday evening, far away in the
country, as I was riding with a gentleman, the proprietor
of the estate around us, I saw a young girl walking home
from church. She was arrayed from head to foot in
virgin white. Her gloves were on, and her parasol was
up. Her hat also was white, and so was the lace, and so
were the bugles which adorned it. She walked with a
stately dignity that was worthy of such a costume, and
worthy also of higher grandeur; for behind her walked an
attendant nymph, carrying the beauty's prayer-book—on
her head. A negro woman carries every burden on her
head, from a tub of water weighing a hundredweight down
to a bottle of physic.

When we came up to her, she turned towards us and
curtsied. She curtsied, for she recognized her 'massa;'
but she curtsied with great dignity, for she recognized
also her own finery. The girl behind with the prayer-
book made the ordinary obeisance, crooking her leg up
at the knee, and then standing upright quicker than
thought.

'Who on earth is that princess?' said I.

'They are two sisters who both work at my mill,'
said my friend. 'Next Sunday they will change places.
Polly will have the parasol and the hat, and Jenny will
carry the prayer-book on her head behind her.'

I was in a shoemaker's shop at St. Thomas, buying
a pair of boots, when a negro entered quickly and in a
loud voice said he wanted a pair of pumps. He was a
labouring man fresh from his labour. He had on an old
hat—what in Ireland men would call a caubeen; he was
in his shirt-sleeves, and was barefooted. As the only
shopman was looking for my boots, he was not attended to
at the moment.

'Want a pair of pumps—directerly,' he roared out in a
very dictatorial voice.

'Sit down for a moment,' said the shopman, 'and I will attend to you.'

He did sit down, but did so in the oddest fashion. He dropped himself suddenly into a chair, and at the same moment rapidly raised his legs from the ground; and as he did so fastened his hands across them just below his knees, so as to keep his feet suspended from his arms. This he contrived to do in such a manner that the moment his body reached the chair his feet left the ground. I looked on in amazement, thinking he was mad.

'Give I a bit of carpet,' he screamed out; still holding up his feet, but with much difficulty.

'Yes, yes,' said the shopman, still searching for the boots.

'Give I a bit of carpet directerly,' he again exclaimed. The seat of the chair was very narrow, and the back was straight, and the position was not easy, as my reader will ascertain if he attempt it. He was half-choked with anger and discomfort.

The shopman gave him the bit of carpet. Most men and women will remember that such bits of carpet are common in shoemakers' shops. They are supplied, I believe, in order that they who are delicate should not soil their stockings on the floor.

The gentleman in search of the pumps had seen that people of dignity were supplied with such luxuries, and resolved to have his value for his money; but as he had on neither shoes nor stockings, the little bit of carpet was hardly necessary for his material comfort.

CHAPTER V.

JAMAICA—COLOURED MEN.

IF in speaking of the negroes I have been in danger of offending my friends at home, I shall be certain in speaking of the coloured men to offend my friends in Jamaica. On this subject, though I have sympathy with them, I have no agreement. They look on themselves as the ascendant race. I look upon those of colour as being so, or at any rate as about to become so.

In speaking of my friends in Jamaica it is not unnatural that I should allude to the pure-blooded Europeans, or European Creoles—to those in whose veins there is no admixture of African blood. 'Similia similibus.' A man from choice will live with those who are of his own habits and his own way of thinking. But as regards Jamaica, I believe that the light of their star is waning, that their ascendency is over—in short, that their work, if not done, is on the decline.

Ascendency is a disagreeable word to apply to any two different races whose fate it may be to live together in the same land. It has been felt to be so in Ireland, when used either with reference to the Saxon Protestant or Celtic Roman Catholic; and it is so with reference to those of various shades of colour in Jamaica. But nevertheless it is the true word. When two rivers come

together, the waters of which do not mix, the one stream
will be the stronger—will overpower the other—will
become ascendant.   And so it is with people and nations.
It may not be pretty-spoken to talk about ascendency;
but sometimes pretty speaking will not answer a man's
purpose.

It is almost unnecessary to explain that by coloured
men I mean those who are of a mixed race—of a breed
mixed, be it in what proportion it may, between the
white European and the black African. Speaking of
Jamaica, I might almost say between the Anglo-Saxon
and the African; for there remains, I take it, but a
small tinge of Spanish blood. Of the old Indian blood
there is, I imagine, hardly a vestige.

Both the white men and the black dislike their coloured
neighbours. It is useless to deny that as a rule such is
the case. The white men now, at this very day, dislike
them more in Jamaica than they do in other parts of the
West Indies, because they are constantly driven to meet
them, and are more afraid of them.

In Jamaica one does come in contact with coloured
men. They are to be met at the Governor's table; they
sit in the House of Assembly; they cannot be refused
admittance to state parties, or even to large assemblies;
they have forced themselves forward, and must be recognized as being in the van. Individuals decry them—will
not have them within their doors—affect to despise them.
But in effect the coloured men of Jamaica cannot be
despised much longer.

It will be said that we have been wrong if we have
ever despised these coloured people, or indeed, if we have
ever despised the negroes, or any other race. I can
hardly think that anything so natural can be very wrong.
Those who are educated and civilized and powerful will
always, in one sense, despise those who are not; and the

most educated and civilized and most powerful will
despise those who are less so. Euphuists may proclaim
against such a doctrine; but experience, I think, teaches
us that it is true. If the coloured people in the West
Indies can overtop contempt, it is because they are acquiring education, civilization, and power. In Jamaica
they are, I hope, in a way to do this.

My theory—for I acknowledge to a theory—is this:
that Providence has sent white men and black men to
these regions in order that from them may spring a race
fitted by intellect for civilization; and fitted also by
physical organization for tropical labour. The negro in
his primitive state is not, I think, fitted for the former;
and the European white Creole is certainly not fitted for
the latter.

To all such rules there are of course exceptions. In
Porto Rico, for instance, one of the two remaining Spanish
colonies in the West Indies, the Peons, or free peasant
labourers, are of mixed Spanish and Indian blood, without,
I believe, any negro element. And there are occasional
negroes whose mental condition would certainly tend to
disprove the former of the two foregoing propositions, were
it not that in such matters exceptional cases prove and
disprove nothing. Englishmen as a rule are stouter than
Frenchmen. Were a French Falstaff and an English
Slender brought into a room together, the above position
would be not a whit disproved.

It is probable also that the future race who shall
inhabit these islands may have other elements than the
two already named. There will soon be here—in the
teeth of our friends of the Anti-Slavery Society—thousands from China and Hindostan. The Chinese and the
Coolies—immigrants from India are always called Coolies
—greatly excel the negro in intelligence, and partake,
though in a limited degree, of the negro's physical abilities

in a hot climate. And thus the blood of Asia will be mixed with that of Africa; and the necessary compound will, by God's infinite wisdom and power, be formed for these latitudes, as it has been formed for the colder regions in which the Anglo-Saxon preserves his energy, and works.

I know it will be said that there have been no signs of a mixture of breed between the negro and the Coolie, and the negro and the Chinese. The instances hitherto are, I am aware, but rare; but then the immigration of these classes is as yet but recent; and custom is necessary, and a language commonly understood, and habits, which the similitude of position will also make common, before such races will amalgamate. That they will amalgamate if brought together, all history teaches us. The Anglo-Saxon and the negro have done so, and in two hundred years have produced a population which is said to amount to a fifth of that of the whole island of Jamaica, and which probably amounts to much more. Two hundred years with us is a long time; but it is not so in the world's history. From 1660 to 1860 A.D. is a vast lapse of years; but how little is the lapse from the year 1660 to the year 1860, dating from the creation of the world; or rather, how small appears such lapse to us! In how many pages is its history written? and yet God's races were spreading themselves over the earth then as now.

Men are in such a hurry. They can hardly believe that that will come to pass of which they have evidence that it will not come to pass in their own days.

But then comes the question, whether the mulatto is more capable of being educated than the negro, and more able to work under a hot sun than the Englishman; whether he does not rather lose the physical power of the one, and the intellectual power of the other. There are those in Jamaica who have known them long, and who

think that as a race they have deteriorated both in mind
and body. I am not prepared to deny this. They probably have deteriorated in mind and body; and nevertheless my theory may be right. Nay, I will go further
and say that such deterioration on both sides is necessary
to the correctness of my theory.

In what compound are we to look for the full strength
of each component part? Should punch be as strong as
brandy, or as sweet as sugar? Neither the one nor the
other. But in order to be good and efficient punch, it
should partake duly of the strength of the spirit and of
the sweetness of the saccharine—according to the skill
and will of the gnostic fabricator, who in mixing knows
his own purposes. So has it ever been also in the admixture of races. The same amount of physical power is not
required for all climates, nor the same amount of mental
energy.

But the mulatto, though he has deteriorated from the
black man in one respect, and from the white in another,
does also excel the black man in one respect, and also
excel the white in another. As a rule, he cannot work
as a negro can. He could not probably endure to labour
in the cane-fields for sixteen hours out of the twenty-four,
as is done by the Cuban slave; but he can work safely
under a tropical sun, and can in the day go through a
fair day's work. He is not liable to yellow fever, as is
the white man, and enjoys as valid a protection from the
effects of heat as the heat of these regions requires.

Nor, as far as we yet know, have Galileos, Shaksperes,
or Napoleons been produced among the mulattos. Few
may probably have been produced who are able even to
form an accurate judgment as to the genius of such men
as these. But that the mulatto race partakes largely of
the intelligence and ambition of their white forefathers, it
is I think useless, and moreover wicked, to deny; wicked,

because the denial arises from an unjust desire to close
against them the door of promotion.

Let any stranger go through the shops and stores of
Kingston, and see how many of them are either owned or
worked by men of colour; let him go into the House of
Assembly, and see how large a proportion of their debates
is carried on by men of colour. I don't think much of
the parliamentary excellence of these debates, as I shall
have to explain by-and-by; but the coloured men at any
rate hold their own against their white colleagues. How
large a portion of the public service is carried on by them;
how well they thrive, though the prejudices of both white
and black are so strong against them!

I just now spoke of these coloured men as mulattos.
I did so because I was then anxious to refer to the exact
and equal division of black and white blood. Of course
it is understood that the mulatto, technically so called, is
the child of parents one of whom is all white and the other
all black; and to judge exactly of the mixed race, one
should judge, probably, from such an equal division.
But no such distinction can be effectually maintained in
speaking, or even in thinking of these people. The
various gradations of coloured blood range from all but
perfect white to all but perfect black; and the dispositions
and capabilities are equally various. In the lower orders,
among those who are nearest to the African stock, no
attempts I imagine are made to preserve an exact line.
One is at first inclined to think that the slightest infusion
of white blood may be traced in the complexion and hair,
and heard in the voice; but when the matter is closely
regarded one often finds it difficult to express an opinion
even to oneself. Colour is frequently not the safest
guide. To an inquirer really endeavouring to separate
the races—should so thankless a task ever be attempted—
the speech, I think, and the intelligence would afford the

sources of information on which most reliance could be placed.

But the distinction between the white and the coloured men is much more closely regarded. And those are the unfortunate among the latter who are tempted, by the closeness of their relationship to Europe, to deny their African parentage. Many do, if not by lip, at any rate by deed, stoutly make such denial; not by lip, for the subject is much too sore for speech, but by every wile by which a white quadroon can seek to deny his ancestry! Such denial is never allowed. The crisp hair, the sallow skin, the known family history, the thick lip of the old remembered granddam, a certain languor in the eye; all or some, or perhaps but one of these tells the tale. But the tale is told, and the life-struggle is made always, and always in vain.

This evil—for it is an evil—arises mainly from the white man's jealousy. He who seeks to pass for other than he is makes a low attempt; all attempts at falsehood must of necessity be low. But I doubt whether such energy of repudiation be not equally low. Why not allow the claim; or seem to allow it, if practicable? ' White art thou, my friend? Be a white man if thou wilt, or rather if thou canst. All we require of thee is that there remains no negro ignorance, no negro cunning, no negro apathy of brain. Forbear those vain attempts to wash out that hair of thine, and make it lank and damp. We will not regard at all, that little wave in thy locks; not even that lisp in thy tongue. But struggle, my friend, to be open in thy speech. Any wave there we cannot but regard. Speak out the thought that is in thee; for if thy thoughts lisp negrowards, our verdict must be against thee.' Is it not thus that we should accept their little efforts?

But we do not accept them so. In lieu thereof, we

admit no claim that can by any evidence be rejected; and, worse than that, we impute the stigma of black blood where there is no evidence to support such imputation. 'A nice fellow, Jones; eh? very intelligent, and well mannered,' some stranger says, who knows nothing of Jones's antecedents. 'Yes, indeed,' answers Smith, of Jamaica; 'a very decent sort of fellow. They do say that he's coloured; of course you know that.' The next time you see Jones, you observe him closely, and can find no trace of the Ethiop. But should he presently descant on purity of blood, and the insupportable impudence of the coloured people, then, and not till then, you would begin to doubt.

But these are evils which beset merely the point of juncture between the two races. With nine-tenths of those of mixed breed no attempts at concealment are by any means possible; and by them, of course, no such attempts are made. They take their lot as it is, and I think that on the whole they make the most of it. They of course are jealous of the assumed ascendency of the white man, and affect to show, sometimes not in the most efficacious manner, that they are his equal in external graces as in internal capacities. They are imperious to the black men, and determined on that side to exhibit and use their superiority. At this we can hardly be surprised. If we cannot set them a better lesson than we do, we can hardly expect the benefit which should arise from better teaching.

But the great point to be settled is this: whether this race of mulattos, quadroons, mustees, and what not, are capable of managing matters for themselves; of undertaking the higher walks of life; of living, in short, as an independent people with a proper share of masterdom; and not necessarily as a servile people, as hewers of wood and drawers of water? If not, it will fare badly for Jamaica, and will probably also fare badly in coming years for the rest of the West Indies. Whether other immigration be allowed or no, of one kind of immigration the supply into Jamaica is becoming less and less. Few European white men now turn thither in quest of fortune. Few Anglo-Saxon adventurers now seek her shores as the future home of their adoption. The white man has been there, and has left his mark. The Creole children of these Europeans of course remain, but their numbers are no longer increased by new comers.

But I think there is no doubt that they are fit— these coloured people, to undertake the higher as well as lower paths of human labour. Indeed, they do undertake them, and thrive well in them now, much to the disgust of the so-esteemed ascendant class. They do make money, and enjoy it. They practise as statesmen, as lawyers, and as doctors in the colony; and, though they have not as yet shone brightly as divines in our English Church, such deficiency may be attributed more to the jealousy of the parsons of that Church than to their own incapacity.

There are, they say, seventy thousand coloured people in the island, and not more than fifteen thousand white people. As the former increase in intelligence, it is not to be supposed that they will submit to the latter. Nor are they at all inclined to submission.

But they have still an up-hill battle before them. They are by no means humble in their gait, and their want of meekness sets their white neighbours against them. They are always proclaiming by their voice and look that they are as good as the white man; but they are always showing by their voice and look, also, that they know that this is a false boast.

And then they are by no means popular with the negro. A negro, as a rule, will not serve a mulatto when he can serve a European or a white Creole. He thinks that the mulatto is too near akin to himself to be worthy of any respect. In his passion he calls him a nigger—and protests that he is not, and never will be like buckra man.

The negroes complain that the coloured men are sly and cunning; that they cannot be trusted as masters; that they tyrannize, bully, and deceive; in short, that they have their own negro faults. There may, doubtless, be some truth in this. They have still a portion of their lesson to learn; perhaps the greater portion. I affirm merely that the lesson is being learned. A race of people with its good and ill qualities is not formed in a couple of centuries.

And if it be fated that the Anglo-Saxon race in these islands is to yield place to another people, and to abandon its ground, having done its appointed work, surely such a decree should be no cause of sorrow. To have done their appointed work, and done it well,—should not this be enough for any men?

But there are they who protest that such ideas as these with reference to this semi-African people are unpatriotic; are unworthy of an Englishman, who should foster the ascendency of his own race and his own country. Such men will have it as an axiom, that when an Englishman has been master once, he should be master always: that his dominion should not give way to strange hands, or his ascendency yield itself to strange races. It is unpatriotic, forsooth, to suggest that these tawny children of the sun should get the better of their British lords, and rule the roast themselves!

Even were it so—should it even be granted that such an idea is unpatriotic, one would then be driven back to ask whether patriotism be a virtue. It is at any rate a virtue in consequence only of the finite aspirations of mankind. To love the universe which God has made,

G

were man capable of such love, would be a loftier attribute than any feeling for one's own country. The Gentile was as dear as the Jew; the Samaritans as much prized as they of Galilee, or as the children of Judah.

The present position and prospects of the children of Great Britain are sufficiently noble, and sufficiently extended. One need not begrudge to others their limited share in the population and government of the world's welfare. While so large a part of North America and Australia remain still savage—waiting the white man's foot—waiting, in fact, for the foot of the Englishman, there can be no reason why we should doom our children to swelter and grow pale within the tropics. A certain work has been ours to do there, a certain amount of remaining work it is still probably our lot to complete. But when that is done; when civilization, commerce, and education shall have been spread; when sufficient of our blood shall have been infused into the veins of those children of the sun; then, I think, we may be ready, without stain to our patriotism, to take off our hats and bid farewell to the West Indies.

And be it remembered that I am here speaking of the general ascendency, not of the political power of these coloured races. It may be that after all we shall still have to send out some white Governor with a white aide-de-camp and a white private secretary—some three or four unfortunate white men to support the dignity of the throne of Queen Victoria's great-grandchild's grandchild. Such may be, or may not be. To my thinking, it would be more for our honour that it should not be so. If the honour, glory, and well-being of the child be dear to the parents, Great Britain should surely be more proud of the United States than of any of her colonies.

We Britishers have a noble mission. The word I know is unpopular, for it has been foully misused; but it is in itself a good word, and none other will supply its place. We have a noble mission, but we are never content with it. It is not enough for us to beget nations, civilize countries, and instruct in truth and knowledge the dominant races of the coming ages. All this will not suffice unless also we can maintain a king over them! What is it to us, or even to them, who may be their king or ruler—or, to speak with a nearer approach to sense, from what source they be governed—so long as they be happy, prosperous, and good? And yet there are men mad enough to regret the United States! Many men are mad enough to look forward with anything but composure to the inevitable, happily inevitable day, when Australia shall follow in the same path.

We have risen so high that we may almost boast to have placed ourselves above national glory. The welfare of the coming world is now the proper care of the Anglo-Saxon race.

The coloured people, I have said, have made their way into society in Jamaica. That is, they have made a certain degree of impression on the millstone; which will therefore soon be perforated through and through, and then crumble to pieces like pumice-stone. Nay, they have been or are judges, attorneys-general, prime ministers, leaders of the opposition, and what not. The men have so far made their way. The difficulty now is with the women.

And in high questions of society here is always the stumbling-block. All manners of men can get themselves into a room together without difficulty, and can behave themselves with moderate forbearance to each other when in it. But there are points on which ladies are harder than steel, stiffer than their brocaded silks, more obdurate than whalebone.

'He wishes me to meet Mrs. So-and-So,' a lady said to me, speaking of her husband, 'because Mr. So-and-

So is a very respectable good sort of man. I have no objection whatever to Mr. So-and-So; but if I begin with her, I know there will be no end.'

'Probably not,' I said; 'when you once commence, you will doubtless have to go on—in the good path.' I confess that the last words were said *sotto voce*. On that occasion the courage was wanting in me to speak out my mind. The lady was very pretty, and I could not endure to be among the unfavoured ones.

'That is just what I have said to Mr. ——; but he never thinks about such things; he is so very imprudent. If I ask Mrs. So-and-So here, how can I keep out Mrs. Such-a-One? They are both very respectable, no doubt; but what were their grandmothers?'

Ah! if we were to think of their grandmothers, it would doubtless be a dark subject. But what, O lady, of their grandchildren? That may be the most important, and also most interesting side from whence to view the family.

'These people marry now,' another lady said to me— a lady not old exactly, but old enough to allude to such a subject; and in the tone of her voice I thought I could catch an idea that she conceived them in doing so to be trenching on the privileges of their superiors. 'But their mothers and grandmothers never thought of looking to that at all. Are we to associate with the children of such women, and teach our daughters that vice is not to be shunned?'

Ah! dear lady—not old, but sufficiently old—this statement of yours is only too true. Their mothers and grandmothers did not think much of matrimony—had but little opportunity of thinking much of it. But with whom did the fault chiefly lie? These very people of whom we are speaking, would they not be your cousins but for the lack of matrimony? Your uncle, your father, your cousins, your grandfather, nay, your very brother, are they not the true criminals in this matter—they who have lived in this unhallowed state with women of a lower race? For the sinners themselves of either sex I would not ask *your* pardon ; but you might forgive the children's children.

The life of coloured women in Jamaica some years since was certainly too often immoral. They themselves were frequently illegitimate, and they were not unwilling that their children should be so also. To such a one it was preferable to be a white man's mistress than the wife of such as herself; and it did not bring on them the same disgrace, this kind of life, as it does on women in England, or even, I may say, on women in Europe, nor the same bitter punishment. Their master, though he might be stern enough and a tyrant, as the owner of slaves living on his own little principality might probably be, was kinder to her than to the other females around her, and in a rough sort of way was true to her. He did not turn her out of the house, and she found it to be promotion to be the mother of his children and the upper servant in his establishment. And in those days, days still so near to us, the coloured woman was a slave herself, unless specially manumitted either in her own generation or in that immediately above her. It is from such alliances as these that the coloured race of Jamaica has sprung.

But all this, if one cannot already boast that it is changed, is quickly changing. Matrimony is in vogue, and the coloured women know their rights, and are inclined to claim them.

Of course among them, as among us at home, and among all people, there are various ranks. There are but few white labourers in Jamaica, and but few negroes who are not labourers. But the coloured people are to be found in all ranks, from that of the Prime Minister—for they have a Prime Minister in Jamaica—down to the worker in the cane-fields. Among their women many are now highly educated, for they send their children to English schools.   Perhaps if I were to say fashionably educated, I might be more strictly correct.   They love dearly to shine; to run over the piano with quick and loud fingers; to dance with skill, which they all do, for they have good figures and correct ears; to know and display the little tricks and graces of English ladies—such tricks and graces as are to be learned between fifteen and seventeen at Ealing, Clapham, and Hornsey.

But the coloured girls of a class below these—perhaps I should say two classes below them—are the most amusing specimens of Jamaica ladies.   I endeavoured to introduce my readers to one at Port Antonio.   They cannot be called pretty, for the upper part of the face almost always recedes; but they have good figures and well-turned limbs.   They are singularly free from *mauvaise honte*, and yet they are not impertinent or ill-mannered.   They are gracious enough with the pale faces when treated graciously, but they can show a very high spirit if they fancy that any slight is shown to them.   They delight to talk contemptuously of niggers.   Those people are dirty niggers, and nasty niggers, and mere niggers.   I have heard this done by one whom I had absolutely taken for a negro, and who was not using loud abusive language, but gently speaking of an inferior class.

With these, as indeed with coloured people of a higher grade, the great difficulty is with their language.   They cannot acquire the natural English pronunciation.   As far as I remember, I have never heard but two negroes who spoke unbroken English; and the lower classes of the coloured people though they are not equally deficient, are still very incapable of plain English articulation.   The ' th' is to them, as to foreigners, an insuperable difficulty. Even Josephine, it may be remembered, was hardly perfect in this respect.

CHAPTER VI.

JAMAICA—WHITE MEN.

IT seems to us natural that white men should hold ascendency over those who are black or coloured. Although we have emancipated our own slaves, and done so much to abolish slavery elsewhere, nevertheless we regard the negro as born to be a servant. We do not realize it to ourselves that it is his right to share with us the high places of the world, and that it should be an affair of individual merit whether we wait on his beck or he on ours. We have never yet brought ourselves so to think, and probably never shall. They still are to us a servile race. Philanthropical abolitionists will no doubt deny the truth of this; but I have no doubt that the conviction is as strong with them—could they analyze their own convictions—as it is with others.

Where white men and black men are together, the white will order and the black will obey, with an obedience more or less implicit according to the terms on which they stand. When those terms are slavery, the white men order with austerity, and the black obey with alacrity. But such terms have been found to be prejudicial to both. Each is brutalized by the contact. The black man becomes brutal and passive as a beast of burden; the white man becomes brutal and ferocious as a beast of prey.

But there are various other terms on which they may

stand as servants and masters. There are those well-understood terms which regulate employment in England and elsewhere, under which the poor man's time is his money, and the rich man's capital his certain means of obtaining labour. As far as we can see these terms, if properly carried out, are the best which human wisdom can devise for the employment and maintenance of mankind. Here in England they are not always properly carried out. At an occasional spot or two things will run rusty for a while. There are strikes; and there are occasional gluts of labour, very distressing to the poor man; and occasional gluts of the thing laboured, very embarrassing to the rich man. But on the whole, seeing that after all the arrangement is only human, here in England it does work pretty well. We intended, no doubt, when we emancipated our slaves in Jamaica, that the affair should work in the same way there.

But the terms there at present are as far removed from the English system as they are from the Cuban, and are almost as abhorrent to justice as slavery itself—as abhorrent to justice, though certainly not so abhorrent to mercy and humanity.

What would a farmer say in England if his ploughman declined to work, and protested that he preferred going to his master's granary and feeding himself and his children on his master's corn? 'Measter, noa; I beez a-tired thick day, and dunna mind to do no wark!' Then the poorhouse, my friend, the poorhouse! And hardly that; starvation first, and nakedness, and all manner of misery. In point of fact our friend the ploughman must go and work, even though his o'erlaboured bones be tired, as no doubt they often are. He knows it, and does it, and in his way is not discontented. And is not this God's ordinance?

His ordinance in England and elsewhere, but not so, apparently, in Jamaica. There we had a devil's ordinance in those days of slavery; and having rid ourselves of that, we have still a devil's ordinance of another sort. It is not perhaps very easy for men to change devil's work into heavenly work at once. The ordinance that at present we have existing there is that *far niente* one of lying in the sun and eating yams—' of eating, not your own yams, you lazy, do-nothing, thieving darkee; but my yams; mine, who am being ruined, root and branch, stock and barrel, house and homestead, wife and bairns, because you won't come and work for me when I offer you due wages; you thieving, do-nothing, lazy nigger.'

' Hush!' will say my angry philanthropist. ' For the sake of humanity, hush! Will coarse abuse and the call-ing of names avail anything? Is he not a man and a brother?' No, my angry philanthropist; while he will not work and will only steal, he is neither the one nor the other, in my estimation, As for his being a brother, that we may say is—fudge; and I will call no professional idler a man.

But the abuse above given is not intended to be looked on as coming out of my own mouth, and I am not, there-fore, to be held responsible for the wording of it. It is inserted there—with small inverted commas, as you see— to show the language with which our angry white friends in Jamaica speak of the extraordinary condition in which they have found themselves placed.

Slowly—with delay that has been awfully ruinous— they now bethink themselves of immigration—immigra-tion from the coast of Africa, immigration from China, Coolie immigrants from Hindostan. When Trinidad and Guiana have helped themselves, then Jamaica bestirs itself. And what then? Then the negroes bestir themselves. ' For heaven's sake let us be looked to! Are we not to be protected from competition? If labourers be brought here, will not these white people again cultivate their grounds? Shall we not be driven from our squatting patches? Shall we not starve; or, almost worse than that, shall we not again fall under Adam's curse? Shall we not again be slaves, in reality, if not in name? Shall we not have to work?'

The negro's idea of emancipation was and is emancipation not from slavery but from work. To lie in the sun and eat breadfruit and yams is his idea of being free. Such freedom as that has not been intended for man in this world; and I say that Jamaica, as it now exists, is still under a devil's ordinance.

One cannot wonder that the white man here should be vituperative in his wrath. Frst came emancipation. He bore that with manful courage; for it must be remembered that even in that he had much to bear. The price he got for his slave was nothing as compared with that slave's actual value. And slavery to him was not repugnant as it is to you and me. One's trade is never repugnant to one's feelings. But so much he did bear with manly courage. He could no longer make slave-grown sugar, but he would not at any rate be compelled to compete with those who could. The protective duties would save him there.

Then free trade became the fashion, and protective duties on sugar were abolished. I beg it may not be thought that I am an advocate for such protection. The West Indians were, I think, thrown over in a scurvy manner, because they were thrown over by their professed friends. But that was, we all know, the way with Sir Robert Peel. Well, free trade in sugar became the law of the land, and then the Jamaica planter found the burden too heavy for his back. The money which had flown in so freely came in such small driblets that he could make no improvement. Portions of his estate went out of cultivation, and then the negro who should have tilled the remainder squatted on it, and said, ' No, massa, me no workee to-day.'

And now, to complete the business, now that Jamaica is at length looking in earnest for immigration—for it has long been looking for immigration with listless dis-earnest —the planter is told that the labour of the black man must be protected. If he be vituperative, who can wonder at it? To speak the truth, he is somewhat vituperative.

The white planter of Jamaica is sore and vituperative and unconvinced. He feels that he has been ill used, and forced to go to the wall; and that now he is there, he is meanly spoken of, as though he were a bore and a nuisance —as one of whom the Colonial Office would gladly rid itself if it knew how. In his heart of hearts there dwells a feeling that after all slavery was not so vile an institution —that that devil as well as some others has been painted too black. In those old days the work was done, the sugar was made, the workmen were comfortably housed and fed, and perhaps on his father's estate were kindly treated. At any rate, such is his present memory. The money came in, things went on pleasantly, and he cannot remember that anybody was unhappy. But now—! Can it be wondered at that in his heart of hearts he should still have a sort of yearning after slavery?

In one sense, at any rate, he has been ill used. The turn in the wheel of Fortune has gone against him, as it went against the hand-loom weavers when machinery became the fashion. Circumstances rather than his own fault have brought him low. Well-disciplined energy in all the periods of his adversity might perhaps have saved him, as it has saved others; but there has been more against him than against others. As regards him himself, the old-fashioned Jamaica planter, the pure blooded white owner of the soil, I think that his day in Jamaica is done. The glory, I fear, has departed from his house. The hand-

loom weavers have been swept into infinite space, and
their children now poke the engine fires, or piece threads
standing in a factory. The children of the old Jamaica
planter must also push their fortunes elsewhere.

It is a thousand pities, for he was, I may still say is,
the prince of planters—the true aristocrat of the West
Indies. He is essentially different as a man from the
somewhat purse-proud Barbadian, whose estate of two
hundred acres has perhaps changed hands half a dozen
times in the last fifty years, or the thoroughly mercantile
sugar manufacturer of Guiana. He has so many of the
characteristics of an English country gentleman that he
does not strike an Englishman as a strange being. He
has his pedigree, and his family house, and his domain
around him. He shoots and fishes, and some few years
since, in the good days, he even kept a pack of hounds.
He is in the commission of the peace, and as such has much
to do. A planter in Demerara may also be a magistrate,
—probably is so; but the fact does not come forward as a
prominent part of his life's history.

In Jamaica too there is scope for a country gentleman.
They have their counties and their parishes; in Barbados
they have nothing but their sugar estates. They have
county society, local balls, and local race-meetings. They
have local politics, local quarrels, and strong old-fashioned
local friendships. In all these things one feels oneself to
be much nearer to England in Jamaica than in any other
of the West Indian islands.

All this is beyond measure pleasant, and it is a thousand
pities that it should not last. I fear, however, that it will
not last—that, indeed, it is not now lasting. That dear
lady's unwillingness to obey her lord's behests, when he
asked her to call on her brown neighbour, nay, the very
fact of that lord's request, both go to prove that this is so.
The lady felt that her neighbour was cutting the very

ground from under her feet. The lord knew 'that old times were changed, old manners gone.' The game was almost up when he found himself compelled to make such a request.

At present, when the old planter sits on the magisterial bench, a coloured man sits beside him; one probably on each side of him. At road sessions he cannot carry out his little project because the coloured men out-vote him. There is a vacancy for his parish in the House of Assembly. The old planter scorns the House of Assembly, and will have nothing to do with it. A coloured man is therefore chosen, and votes away the white man's taxes. And then things worse and worse arise; not only coloured men get into office, but black men also. What is our old aristocratic planter to do with a negro churchwarden on one side, and a negro coroner on another? 'Fancy what our state is,' a young planter said to me; 'I dare not die, for fear I should be sat upon by a black man!'

I know that it will be thought by many, and probably said by some, that these are distinctions to which we ought not to allude. But without alluding to them in one's own mind it is impossible to understand the state of the country; and without alluding to them in speech it is impossible to explain the state of the country. The fact is, that in Jamaica, at the present day, the coloured people do stand on strong ground, and that they do not so stand with the goodwill of the old aristocracy of the country. They have forced their way up, and now loudly protest that they intend to keep it. I think that they will keep it, and that on the whole it will be well for us Anglo-Saxons to have created a race capable of living and working in the climate without inconvenience.

It is singular, however, how little all this is understood in England. There it is conceived that white men and coloured men, white ladies and coloured ladies, meet together and amalgamate without any difference. The Duchess of This and Lord That are very happy to have at their table some intelligent dark gentleman, or even a well-dressed negro, though he may not perhaps be very intelligent. There is some little excitement in it, some change from the common ; and perhaps also an easy opportunity of practising on a small scale those philanthropic views which they preach with so much eloquence. When one hobnobs over a glass of champagne with a dark gentleman, he is in some sort a man and a brother. But the duchess and the lord think that because the dark gentleman is to their taste, he must necessarily be as much to the taste of the neighbours among whom he has been born and bred ; of those who have been accustomed to see him from his childhood.

There never was a greater mistake. A coloured man may be a fine prophet in London ; but he will be no prophet in Jamaica, which is his own country ; no prophet at any rate among his white neighbours.

I knew a case in which a very intelligent—nay, I believe, a highly-educated young coloured gentleman, was sent out by certain excellent philanthropic big-wigs to fill an official situation in Jamaica. He was a stranger to Jamaica, never having been there before. Now, when he was so sent out, the home big-wigs alluded to intimated to certain other big-wigs in Jamaica that their dark protégé would be a great acquisition to the society of the place. I mention this to show the ignorance of those London big-wigs, not as to the capability of the young gentleman which probably was not over-rated, but as to the manners and life of the place. I imagine that the gentleman has hardly once found himself in that society which it was supposed he would adorn. The time, however, will probably come when he and others of the same class will have sufficient society of their own.

I have said elsewhere that the coloured people in Jamaica have made their way into society; and in what I now say I may seem to contradict myself. Into what may perhaps be termed public society they have made their way. Those who have seen the details of colonial life will know that there is a public society to which people are admitted or not admitted, according to their acknowledged rights. Governor's parties, public balls, and certain meetings which are semi-official and semi-social, are of this nature. A Governor in Jamaica would, I imagine, not conceive himself to have the power of excluding coloured people from his table, even if he wished it. But in Barbados I doubt whether a Governor could, if he wished it, do the reverse.

So far coloured people in Jamaica have made their footing good; and they are gradually advancing beyond this. But not the less as a rule are they disliked by the old white aristocracy of the country; in a strong degree by the planters themselves, but in a much stronger by the planters' wives.

So much for my theory as to the races of men in Jamaica, and as to the social condition of the white and coloured people with reference to each other. Now I would say a word or two respecting the white man as he himself is, without reference either to his neighbour or to his prospects.

A better fellow cannot be found anywhere than a gentleman of Jamaica, or one with whom it is easier to live on pleasant terms. He is generally hospitable, affable, and generous; easy to know, and pleasant when known; not given perhaps to much deep erudition, but capable of talking with ease on most subjects of conversation; fond of society, and of pleasure, if you choose to call it so; but not generally addicted to low pleasures. He is often witty, and has a sharp side to his tongue if occasion be given him to use it. He is not generally, I think, a hard-working man. Had he been so, the country perhaps would not have been in its present condition. But he is bright and clever, and in spite of all that he has gone through, he is at all times good-humoured.

No men are fonder of the country to which they belong, or prouder of the name of Great Britain than these Jamaicans. It has been our policy—and, as regards our larger colonies, the policy I have no doubt has been beneficial—to leave our dependencies very much to themselves; to interfere in the way of governing as little as might be; and to withdraw as much as possible from any participation in their internal concerns. This policy is anything but popular with the white aristocracy of Jamaica. They would fain, if it were possible, dispense altogether with their legislature, and be governed altogether from home. In spite of what they have suffered, they are still willing to trust the statesmen of England, but are most unwilling to trust the statesmen of Jamaica.

Nothing is more peculiar than the way in which the word 'home' is used in Jamaica, and indeed all through the West Indies. With the white people, it always signifies England, even though the person using the word has never been there. I could never trace the use of the word in Jamaica as applied by white men or white women to the home in which they lived, not even though that home had been the dwelling of their fathers as well as of themselves. The word 'home' with them is sacred, and means something holier than a habitation in the tropics. It refers always to the old country.

In this respect, as in so many others, an Englishman differs greatly from a Frenchman. Though we English, as a rule, are much more given to colonize than our neighbours; though we spread ourselves over the face of the globe, while they have established comparatively but few settlements in the outer world; nevertheless, when we leave our country, we almost always do so with some idea, be

it ever so vague, that we shall return to it again, and
again make it our home. But the Frenchman divests
himself of any such idea. He also loves France, or at any
rate loves Paris; but his object is to carry his Paris with
him; to make a Paris for himself, whether it be in a sugar
island among the Antilles, or in a trading town upon the
Levant.

And in some respects the Frenchman is the wiser man.
He never looks behind him with regret. He does his best
to make his new house comfortable. The spot on which
he fixes is his home, and so he calls it, and so regards it.
But with an Englishman in the West Indies—even with
an English Creole—England is always his home.

If the people in Jamaica have any prejudice, it is on
the subject of heat. I suppose they have a general idea
that their island is hotter than England; but they never
reduce this to an individual idea respecting their own
habitation.

'Come and dine with me,' a man says to you; 'I can
give you a cool bed.' The invitation at first sounded
strange to me, but I soon got used to it; I soon even
liked it, though I found too often that the promise was
not kept. How could it be kept while the quicksilver
was standing at eighty-five in the shade?

And each man boasts that his house is ten degrees
cooler than that of his neighbour; and each man, if you
contest the point, has a reason to prove why it must be so.

But a stranger, at any rate round Kingston, is apt to
put the matter in a different light. One place may be
hotter than another, but cool is a word which he never
uses. On the whole, I think that the heat of Kingston,
Jamaica, is more oppressive than that of any other place
among the British West Indies. When one gets down
to the Spanish coast, then, indeed, one can look back even
to Kingston with regret.

CHAPTER VII.

JAMAICA—SUGAR.

THAT Jamaica was a land of wealth, rivalling the East in its means of riches, nay, excelling it as a market for capital, as a place in which money might be turned; and that it now is a spot on the earth almost more poverty-stricken than any other—so much is known almost to all men. That this change was brought about by the manumission of the slaves, which was completed in 1838, of that also the English world is generally aware. And there probably the usual knowledge about Jamaica ends. And we may also say that the solicitude of Englishmen at large goes no further. The families who are connected with Jamaica by ties of interest are becoming fewer and fewer. Property has been abandoned as good for nothing, and nearly forgotten; or has been sold for what wretched trifle it would fetch; or left to an overseer, who is hardly expected to send home proceeds—is merely ordered imperatively to apply for no subsidies. Fathers no longer send their younger sons to make their fortunes there. Young English girls no longer come out as brides. Dukes and earls do not now govern the rich gem of the West, spending their tens of thousands in royal magnificence, and laying by other tens of thousands for home consumption. In lieu of this, some governor by profession, unfortunate for the moment, takes Jamaica with a groan, as a stepping-stone to some better Barataria—New Zealand perhaps, or Frazer River; and by strict economy tries to save the price of his silver forks. Equerries, aides-de-camp, and private secretaries no longer flaunt it about Spanish Town. The flaunting about Spanish Town is now of a dull sort. Ichabod! The glory of that house is gone. The palmy days of that island are over.

Those who are failing and falling in the world excite but little interest; and so it is at present with Jamaica. From time to time we hear that properties which used to bring five thousand pounds a year, are not now worth five hundred pounds in fee simple. We hear it, thank our stars that we have not been brought up in the Jamaica line, and there's an end of it. If we have young friends whom we wish to send forth into the world, we search the maps with them at our elbows; but we put our hands over the West Indies—over the first fruits of the courage and skill of Columbus—as a spot tabooed by Providence. Nay, if we could, we would fain forget Jamaica altogether.

But there it is; a spot on the earth not to be lost sight of or forgotten altogether, let us wish it ever so much. It belongs to us, and must be in some sort thought of and managed, and, if possible, governed. Though the utter sinking of Jamaica under the sea might not be regarded as a misfortune, it is not to be thought of that it should belong to others than Britain. How should we look at the English politician who would propose to sell it to the United States; or beg Spain to take it as an appendage to Cuba? It is one of the few sores in our huge and healthy carcase; and the sore has been now running so long, that we have almost given over asking whether it be curable.

This at any rate is certain—it will not sink into the sea, but will remain there, inhabited, if not by white men, then by coloured men or black; and must, unfortunately, be governed by us English.

We have indulged our antipathy to cruelty by abolishing slavery. We have made the peculiar institution an impossibility under the British crown. But in doing so we overthrew one particular interest; and, alas! we overthrew also, and necessarily so, the holders of that interest. As for the twenty millions which we gave to the slave-owners, it was at best but as though we had put down awls and lasts by Act of Parliament, and, giving the shoemakers the price of their tools, told them they might make shoes as best they could without them; failing any such possibility, that they might live on the price of their lost articles. Well; the shoemakers did their best, and continued their trade in shoes under much difficulty.

But then we have had another antipathy to indulge, and have indulged it—our antipathy to protection. We have abolished the duty on slave-grown sugar; and the shoemakers who have no awls and lasts have to compete sadly with their happy neighbours, possessed of these useful shoemaking utensils.

Make no more shoes, but make something in lieu of shoes, we say to them. The world wants not shoes only; —make hats. Give up your sugar, and bring forth produce that does not require slave labour. Could the men of Jamaica with one voice speak out such words as the experience of the world might teach them, they would probably answer thus:—'Yes; in two hundred years or so we will do so. So long it will take to alter the settled trade and habit of a community. In the mean time, for ourselves, our living selves, our late luxurious homes, our idle, softly-nurtured Creole wives, our children coming and to come—for ourselves—what immediate compensation do you intend to offer us, Mr. Bull?'

Mr. Bull, with sufficient anger at such importunity; with sufficient remembrance of his late twenty millions of pounds sterling; with some plain allusions to that payment, buttons up his breeches-pocket and growls angrily.

Abolition of slavery is good, and free trade is good. Such little insight as a plain man may have into the affairs around him seems to me to suffice for the expression of such opinion. Nor will I presume to say that those who proposed either the one law or the other were premature. To get a good law passed and out of hand is always desirable. There are from day to day so many new impediments! But the law having been passed, we should think somewhat of the sufferers.

Planters in Jamaica assert that when the abolition of slavery was hurried on by the termination of the apprentice system before the time first stipulated, they were promised by the government at home that their interests should be protected by high duties on slave-grown sugar. That such pledge was ever absolutely made, I do not credit. But that, if made, it could be worth anything, no man looking to the history of England could imagine. What minister can pledge his successors? In Jamaica it is said that the pledge was given and broken by the same man—by Sir Robert Peel. But when did Sir Robert Peel's pledge in one year bind even his own conduct in the next?

The fact perhaps is this, that no one interest can ever be allowed to stand in the way of national progress. We could not stop machinery for the sake of the hand-loom weavers. The poor hand-loom weavers felt themselves aggrieved; knew that the very bread was taken from their mouths, their hard-earned cup from their lips. They felt, poor weavers! that they could not take themselves in middle life to poking fires and greasing wheels. Time, the eater of things, has now pretty well eaten the hand-loom weavers—them and their miseries. Must it not be so also with the Jamaica planters?

In the mean time the sight, as regards the white man, is a sad one to see ; and almost the sadder in that the last three or four years have been in a slight degree prosperous to the Jamaica sugar-grower ; so that this question of producing sugar in that island at a rate that will pay for itself is not quite answered. The drowning man still clings by a rope's end, though it be but by half an inch, and that held between his teeth. Let go, thou unhappy one, and drown thyself out of the way! Is it not thus that Great Britain, speaking to him from the high places in Exeter Hall, shouts to him in his death struggles?

Are Englishmen in general aware that half the sugar estates in Jamaica, and I believe more than half the coffee plantations, have gone back into a state of bush?— that all this land, rich with the richest produce only some thirty years since, has now fallen back into wilderness ?—that the world has hereabouts so retrograded?— that chaos and darkness have reswallowed so vast an extent of the most bountiful land that civilization had ever mastered, and that too beneath the British government?

And of those who are now growing canes in Jamaica a great portion are gentlemen who have lately bought their estates for the value of the copper in the sugar-boilers, and of the metal in the rum-stills. If to this has been added anything like a fair value for wheels in the machinery, the estate has not been badly sold.

Some estates there are, and they are not many, which are still worked by the agents—attorneys is the proper word—of rich proprietors in England ; of men so rich that they have been able to bear the continual drain of properties that for years have been always losing—of men who have had wealth and spirit to endure this. It is hardly necessary to say that they are few ; and that many whose spirit has been high, but wealth insufficient, have gone grievously to the wall in the attempt.

And there are still some who, living on the spot, have hitherto pulled through it all; who have watched houses falling and the wilderness progressing, and have still stuck to their homes and their work; men whose properties for ten years, counting from the discontinuance of protection, have gradually grown less and less beneath their eyes, till utter want has been close to them. And yet they have held on. In the good times they may have made five hundred hogsheads of sugar every year. It has come to that with them that in some years they have made but thirty. But they have made that thirty and still held on. All honour at least to them! For their sake, if for that of no others, we would be tempted to pray that these few years of their prosperity may be prolonged and grow somewhat fatter.

The exported produce of Jamaica consists chiefly of sugar and rum. The article next in importance is coffee. Then they export also logwood, arrowroot, pimento, and ginger: but not in quantities to make them of much national value. Mahogany is also cut here, and fustic. But sugar and rum are still the staples of the island. Now all the world knows that rum and sugar are made from the same plant.

And yet every one will tell you that the cane can hardly be got to thrive in Jamaica without slave labour; will tell you, also, that the land of Jamaica is so generous that it will give forth many of the most wonderful fruits of the world, almost without labour. Putting these two things together, would not any simple man advise them to abandon sugar? Ah! he would be very simple if he were to do so with a voice that could make itself well heard, and should dare to do so in Jamaica.

Men there are generally tolerant of opinion on most matters, and submit to be talked to on their own short-comings and colonial mismanagement with a decent grace.

You may advise them to do this, and counsel them to do that, referring to their own immediate concerns, without receiving that rebuke which your interference might probably deserve; but do not try their complaisance too far: do not advise them to give over making sugar. If you give such advice in a voice loud enough to be heard, the island will soon be too hot to hold you. Sugar is loved there, whether wisely loved or not. If not wisely, then too well.

When I hear a Jamaica planter talking of sugar, I cannot but think of Burns, and his muse that had made him poor and kept him so. And the planter is just as ready to give up his canes as the poet was to abandon his song.

The production of sugar and the necessary concomitant production of rum—for in Jamaica the two do necessarily go together—is not, one would say, an alluring occupation. I do not here intend to indulge my readers with a detailed description of the whole progress, from the planting or ratooning of the cane till the sugar and the rum are shipped. Books there are, no doubt, much wiser than mine in which the whole process is developed. But I would wish this much to be understood, that the sugar-planter, as things at present are, must attend to and be master of, and practically carry out three several trades. He must be an agriculturist, and grow his cane; and like all agriculturists must take his crop from the ground and have it ready for use; as the wheat grower does in England, and the cotton grower in America. But then he must also be a manufacturer, and that in a branch of manufacture which requires complicated machinery. The wheat grower does not grind his wheat and make it into bread. Nor does the cotton grower fabricate calico. But the grower of canes must make sugar. He must have his boiling-houses, and trash-houses; his water power and his steam power; he must dabble in machinery, and, in fact, be a Manchester manufacturer as well as a Kent farmer. And then, over and beyond this, he must be a distiller. The sugar leaves him fit for your puddings, and the rum fit for your punch—always excepting the slight article of adulteration which you are good enough to add afterwards yourselves. Such a complication of trades would not be thought very alluring to a gentleman farmer in England.

And yet the Jamaica proprietor holds faithfully by his sugar-canes.

It has been said that sugar is an article which for its proper production requires slave labour. That this is absolutely so is certainly not the fact, for very good sugar is made in Jamaica without it. That thousands of pounds could be made with slaves where only hundreds are made —or, as the case may be, are lost—without it, I do not doubt. The complaint generally resolves itself to this, that free labour in Jamaica cannot be commanded; that it cannot be had always, and up to a certain given quantity at a certain moment; that labour is scarce, and therefore high priced, and that labour being high priced, a negro can live on half a day's wages, and will not therefore work the whole day—will not always work any part of the day at all, seeing that his yams, his breadfruit, and his plantains are ready to his hands. But the slaves!— Oh! those were the good times!

I have in another chapter said a few words about the negroes as at present existing in Jamaica, I also shall say a few words as to slavery elsewhere; and I will endeavour not to repeat myself. This much, however, is at least clear to all men, that you cannot eat your cake and have it. You cannot abolish slavery to the infinite good of your souls, your minds, and intellects, and yet retain it for the good of your pockets. Seeing that these men are free, it is worse than useless to begrudge them the use of their freedom. If I have means to lie in the sun and meditate idle, why, O my worthy taskmaster! should you expect me to pull out at thy behest long reels of cotton, long reels of law jargon, long reels of official verbosity, long reels of gossamer literature. Why, indeed? Not having means so to lie, I do pull out the reels, taking such wages as I can get, and am thankful. But my friend and brother over there, my skin-polished, shining, oil-fat negro, is a richer man than I. He lies under his mango-tree, and eats the luscious fruit in the sun; he sends his black urchin up for a breadfruit, and behold the family table is spread. He pierces a cocoa-nut, and, lo! there is his beverage. He lies on the grass surrounded by oranges, bananas, and pine-apples. O my hard task-master of the sugar-mill, is he not better off than thou? why should he work at thy order? 'No, massa, me weak in me belly; me no workee to-day; me no like workee just 'em little moment.' Yes, Sambo has learned to have his own way; though hardly learned to claim his right without lying.

That this is all bad—bad nearly as bad can be—bad perhaps as anything short of slavery, all men will allow. It will be quite as bad in the long run for the negro as for the white man—worse, indeed; for the white man will by degrees wash his hands of the whole concern. But as matters are, one cannot wonder that the black man will not work. The question stands thus: cannot he be made to do so? Can it not be contrived that he shall be free, free as is the Englishman, and yet compelled, as is the Englishman, to eat his bread in the sweat of his brow?

I utterly disbelieve in statistics as a science, and am never myself guided by any long-winded statement of figures from a Chancellor of the Exchequer or such like big-wig. To my mind it is an hallucination. Such statements are 'ignes fatui.' Figures, when they go beyond six in number, represent to me not facts, but dreams, or sometimes worse than dreams. I have therefore no right myself to offer statistics to the reader. But it was stated in the Census taken in 1844 that there were sixteen thousand white people in the island, and about three hundred thousand blacks. There were also about seventy thousand coloured people. Putting aside for the moment the latter as a middle class, and regarding the black as the free servants of the white, one would say that labour should not be so deficient. But what if your free servants don't work; unfortunately know how to live without working?

The political question that presses upon one in viewing Jamaica, is certainly this—Will the growth of sugar pay in Jamaica, or will it not? I have already stated my conviction that a change is now taking place in the very blood and nature of the men who are destined to be the dominant classes in these western tropical latitudes. That the white man, the white Englishman, or white English Creole, will ever again be a thoroughly successful sugar grower in Jamaica I do not believe. That the brown man may be so is very probable; but great changes must first be made in the countries around him.

While the 'peculiar institution' exists in Cuba, Brazil, Porto Rico, and the Southern States, it cannot, I think, come to pass. A plentiful crop in Cuba may in any year bring sugar to a price which will give no return whatever to the Jamaica grower. A spare crop in Jamaica itself will have the same result; and there are many causes for spare crops; drought, for instance, and floods, and abounding rats, and want of capital to renew and manure the plants. At present the trade will only give in good years a fair profit to those who have purchased their land almost for nothing. A trade that cannot stand many misfortunes can hardly exist prosperously. This trade has stood very many; but I doubt whether it can stand more.

The 'peculiar institution,' however, will not live for
ever.   The time must come when abolition will be popular even in Louisiana.   And when it is law there, it will
be the law in Cuba also.   If that day shall have arrived
before the last sugar-mill in the island shall have been
stopped, Jamaica may then compete with other free
countries.   The world will not do without sugar, let it be
produced by slaves or free men.

But though a man may venture to foretell the abolition
of slavery in the States, and yet call himself no prophet,
he must be a wiser man than I who can foretell the time.
It will hardly be to-morrow ; nor yet the next day.   It
will scarcely come so that we may see it.   Before it does
come it may easily be that the last sugar-mill in poor
Jamaica will in truth have stopped.

CHAPTER VIII.

JAMAICA—EMPEROR SOULOUQUE.

We all remember the day when Mr. Smith landed at Newhaven and took up his abode quietly at the inn there. Poor Mr. Smith! In the ripeness of time he has betaken himself a stage further on his long journey, travelling now probably without disguise, either that of a citizen King or of a citizen Smith.

And now, following his illustrious example, the ex-Emperor Soulouque has sought the safety always to be found on English territories by sovereigns out of place. In January, 1859, his Highness landed at Kingston, Jamaica, having made his town of Port au Prince and his kingdom of Hayti somewhat too hot to hold him.

All the world probably knows that King Soulouque is a black man. One blacker never endured the meridian heat of a tropical sun.

The island which was christened Hispaniola by Columbus, has resumed its ancient name of Hayti. It is, however, divided into two kingdoms—two republics one may now say. That to the east is generally called St. Domingo, having borrowed the name given by Columbus to a town. This is by far the larger, but at the same time the poorer division of the island. That to the west is now called Hayti, and over this territory Soulouque reigned as emperor. He reigned as emperor, and was so styled, having been elected as President; in which little change in his state he has been imitated by a neighbour of ours with a success almost equal to his own.

For some dozen years the success of Soulouque was very considerable. He has had a dominion which has been almost despotic; and has, so rumour says, invested some three or four hundred thousand pounds in European funds. In this latter point his imitator has, I fear, hardly equalled him.

But a higher ambition fired the bosom of Soulouque, and he sighed after the territories of his neighbours—not generously to bestow them on other kings, but that he might keep them on his own behoof. Soulouque desired to be emperor of the whole island, and he sounded his trumpet and prepared his arms. He called together his army, and put on the boots of Bombastes. He put on the boots of Bombastes and bade his men meet him—at the Barley-mow or elsewhere.

But it seems that his men were slow in coming to the rendezvous. Nothing that Soulouque could say, nothing that he could do, no admonitions through his sternest government ministers, no reading of the mutiny act by his commanders and generals, would induce them actually to make an assault at arms. Then Soulouque was angry, and in his anger he maltreated his army. He put his men into pits, and kept them there without food; left them to be eaten by vermin—to be fed upon while they could not feed; and played, upon the whole, such a melo-drama of autocratic tricks and fantasies as might have done honour to a white Nero. Then at last black human nature could endure no more, and Soulouque, dreading a pit for his own majesty, was forced to run.

In one respect he was more fortunate than Mr. Smith. In his dire necessity an English troop-ship was found to be at hand. The 'Melbourne' was steaming home from

Jamaica, and the officer in command having been appealed to for assistance, consented to return to Kingston with the royal suite. This she did; and on the 22nd of January, Soulouque, with his wife and daughter, his prime minister, and certain coal-black maids of honour, was landed at the quays.

When under the ægis of British protection the ex-emperor was of course safe. But he had not exactly chosen a bed of roses for himself in coming to Jamaica. It might be probable that a bed of roses was not easily to be found at the moment. At Kingston there were collected many Haytians, who had either been banished by Soulouque in the plenitude of his power, or had run from him as he was now running from his subjects. There were many whose brothers and fathers had been destroyed in Hayti, whose friends had perished under the hands of the tyrant's executioner, for whom pits would have been prepared had they not vanished speedily. These refugees had sought safety also in Jamaica, and for them a day of triumph had now arrived. They were not the men to allow an opportunity for triumph to pass without enjoying it.

These were mostly brown men—men of a mixed race; men, and indeed women also. With Soulouque and his government such had found no favour. He had been glad to welcome white residents in his kingdom, and of course had rejoiced in having black men as his subjects. But of the coloured people he had endeavoured in every way to rid himself. He had done so to a great extent, and many of them were now ready to welcome him at Kingston.

Kingston does not rejoice in public equipages of much pretension; nor are there to be hired many carriages fit for the conveyance of royalty, even in its decadence. Two small, wretched vehicles were however procured, such as ply in the streets there, and carry passengers to the Spanish

Town railway at sixpence a head. In one of these sat
Soulouque and his wife, with a British officer on the box
beside the driver, and with two black policemen hanging
behind. In another, similarly guarded, were packed the
Countess Olive—that being the name of the ex-emperor's
daughter—and her attendants. And thus, travelling by
different streets, they made their way to their hotel.

One would certainly have wished, in despite of those
wretched pits, that they had been allowed to do so without annoyance; but such was not the case. The banished
Haytians had it not in their philosophy to abstain from
triumphing on a fallen enemy. They surrounded the
carriages with a dusky cloud, and received the fugitives
with howls of self-congratulation at their abasement. Nor
was this all. When the royal party was duly lodged at
the Date-Tree tavern, the ex-Haytians lodged themselves
opposite. There they held a dignity ball in token of
their joy; and for three days maintained their position in
order that poor Soulouque might witness their rejoicings.

'They have said a mass over him, the wretched being!'
said the landlady of my hotel to me, triumphantly.

'Said a mass over him?'

'Yes, the black nigger;—king, indeed! said a mass over
him 'cause he's down. Thank God for that! And pray
God keep him so. Him king indeed, the black nigger!'
All which could not have been comfortable for poor
Soulouque.

The royal party had endeavoured in the first instance
to take up their quarters at this lady's hotel, or lodging-
house, as they are usually called. But the patriotic sister
of Mrs. Seacole would listen to no such proposition. 'I
won't keep a house for black men,' she said to me. 'As
for kings, I would despise myself to have a black king.
As for that black beast and his black women—Bah!'
Now this was certainly magnanimous, for Soulouque would

have been prepared to pay well for his accommodation. But the ordinary contempt which the coloured people have for negroes was heightened in this case by the presumption of black royalty—perhaps also by loyalty. ' Queen Victoria is my king,' said Mrs. Seacole's sister.

I must confess that I endeavoured to excite her loyalty rather than her compassion. A few friends were to dine with me that day ; and where would have been my turtle soup had Soulouque and his suite taken possession of the house ?

The deposed tyrant, when he left Hayti, published a short manifesto, in which he set forth that he, Faustin the First, having been elected by the free suffrages of his fellow countrymen, had endeavoured to govern them well, actuated by a pure love of his country; that he had remained at his post as long as his doing so had been pleasing to his countrymen; but that now, having discovered by sure symptoms that his countrymen desired to see him no longer on the throne, he voluntarily and immediately abdicated his seat. From henceforth he could only wish well to the prosperity of Hayti.

Free suffrages of his people! Ah, me! Such farces strike us but as farces when Hayti and such like lands are concerned. But when they come nearer to us they are very sad.

Soulouque is a stout, hale man, apparently of sixty-five or sixty-eight years of age. It is difficult to judge of the expression of a black man's face unless it be very plainly seen ; but it appeared to me to be by no means repulsive. He has been, I believe, some twelve years Emperor of Hayti, and as he has escaped with wealth, he cannot be said to have been unfortunate.

CHAPTER IX.

JAMAICA—THE GOVERNMENT.

QUEEN, Lords, and Commons, with the full paraphernalia of triple readings, adjournments of the house, and counting out, prevails in Jamaica as it does in Great Britain.

By this it will be understood that there is a Governor, representing the Crown, whose sanction or veto is of course given, as regards important measures, in accordance with instructions from the Colonial Office. The Governor has an Executive Committee, which tallies with our Cabinet. It consists at present of three members, one of whom belongs to the upper House and two to the lower. The Governor may appoint a fourth member if it so please him. These gentlemen are paid for their services, and preside over different departments, as do our Secretaries of State, &c. And there is a Most Honourable Privy Council, just as we have at home. Of this latter, the members may or may not support the Governor, seeing that they are elected for life.

The House of Lords is represented by the Legislative Council. This quasi-peerage is of course not hereditary, but the members sit for life, and are nominated by the Governor. They are seventeen in number. The Legislative Council can of course put a veto on any bill.

The House of Assembly stands in the place of the

House of Commons. It consists of forty-seven members, two being elected by nineteen parishes, and three each by three other parishes, those, namely, which contain the towns of Kingston, Spanish Town, and Port Royal.

In one respect this House of Commons falls short of the privileges and powers of our House at home. It cannot suggest money bills. No honourable member can make a proposition that so much a year shall be paid for such a purpose. The government did not wish to be driven to exercise the invidious power of putting repeated vetos on repeated suggestions for semi-public expenditure; and therefore this power has been taken away. But any honourable member can bring before the House a motion to the effect that the Governor be recommended himself to propose, by one of the Executive Committee, such or such a money bill; and then if the Governor decline, the House can refuse to pass his supplies, and can play the 'red devil' with his Excellency. So that it seems to come pretty nearly to the same thing.

At home in England, Crown Lords and Commons really seem to do very well. Some may think that the system wants a little shove this way, some the other. Reform may, or may not, be more or less needed. But on the whole we are governed honestly, liberally, and successfully; with at least a greater share of honesty, liberality, and success than has fallen to the lot of most other people. Each of the three estates enjoys the respect of the people at large, and a seat, either among the Lords or the Commons, is an object of high ambition. The system may therefore be said to be successful.

But it does not follow that because it answers in England it should answer in Jamaica; that institutions which suit the country which is perhaps in the whole world the furthest advanced in civilization, wealth, and public honesty, should suit equally well an island which is unfortunately very far from being advanced in those good qualities; whose civilization, as regards the bulk of the population, is hardly above that of savages, whose wealth has vanished, and of whose public honesty—I will say nothing. Of that I myself will say nothing, but the Jamaicans speak of it in terms which are not flattering to their own land.

I do not think that the system does answer in Jamaica. In the first place, it must be remembered that it is carried on there in a manner very different from that exercised in our other West-Indian colonies. In Jamaica any man may vote who pays either tax or rent; but by a late law he must put in his claim to vote on a ten shilling stamp. There are in round numbers three hundred thousand blacks, seventy thousand coloured people, and fifteen thousand white; it may therefore easily be seen in what hands the power of electing must rest. Now in Barbados no coloured man votes at all. A coloured man or negro is doubtless qualified to vote if he own a freehold; but then, care is taken that such shall not own freeholds. In Trinidad, the legislative power is almost entirely in the hands of the Crown. In Guiana, which I look upon as the best governed of them all, this is very much the case.

It is not that I would begrudge the black man the right of voting because he is black, or that I would say that he is and must be unfit to vote, or unfit even to sit in a house of assembly; but the amalgamation as at present existing is bad. The objects sought after by a free and open representation of the people are not gained unless those men are as a rule returned who are most respected in the commonwealth, so that the body of which they are the units may be respected also. This object is not achieved in Jamaica, and consequently the House of Assembly is not respected. It does not contain the men of most weight and condition in the island, and is contemptuously spoken of even in Jamaica itself, and even by its own members.

Some there are, some few, who have gotten themselves to be elected, in order that things which are already bad may not, if such can be avoided, become worse. They, no doubt, are those who best do their duty by the country in which their lot lies. But, for the most part, those who should represent Jamaica will not condescend to take part in the debates, nor will they solicit the votes of the negroes.

It would appear from these observations as though I thought that the absolute ascendency of the white man should still be maintained in Jamaica. By no means. Let him be ascendant who can—in Jamaica or elsewhere —who honestly can. I doubt whether such ascendency, the ascendency of Europeans and white Creoles, can be longer maintained in this island. It is not even now maintained; and for that reason chiefly I hold that this system of Lords and Commons is not compatible with the present genius of the place. Let coloured men fill the public offices, and enjoy the sweets of official pickings. I would by no means wish to interfere with any good things which fortune may be giving them in this respect. But I think there would be greater probability of their advancing in their new profession honestly and usefully, if they could be made to look more to the Colonial Office at home, and less to the native legislature.

At home, no member of the House of Commons can hold a government contract. The members of the House of Assembly in Jamaica have no such prejudicial embargo attached to the honour of their seats. They can hold the government contracts; and it is astonishing how many of them are in their hands.

The great point which strikes a stranger is this, that the House of Assembly is not respected in the island.

Jamaicans themselves have no confidence in it. If the white men could be polled, the majority I think would prefer to be rid of it altogether, and to be governed, as Trinidad is governed, by a Governor with a council; of course with due power of reference to the Colonial Office.

Let any man fancy what England would be if the House of Commons were ludicrous in the eyes of Englishmen; if men ridiculed or were ashamed of all their debates. Such is the case as regards the Jamaica House of Commons.

In truth, there is not room for a machinery so complicated in this island. The handful of white men can no longer have it all their own way; and as for the negroes —let any warmest advocate of the 'man and brother' position say whether he has come across three or four of the class who are fit to enact laws for their own guidance and the guidance of others.

It pains me to write words which may seem to be opposed to humanity and a wide philanthropy; but a spade is a spade, and it is worse than useless to say that it is something else.

The proof of the truth of what I say with reference to this system of Lords and Commons is to be found in the eating of the pudding. It may not perhaps be fair to adduce the prosperity of Barbados, and to compare it with the adversity of Jamaica, seeing that local circumstances were advantageous to Barbados at the times of emancipation and equalization of the sugar duties. Barbados was always able to command a plentiful supply of labour. But it is quite fair to compare Jamaica with Guiana or Trinidad. In both these colonies the negro was as well able to shirk his work as in Jamaica.

And in these two colonies the negro did shirk his work, just as he did in Jamaica; and does still to a great extent.

The limits of these colonies are as extensive as Jamaica is, and the negro can squat. They are as fertile as Jamaica is, and the negro can procure his food almost without trouble. But not the less is it a fact that the exportation of sugar from Guiana and Trinidad now exceeds the amount exported in the time of slavery, while the export-ation from Jamaica is almost as nothing.

But in Trinidad and Guiana they have no House of Commons, with Mr. Speaker, three readings, motions for adjournment, and unlimited powers of speech. In those colonies the governments— acting with such assistance as was necessary—have succeeded in getting foreign labour. In Jamaica they have as yet but succeeded in talking about it. In Guiana and Trinidad they make much sugar, and boast loudly of making more. In Jamaica they make but very little, and have not self-confidence enough left with them to make any boast whatsoever.

With all the love that an Englishman should have for a popular parliamentary representation, I cannot think it adapted to a small colony, even were that colony not from circumstances so peculiarly ill fitted for it as is Jamaica. In Canada and Australia it is no doubt very well; the spirit of a fresh and energetic people struggling on into the world's eminence will produce men fit for debating, men who can stand on their legs without mak-ing a house of legislature ridiculous. But what could Lords and Commons do in Malta, or in Jersey? What would they do in the Scilly Islands? What have they been doing in the Ionian Islands? And, alas! what have they done in Jamaica?

Her roads are almost impassable, her bridges are broken down, her coffee plantations have gone back to bush, her sugar estates have been sold for the value of the sugar-boilers. Kingston as a town is the most deplorable that man ever visited, unless it be that Spanish Town is worse.

And yet they have Lords and Commons with all but unlimited powers of making motions! It has availed them
nothing, and I fear will avail them nothing.

This I know may be said, that be the Lords and Commons there for good or evil, they are to be moved neither
by men nor gods. It is I imagine true, that no power
known to the British empire could deprive Jamaica of
her constitution. It has had some kind of a house of
assembly since the time of Charles II.; nay, I believe,
since the days of Cromwell; which by successive doctor-
ing has grown to be such a parody, as it now is, on our
home mode of doing business. How all this may now
be altered and brought back to reason, perhaps no man
can say. Probably it cannot be altered till some further
smash shall come; but it is not on that account the less
objectionable.

The House of Assembly and the Chamber of the
Legislative Council are both situated in the same square
with the Governor's mansion in Spanish Town. The
desolateness of this place I have attempted to describe
elsewhere, and yet, when I was there, Parliament was
sitting! What must the place be during the nine months
when Parliament does not sit? They are yellow buildings, erected at considerable expense, and not without
some pretence. But nevertheless, they are ugly—ugly from
their colour, ugly from the heat, and ugly from a certain
heaviness which seems natural to them and to the place.

The house itself in which the forty-seven members sit
is comfortable enough, and not badly adapted for its
purposes. The Speaker sits at one end all in full fig, with
a clerk at the table below; opposite to him, two-thirds
down the room, a low bar, about four feet high, runs
across it. As far as this the public are always admitted;
and when any subject of special interest is under discus-
sion twelve or fifteen persons may be seen there assembled.

Then there is a side room opening from the house, into which members take their friends. Indeed it is, I believe, generally open to any one wearing a decent coat. There is the Bellamy of the establishment, in which honourable members take such refreshment as the warmth of the debate may render necessary. Their tastes seemed to me to be simple, and to addict themselves chiefly to rum and water.

I was throwing away my cigar as I entered the precincts of the house. 'Oh, you can smoke,' said my friend to me; 'only, when you stand at the doorway, don't let the Speaker's eye catch the light; but it won't much matter.' So I walked on, and stood at the side door, smoking my cigar indeed, but conscious that I was desecrating the place.

I saw five or six coloured gentlemen in the house, and two negroes—sitting in the house as members. As far as the two latter men were concerned, I could not but be gratified to see them in the fair enjoyment of the objects of a fair ambition. Had they not by efforts of their own made themselves greatly superior to others of their race, they would not have been there. I say this, fearing that it may be thought that I begrudge a black man such a position. I begrudge the black men nothing that they can honestly lay hands on; but I think that we shall benefit neither them nor ourselves by attempting with a false philanthropy to make them out to be other than they are.

The subject under debate was a railway bill. The railway system is not very extended in the island; but there is a railway, and the talk was of prolonging it. Indeed, the house I believe had on some previous occasion decided that it should be prolonged, and the present fight was as to some particular detail. What that detail was I did not learn, for the business being performed was a continual series of motions for adjournment carried on by a victorious minority of three.

It was clear that the conquered majority of—say thirty —was very angry. For some reason, appertaining probably to the tactics of the house, these thirty were exceedingly anxious to have some special point carried and put out of the way that night, but the three were inexorable. Two of the three spoke continually, and ended every speech with a motion for adjournment.

And then there was a disagreement among the thirty. Some declared all this to be 'bosh,' proposed to leave the house without any adjournment, play whist, and let the three victors enjoy their barren triumph. Others, made of sterner stuff, would not thus give way. One after another they made impetuous little speeches, then two at a time, and at last three. They thumped the table, and called each other pretty names, walked about furiously, and devoted the three victors to the infernal gods.

And then one of the black gentlemen arose, and made a calm, deliberate little oration. The words he spoke were about the wisest which were spoken that night, and yet they were not very wise. He offered to the house a few platitudes on the general benefit of railways, which would have applied to any railway under the sun, saying that eggs and fowls would be taken to market; and then he sat down. On his behalf I must declare that there were no other words of such wisdom spoken that night. But this relief lasted only for three minutes.

After a while two members coming to the door declared that it was becoming unbearable, and carried me away to play whist. 'My place is close by,' said one, 'and if the row becomes hot we shall hear it. It is dreadful to stay there with such an object, and with the certainty of missing one's object after all.' As I was inclined to agree with him, I went away and played whist.

But soon a storm of voices reached our ears round the card-table. 'They are hard at it now,' said one honour-

able member. 'That's So-and-So, by the screech.' The
yell might have been heard at Kingston, and no doubt
was.

'By heavens they are at it,' said another. 'Ha, ha,
ha! A nice house of assembly, isn't it?'

'Will they pitch into one another?' I asked, thinking
of scenes of which I had read of in another country; and
thinking also, I must confess, that an absolute bodily
scrimmage on the floor of the house might be worth
seeing.

'They don't often do that,' said my friend. 'They
trust chiefly to their voices; but there's no knowing.'

The temptation was too much for me, so I threw down
my cards and rushed back to the Assembly. When I
arrived the louder portion of the noise was being made
by one gentleman who was walking round and round the
chamber, swearing in a loud voice that he would resign
the very moment the Speaker was seated in the chair;
for at that time the house was in committee. The louder
portion of the noise, I say, for two other honourable members were speaking, and the rest were discussing the matter
in small parties.

'Shameful, abominable, scandalous, rascally!' shouted
the angry gentleman over and over again, as he paced
round and round the chamber. 'I'll not sit in such a
house; no man should sit in such a house. By G—, I'll
resign as soon as I see the Speaker in that chair. Sir,
come and have a drink of rum and water.'

In his angry wanderings his steps had brought him to
the door at which I was standing, and these last words
were addressed to me. 'Come and have a drink of rum
and water,' and he seized me with a hospitable violence
by the arm. I did not dare to deny so angry a legislator,
and I drank the rum and water. Then I returned to my
cards.

It may be said that nearly the same thing does sometimes occur in our own House of Commons—always omitting the threats of resignation and the drink. With us at home a small minority may impede the business of the house by adjournments, and members sometimes become loud and angry. But in Jamaica the storm raged in so small a teapot! The railway extension was to be but for a mile or two, and I fear would hardly benefit more than the eggs and fowls for which the dark gentleman pleaded.

In heading this chapter I have spoken of the government, and it may be objected to me that in writing it I have written only of the legislature, and not at all of the mode of governing. But in truth the mode of government depends entirely on the mode of legislature.

As regards the Governor himself and his ministers, I do not doubt that they do their best; but I think that their best might be much better if their hands were not so closely tied by this teapot system of Queen, Lords, and Commons.

CHAPTER X.

CUBA.

CUBA is the largest and the most westerly of the West Indian islands. It is in the shape of a half-moon, and with one of its horns nearly lies across the mouth of the Gulf of Mexico. It belongs to the Spanish crown, of which it is by far the most splendid appendage. So much for facts —geographical and historical.

The journey from Kingston to Cien Fuegos, of which I have said somewhat in my first chapter, was not completed under better auspices than those which witnessed its commencement. That perfidious bark, built in the eclipse, was bad to the last, and my voyage took nine days instead of three. My humble stock of provisions had long been all gone, and my patience was nearly at as low an ebb. Then, as a finale, the Cuban pilot who took us in hand as we entered the port, ran us on shore just under the Spanish fort, and there left us. From this position it was impossible to escape, though the shore lay close to us, inasmuch as it is an offence of the gravest nature to land in those ports without the ceremony of a visit from the medical officer ; and no medical officer would come to us there. And then two of our small crew had been taken sick, and we had before us in our mind's eye all the pleasures of quarantine.

A man, and especially an author, is thankful for calamities if they be of a tragic dye. It would be as good as a small fortune to be left for three days without food or water, or to run for one's life before a black storm on unknown seas in a small boat. But we had no such luck as this. There was plenty of food, though it was not very palatable; and the peril of our position cannot be insisted on, as we might have thrown a baby on shore from the vessel, let alone a biscuit. We did what we could to get up a catastrophe among the sharks, by bathing off the ship's sides. But even this was in vain. One small shark we did see. But in lieu of it eating us, we ate it. In spite of the popular prejudice, I have to declare that it was delicious.

But at last I did find myself in the hotel at Cien Fuegos. And here I must say a word in praise of the civility of the Spanish authorities of that town—and, indeed, of those gentlemen generally wherever I chanced to meet them. They welcome you with easy courtesy; offer you coffee or beer; assure you at parting that their whole house is at your disposal; and then load you—at least they so loaded me—with cigars.

' My friend,' said the captain of the port, holding in his hand a huge parcel of these articles, each about seven inches long—' I wish I could do you a service. It would make me happy for ever if I could truly serve you.'

' Señor, the service you have done me is inestimable in allowing me to make the acquaintance of Don ——.'

' But at least accept these few cigars;' and then he pressed the bundle into my hand, and pressed his own hand over mine. ' Smoke one daily after dinner; and when you procure any that are better, do a fastidious old smoker the great kindness to inform him where they are to be found.'

This treasure to which his fancy alluded, but in the

existence of which he will never believe, I have not yet discovered.

Cien Fuegos is a small new town on the southern coast of Cuba, created by the sugar trade, and devoted, of course, to commerce. It is clean, prosperous, and quickly increasing. Its streets are lighted with gas, while those in the Havana still depend upon oil-lamps. It has its opera, its governor's house, its alaméda, its military and public hospital, its market-place, and railway station; and unless the engineers deceive themselves, it will in time have its well. It has also that institution which in the eyes of travellers ranks so much above all others, a good and clean inn.

My first object after landing was to see a slave sugar estate. I had been told in Jamaica that to effect this required some little management; that the owners of the slaves were not usually willing to allow strangers to see them at work; and that the manufacture of sugar in Cuba was as a rule kept sacred from profane eyes. But I found no such difficulty. I made my request to an English merchant at Cien Fuegos, and he gave me a letter of introduction to the proprietor of an estate some fifteen miles from the town; and by their joint courtesy I saw all that I wished.

On this property, which consisted altogether of eighteen hundred acres—the greater portion of which was not yet under cultivation—there were six hundred acres of cane pieces. The average year's produce was eighteen hundred hogsheads, or three hogsheads to the acre. The hogshead was intended to represent a ton of sugar when it reached the market, but judging from all that I could learn, it usually fell short of it by more than a hundredweight. The value of such a hogshead at Cien Fuegos was about twenty-five pounds. There were one hundred and fifty negro men on the estate, the average cash value of each man being three hundred and fifty pounds; most of the men had their wives. In stating this it must not be supposed that either I or my informant insist much on the validity of their marriage ceremony; any such ceremony was probably of rare occurrence. During the crop time, at which period my visit was made, and which lasts generally from November till May, the negroes sleep during six hours out of the twenty-four, have two for their meals, and work for sixteen! No difference is made on Sunday. Their food is very plentiful, and of a good and strong description. They are sleek and fat and large, like well-preserved brewers' horses; and with reference to them, as also with reference to the brewers' horses, it has probably been ascertained what amount of work may be exacted so as to give the greatest profit. During the remainder of the year the labour of the negroes averages twelve hours a day, and one day of rest in the week is usually allowed to them.

I was of course anxious to see what was the nature of the coercive measures used with them. But in this respect my curiosity was not indulged. I can only say that I saw none, and saw the mark and signs of none. No doubt the whip is in use, but I did not see it. The gentleman whose estate I visited had no notice of our coming, and there was no appearance of anything being hidden from us. I could not, however, bring myself to inquire of him as to their punishment.

The slaves throughout the island are always as a rule baptized. Those who are employed in the town and as household servants appear to be educated in compliance with, at any rate the outward doctrines of, the Roman Catholic church. But with the great mass of the negroes —those who work on the sugar-canes—all attention to religion ends with their baptism. They have the advantage, whatever it may be, of that ceremony in infancy; and from that time forth they are treated as the beasts of the stall.

From all that I could hear, as well as from what I could see, I have reason to think that, regarding them as beasts, they are well treated. Their hours of labour are certainly very long—so long as to appear almost impossible to a European workman. But under the system, such as it is, the men do not apparently lose their health, though, no doubt, they become prematurely old, and as a rule die early. The property is too valuable to be neglected or ill used. The object of course is to make that property pay; and therefore a present healthy condition is cared for, but long life is not regarded. It is exactly the same with horses in this country.

When all has been said that can be said in favour of the slave-owner in Cuba, it comes to this—that he treats his slaves as beasts of burden, and so treating them, does it skilfully and with prudence. The point which most shocks an Englishman is the absence of all religion, the ignoring of the black man's soul. But this, perhaps, may be taken as an excuse, that the white men here ignore their own souls also. The Roman Catholic worship seems to be at a lower ebb in Cuba than almost any country in which I have seen it.

It is singular that no priest should even make any effort on the subject with regard to the negroes; but I am assured that such is the fact. They do not wish to do so; nor will they allow of any one asking them to make the experiment. One would think that had there been any truth or any courage in them, they would have declared the inutility of baptism, and have proclaimed that negroes have no souls. But there is no truth in them; neither is there any courage.

The works at the Cuban sugar estate were very different from those I had seen at Jamaica. They were on a much larger scale, in much better order, overlooked by a larger proportion of white men, with a greater amount of skilled labour.   The evidences of capital were very plain in Cuba ; whereas, the want of it was frequently equally plain in our own island.

Not that the planters in Cuba are as a rule themselves very rich men.   The estates are deeply mortgaged to the different merchants at the different ports, as are those in Jamaica to the merchants of Kingston.   These merchants in Cuba are generally Americans, Englishmen, Germans, Spaniards from the American Republics—anything but Cubans ; and the slave-owners are but the go-betweens who secure the profits of the slave-trade for the merchants.

My friend at the estate invited us to a late breakfast after having shown me what I came to see.   ' You have taken me so unawares,' said he, ' that we cannot offer you much except a welcome.'   Well, it was not much—for Cuba perhaps.   A delicious soup, made partly of eggs, a bottle of excellent claret, a paté de foie gras, some game deliciously dressed, and half a dozen kinds of vegetables ; that was all.   I had seen nothing among the slaves which in any way interfered with my appetite, or with the cup of coffee and cigar which came after the little nothings above mentioned.

We then went down to the railway station.   It was a peculiar station I was told, and the tickets could not be paid for till we reached Cien Fuegos.   But, lo ! on arriving at Cien Fuegos there was nothing more to pay. ' It has all been done,' said some one to me.

If one was but convinced that those sleek, fat, smiling bipeds were but two legged beasts of burden, and nothing more, all would have been well at the estate which we visited.

All Cuba was of course full of the late message from

the President of the United States, which at the time of my visit was some two months old there. The purport of what Mr. Buchanan said regarding Cuba may perhaps be expressed as follows :—' Circumstances and destiny absolutely require that the United States should be the masters of that island. That we should take it by fili-bustering or violence is not in accordance with our national genius. It will suit our character and honesty much better that we should obtain it by purchase. Let us therefore offer a fair price for it. If a fair price be refused, that of course will be a casus belli. Spain will then have injured us, and we may declare war. Under these circumstances we should probably obtain the place without purchase ; but let us hope better things.' This is what the President has said, either in plain words or by inference equally plain.

It may easily be conceived with what feeling such an announcement has been received by Spain, and those who hold Spanish authority in Cuba. There is an outspoken insolence in the threat, which, by a first-class power, would itself have been considered a cause for war. But Spain is not a first-class power, and like the other weak ones of the earth, must either perish or live by adhering to and obeying those who will protect her. Though too ignoble to be strong, she has been too proud to be obedient. And as a matter of course she will go to the wall.

A scrupulous man who feels that he would fain regulate his course in politics by the same line as that used for his ordinary life, cannot but feel angry at the loud tone of America's audacious threat. But even such a one knows that that threat will sooner or later be carried out, and that humanity will benefit by its accomplishment. Per-haps it may be said that scrupulous men should have but little dealing in state policy.

K 2

The plea under which Mr. Buchanan proposes to quarrel
with Spain, if she will not sell that which America wishes
to buy, is the plea under which Ahab quarrelled with
Naboth. A man is, individually, disgusted that a President of the United States should have made such an
utterance. But looking at the question in a broader point
of view, in one which regards future ages rather than the
present time, one can hardly refrain from rejoicing at any
event which will tend to bring about that which in itself is
so desirable.

We reprobate the name of filibuster, and have a holy
horror of the trade. And it is perhaps fortunate that
with us the age of individual filibustering is well-nigh
gone by. But it may be fair for us to consider whether
we have not in our younger days done as much in this
line as have the Americans—whether Clive, for instance,
was not a filibuster—or Warren Hastings. Have we not
annexed, and maintained, and encroached; protected, and
assumed, and taken possession in the East—doing it all of
course for the good of humanity? And why should we
begrudge the same career to America?

That we do begrudge it is certain. That she purchased
California and took Texas went at first against the grain
with us; and Englishmen, as a rule, would wish to
maintain Cuba in the possession of Spain. But what
Englishman who thinks about it will doubt that California and Texas have thriven since they were annexed,
as they never could have thriven while forming part of
the Mexican empire—or can doubt that Cuba, if delivered
up to the States, would gain infinitely by such a change
of masters?

Filibustering, called by that or some other name, is
the destiny of a great portion of that race to which we
Englishmen and Americans belong. It would be a bad
profession probably for a scrupulous man. With the

unscrupulous man, what stumbling-blocks there may be
between his deeds and his conscience is for his consideration and for God's judgment. But it will hardly suit
us as a nation to be loud against it. By what other
process have poor and weak races been compelled to give
way to those who have power and energy? And who
have displaced so many of the poor and weak, and spread
abroad so vast an energy, such an extent of power as we
of England?

The truth may perhaps be this :—that a filibuster needs
expect no good word from his fellow-mortals till he has
proved his claim to it by success.

From such information as I could obtain, I am of
opinion that the Cubans themselves would be glad enough
to see the transfer well effected. How, indeed, can it be
otherwise? At present they have no national privilege
except that of undergoing taxation. Every office is held
by a Spaniard. Every soldier in the island—and they
say that there are twenty-five thousand—must be a
Spaniard. The ships of war are commanded and manned
by Spaniards. All that is shown before their eyes of
brilliancy and power and high place is purely Spanish.
No Cuban has any voice in his own country. He can
never have the consolation of thinking that his tyrant is
his countryman, or reflect that under altered circumstances it might possibly have been his fortune to
tyrannize. What love can he have for Spain? He
cannot even have the poor pride of being slave to a
great lord. He is the lacquey of a reduced gentleman,
and lives on the vails of those who despise his master.
Of course the transfer would be grateful to him.

But no Cuban will himself do anything to bring it
about. To wish is one thing; to act is another. A man
standing behind his counter may feel that his hand is
restricted on every side, and his taxes alone unrestricted ;

but he must have other than Hispano-Creole blood in
his veins if he do more than stand and feel. Indeed,
wishing is too strong a word to be fairly applicable to
his state of mind. He would be glad that Cuba should
be American ; but he would prefer that he himself should
lie in a dormant state while the dangerous transfer is
going on.

I have ventured to say that humanity would certainly
be benefited by such a transfer. We, when we think of
Cuba, think of it almost entirely as a slave country.
And, indeed, in this light, and in this light only, is it
peculiar, being the solitary land into which slaves are
now systematically imported out of Africa. Into that
great question of guarding the slave coast it would be
futile here to enter ; but this I believe is acknowledged,
that if the Cuban market be closed against the trade, the
trade must perish of exhaustion. At present slaves are
brought into Cuba in spite of us ; and, as we all know,
can be brought in under the American stars and stripes.
But no one accuses the American Government of systematically favouring an importation of Africans into their
own States. When Cuba becomes one of them the trade
will cease. The obstacle to that trade which is created
by our vessels of war on the coast of Africa may, or may
not, be worth the cost. But no man who looks into the
subject will presume to say that we can be as efficacious
there as the Americans would be if they were the owners
of the present slave-market.

I do not know whether it be sufficiently understood in
England, that though slavery is an institution of the
United States, the slave-trade, as commonly understood
under that denomination, is as illegal there as in England.
That slavery itself would be continued in Cuba under the
Americans—continued for a while—is of course certain.
So is it in Louisiana and the Carolinas. But the horrors

of the middle passage, the kidnapping of negroes, the African wars which are waged for the sake of prisoners, would of necessity come to an end.

But this slave-trade is as opposed to the laws of Spain and its colonies as it is to those of the United States or of Great Britain. This is true; and were the law carried out in Cuba as well as it is in the United States, an Englishman would feel disinclined to look on with calmness at the violent dismemberment of the Spanish empire. But in Cuba the law is broken systematically. The Captain-General in Cuba will allow no African to be imported into the island—except for a consideration. It is said that the present Captain-General receives only a gold doubloon, or about three pounds twelve shillings, on every head of wool so brought in; and he has therefore the reputation of being a very moderate man. O'Donnel required twice as large a bribe. Valdez would take nothing, and he is spoken of as the foolish Governor. Even he, though he would take no bribe, was not allowed to throw obstacles in the way of the slave-trade. That such a bribe is usually demanded, and as a matter of course paid, is as well known—ay, much better known, than any other of the island port duties. The fact is so notorious to all men, that it is almost as absurd to insist on it as it would be to urge that the income of the Queen of England is paid from the taxes. It is known to every one, and among others is known to the government of Spain. Under these circumstances, who can feel sympathy with her, or wish that she should retain her colony? Does she not daily show that she is unfit to hold it?

There must be some stage in misgovernment which will justify the interference of by-standing nations, in the name of humanity. That rule in life which forbids a man to come between a husband and his wife is a good rule. But nevertheless, who can stand by quiescent and see a brute half murder the poor woman whom he should protect?

And in other ways, and through causes also, humanity would be benefited by such a transfer. We in England are not very fond of a republic. We would hardly exchange our throne for a president's chair, or even dispense at present with our House of Peers or our Bench of Bishops. But we can see that men thrive under the stars and stripes; whereas they pine beneath the red and yellow flag of Spain. This, it may be said, is attributable to the race of the men rather than to the government. But the race will be improved by the infusion of new blood. Let the world say what chance there is of such improvement in the Spanish government.

The trade of the country is falling into the hands of foreigners—into those principally of Americans from the States. The Havana will soon become as much American as New Orleans. It requires but little of the spirit of prophecy to foretell that the Spanish rule will not be long obeyed by such people.

On the whole I cannot see how Englishmen can refrain from sympathizing with the desire of the United States to become possessed of this fertile island. As far as we ourselves are concerned, it would be infinitely for our benefit. We can trade with the United States when we can hardly do so with Spain. Moreover, if Jamaica and the smaller British islands can ever again hold up their heads against Cuba as sugar-producing colonies, it will be when the slave-trade has been abolished. Till such time it can never be.

And then where are our professions for the amelioration, and especially for the Christianity of the human race? I have said what is the religious education of the slaves in Cuba. I may also say that in this island no place of Protestant worship exists, or is possible. The

Roman Catholic religion is alone allowed, and that is at its very lowest point. 'The old women of both sexes go to mass,' a Spaniard told me; 'and the girls when their clothes are new.'

But above all things it behoves us to rid ourselves of the jealousy which I fear we too often feel towards American pretension. 'Jonathan is getting bumptious,' we are apt to say; 'he ought to have ——' this and that other punishment, according to the taste of the offended Englishman.

Jonathan is becoming bumptious, no doubt. Young men of genius, when they succeed in life at comparatively early years, are generally afflicted more or less with this disease. But one is not inclined to throw aside as useless, the intellect, energy, and genius of youth because it is not accompanied by modesty, grace, and self-denial. Do we not, in regard to all our friends, take the good that we find in them, aware that in the very best there will be some deficiency to forgive? That young barrister who is so bright, so energetic, so useful, is perhaps *soi-disant* more than a little. One cannot deny it. But age will cure that. Have we a right to expect that he should be perfect?

And are the Americans the first bumptious people on record? Has no other nation assumed itself to be in advance of the world; to be the apostle of progress, the fountain of liberty, the rock-spring of manly work? If the Americans were not bumptious, how unlike would they be to the parent that bore them!

The world is wide enough for us and for our offspring, and we may be well content that we have it nearly all between us. Let them fulfil their destiny in the West, while we do so in the East. It may be that there also we may establish another child who in due time shall also run alone, shall also boast somewhat loudly of its own doings. It is a proud reflection that we alone, of all people, have such children; a proud reflection, and a joyous one; though the weaning of the baby will always be in some respects painful to the mother.

Nowhere have I met a kinder hospitality than I did at Cien Fuegos, whether from Spaniards, Frenchmen, Americans, or Englishmen; for at Cien Fuegos there are men of all these countries. But I must specify my friend Mr. M——. Why should such a man be shut up for life at such an outlandish place? Full of wit, singing an excellent song, telling a story better, I think, than any other man to whom I have ever listened, speaking four or five languages fluently, pleasant in manner, hospitable in heart, a thorough good fellow at all points, why should he bury himself at Cien Fuegos? 'Auri sacra fames.' It is the presumable reason for all such burials. English reader, shouldst thou find thyself at Cien Fuegos in thy travels, it will not take thee long to discover my friend M——. He is there known to every one. It will only concern thee to see that thou art worthy of his acquaintance.

From Cien Fuegos I went to the Havana, the metropolis, as all the world knows, of Cuba. Our route lay by steamer to Batavano, and thence by railway. The communication round Cuba—that is from port to port—is not ill arranged or ill conducted. The boats are American built, and engineered by Englishmen or Americans. Breakfast and dinner are given on board, and the cost is included in the sum paid for the fare. The provisions are plentiful, and not bad, if oil can be avoided. As everything is done to foster Spain, Spanish wine is always used, and Spanish ware, and, above all things, Spanish oil. Now Spain does not send her best oil to her colonies. I heard great complaint made of the fares charged on board these boats. The fares when compared with those charged in America doubtless are high; but I do not know that any one has a right to expect that he shall travel as cheaply in Cuba as in the States.

I had heard much of the extravagant charges made for all kinds of accommodation in Cuba; at hotels, in the shops, for travelling, for chance work, and the general wants of a stranger. I found these statements to be much exaggerated. Railway travelling by the first class is about $3\frac{1}{2}d.$ a mile, which is about $1d.$ a mile more than in England. At hotels the charge is two and a half or three dollars a day. The former sum is the more general. This includes a cup of coffee in the morning, a very serious meal at nine o'clock, together with fairly good Catalan wine, dinner at four, with another cup of coffee, and more wine *ad libitum;* bed, and attendance. Indeed, a man may go out of his hotel, without inconvenience, paying nothing beyond the regular daily charge. Extras are dear. I, for instance, having in my ignorance asked for a bottle of champagne, paid for it seventeen shillings. A friend dining with one also, or breakfasting, is an expensive affair. The two together cost considerably more than one's own total daily payment. Thus, as one pays at an hotel whether one's dinner be eaten or no, it becomes almost an insane expense for friends at different hotels to invite each other.

But let it not be supposed that I speak in praise of the hotels at the Havana. Far be it from me to do so. I only say that they are not dear. I found it impossible to command the luxury of a bedroom to myself. It was not the custom of the country they told me. If I chose to pay five dollars a day, just double the usual price, I could be indulged as soon—as circumstances would admit of it; which was intended to signify that they would be happy to charge me for the second bed as soon as the time should come that they had no one else on whom to levy the rate. And the dirt of that bedroom!

I had been unable to get into either of the hotels at the Havana to which I had been recommended, every corner in each having been appropriated. In my grief at the dirt of my abode, and at the too near vicinity of my Spanish neighbour—the fellow-occupant of my chamber was from Spain—I complained somewhat bitterly to an American acquaintance, who had, as I thought, been more lucky in his inn.

'One companion!' said he; 'why, I have three; one walks about all night in a bedgown, a second snores, and the other is dying!'

A friend of mine, an English officer, was at another house. He also was one of four; and it so occurred that he lost thirty pounds out of his sac de nuit. On the whole I may consider myself to have been lucky.

Labour generally is dear, a workman getting a dollar or four shillings and twopence, where in England a man might earn perhaps half a crown. A porter therefore for whom sixpence might suffice in England will require a shilling. A volante—I shall have a word to say about volantes by-and-by—for any distance within the walls costs eightpence. Outside the walls the price seems to be unconscionably higher. Omnibuses which run over two miles charge some fraction over sixpence for each journey. I find that a pair of boots cost me twenty-five shillings. In London they would cost about the same. Those procured in Cuba, however, were worth nothing, which certainly makes a difference. Meat is eightpence the English pound. Bread is somewhat dearer than in England, but not much.

House-rent may be taken as being nearly four times as high as it is in any decent but not fashionable part of London, and the wages of house-servants are twice as high as they are with us. The high prices in the Havana are such therefore as to affect the resident rather than the stranger. One article, however, is very costly; but as it concerns a luxury not much in general use among the inhabitants, this is not surprising. If a man will have his linen washed, he will be made to pay for it.

There is nothing attractive in the town of Havana; nothing whatever to my mind, if we except the harbour. The streets are narrow, dirty, and foul. In this respect there is certainly much difference between those within and without the wall. The latter are wider, more airy, and less vile. But even in them there is nothing to justify the praises with which the Havana is generally mentioned in the West Indies. It excels in population, size, and no doubt in wealth, any other city there; but this does not imply a great eulogium. The three principal public buildings are the Opera House, the Cathedral, and the palace of the Captain-General. The former has been nearly knocked down by an explosion of gas, and is now closed. I believe it to be an admirable model for a second-rate house. The cathedral is as devoid of beauty, both externally and internally, as such an edifice can be made. To describe such a building would be an absurd waste of time and patience. We all know what is a large Roman Catholic church, built in the worst taste, and by a combination of the lowest attributes of Gothic and Latin architecture. The palace, having been built for a residence, does not appear so utterly vile, though it is the child of some similar father. It occupies one side of a public square or pláza, and from its position has a moderately-imposing effect. Of pictures in the Havana there are none of which mention should be made.

But the glory of the Havana is the Paseo—the glory so called. This is the public drive and fashionable lounge of the town—the Hyde Park, the Bois de Boulogne, the Cascine, the Corso, the Alaméda. It is for their hour on the Paseo that the ladies dress themselves, and the gentlemen prepare their jewelry. It consists of a road running outside a portion of the wall, of the extent perhaps of half a mile, and ornamented with seats and avenues of trees, as are the Boulevards at Paris. If it is to be compared with any other resort of the kind in the West Indies, it certainly must be owned there is nothing like it; but a European on first seeing it cannot understand why it is so eulogized. Indeed, it is probable that if he first goes thither alone, as was the case with me, he will pass over it, seeking for some other Paseo.

But then the glory of the Paseo consists in its volantes. As one boasts that one has swum in a gondola, so will one boast of having sat in a volante. It is the pride of Cuban girls to appear on the Paseo in these carriages on the afternoons of holidays and Sundays; and there is certainly enough of the picturesque about the vehicle to make it worthy of some description. It is the most singular of carriages, and its construction is such as to give a flat contradiction to all an Englishman's preconceived notions respecting the power of horses.

The volante is made to hold two sitters, though there is sometimes a low middle seat which affords accommodation to a third lady. We will commence the description from behind. There are two very huge wheels, rough, strong, high, thick, and of considerable weight. The axles generally are not capped, but the nave shines with coarse polished metal. Supported on the axle-tree, and swinging forward from it on springs, is the body of a cabriolet, such as ordinary cabriolets used to be, with the seat, however, somewhat lower, and with much more room for the feet. The back of this is open, and generally a curtain hangs down over the open space. A metal bar, which is polished so as to look like silver, runs across the foot-board and supports the feet. The body, it must be understood, swings forward from these high wheels, so that the whole of the weight, instead of being supported, hangs from it. Then there are a pair of shafts, which, counting from the back of the carriage to the front where they touch the horse at the saddle, are about fourteen feet in length. They do not go beyond the saddle, or the tug depending from the saddle in which they hang. From this immense length it comes to pass that there is a wide interval, exceeding six feet, between the carriage and the horse's tail; and it follows also, from the construction of the machine, that a large portion of the weight must rest on the horse's back.

In addition to this, the unfortunate horse has ordinarily to bear the weight of a rider. For with a volante your servant rides, and does not drive you. With the fashionable world on the Paseo a second horse is used—what we should call an outrider—and the servant sits on this. But as regards those which ply in the town, there is but one horse. How animals can work beneath such a yoke was to me unintelligible.

The great point in the volante of fashion is the servant's dress. He is always a negro, and generally a large negro. He wears a huge pair—not of boots, for they have no feet to them—of galligaskins I may call them, made of thick stiff leather, but so as to fit the leg exactly. The top of them comes some nine inches above the knee, so that when one of these men is seen seated at his ease, the point of his boot nearly touches his chin. They are fastened down the sides with metal fastenings, and at the bottom there is a huge spur. The usual dress of these men, over and above their boots, consists of white breeches, red jackets ornamented with gold lace, and broad-brimmed straw hats. Nothing can be more awkward, and nothing more barbaric than the whole affair; but nevertheless there is about it a barbaric splendour, which has its effect. The great length of the equipage, and the distance of the horse from his work, is what chiefly strikes an Englishman.

The carriage usually holds, when on the Paseo, two or three ladies. Their great object evidently has been to expand their dresses, so that they may group well together, and with a good result as regards colour. It must be confessed that in this respect they are generally successful. They wear no head-dress when in their carriages, and indeed may generally be seen out of doors with their hair uncovered. Though they are of Spanish descent, the mantilla is unknown here. Nor could I trace much similarity to Spanish manner in other particulars. The ladies do not walk like Spanish women—at least not like the women of Andalusia, with whom one would presume them to have had the nearest connection. The walk of the Andalusian women surpasses that of any other, while the Cuban lady is not graceful in her gait. Neither can they boast the brilliantly dangerous beauty of Seville. In Cuba they have good eyes, but rarely good faces. The forehead and the chin too generally recede, leaving the nose with a prominence that is not agreeable. But as my gallantry has not prevented me from speaking in this uncourteous manner of their appearance, my honesty bids me add, that what they lack in beauty they make up in morals, as compared with their cousins in Europe. For travelling *en garçon*, I should probably prefer the south of Spain. But were I doomed to look for domesticity in either clime—and God forbid that such a doom should be mine!—I might perhaps prefer a Cuban mother for my children.

But the volante is held as very precious by the Cuban ladies. The volante itself, I mean—the actual vehicle. It is not intrusted, as coaches are with us, to the dusty mercies of a coach-house. It is ordinarily kept in the hall, and you pass it by as you enter the house; but it is by no means uncommon to see it in the dining-room. As the rooms are large and usually not full of furniture, it does not look amiss there.

The amusements of the Cubans are not very varied, and are innocent in their nature ; for the gambling as carried on there I regard rather as a business than an amusement. They greatly love dancing, and have dances of their own and music of their own, which are peculiar, and difficult to a stranger. Their tunes are striking, and very pretty. They are fond of music generally, and maintain a fairly good opera company at the Havana. In the pláza there— the square, namely, in front of the Captain-General's house—a military band plays from eight to nine every evening. The place is then thronged with people, but by far the majority of them are men.

It is the custom at all the towns in Cuba for the family, when at home, to pass their evening seated near the large low open window of their drawing-rooms ; and as these windows almost always look into the streets, the whole internal arrangement is seen by every one who passes. These windows are always protected by iron bars, as though they were the windows of a prison; in other respects they are completely open.

Four chairs are to be seen ranged in a row, and four more opposite to them, running from the window into the room and placed close together. Between these is generally laid a small piece of carpet. The majority of these chairs are made to rock ; for the Creole lady always rocks herself. I have watched them going through the accustomed motion with their bodies, even when seated on chairs with stern immovable legs. This is the usual evening living-place of the family ; and I never yet saw an occupant of one of these chairs with a book in her hand, or in his. I asked an Englishman, a resident in the Havana, whether he had ever done so. ‘ A book !’ he

L

answered; ' why, the girls can't read, in your sense of the word reading.'

The young men, and many of those who are no longer young, spend their evenings, and apparently a large portion of their days, in eating ices and playing billiards. The accommodation in the Havana for these amusements is on a very large scale.

The harbour at the Havana is an interesting sight. It is in the first place very picturesque, which to the ordinary visitor is the most important feature. But it is also commodious, large, and safe. It is approached between two forts. That to the westward, which is the principal defence, is called the Morro. Here also stands the lighthouse. No Englishman omits to hear, as he enters the harbour, that these forts were taken by the English in Albemarle's time. Now it seems to me, they might very easily be taken by any one who chose to spend on them the necessary amount of gunpowder. But then I know nothing about forts.

This special one of the Morro I did take; not by gunpowder, but by stratagem. I was informed that no one was allowed to see it since the open defiance of the island contained in the last message of the United States President. But I was also informed—whisperingly, in the ear—that a request to see the lighthouse would be granted, and that as I was not an American, the fort should follow. It resulted in a little black boy taking me over the whole edifice—an impudent little black boy, who filled his pockets with stones and pelted the sentries. The view of the harbour from the lighthouse is very good and quite worth the trouble of the visit. The fort itself I did not understand, but a young English officer, who was with me, pooh-poohed it as a thing of nothing. But then young English officers pooh-pooh everything. Here again I must add that nothing can exceed the courtesy of all Spanish officials. If they could only possess honesty and energy as well as courtesy !

By far the most interesting spot in the Havana is the Quay, to which the vessels are fastened end-ways, the bow usually lying against the quay. In other places the side of the vessel is, I believe, brought to the wharf. Here there are signs of true life. One cannot but think how those quays would be extended, and that life increased, if the place were in the hands of other people.

I have said that I regarded gambling in Cuba not as an amusement, but an occupation. The public lotteries offer the daily means to every one for gratifying this passion. They are maintained by the government, and afford a profit, I am told, of something over a million dollars per annum. In all public places tickets are hawked about. One may buy a whole ticket, half, a quarter, an eighth, or a sixteenth. It is done without any disguise or shame, and the institution seemed, I must say, to be as popular with the Europeans living there, as with the natives. In the eyes of an Englishman new from Great Britain, with his prejudices still thick upon him, this great national feature loses some of its nobility and grandeur.

This, together with the bribery, which is so universal, shows what is the spirit of the country. For a government supported by the profits of a gambling-hell, and for a Governor enriched by bribes on slaves illegally imported, what Englishman can feel sympathy ? I would fain hope that there is no such sympathy felt in England.

I have been answered, when expressing indignation at the system, by a request that I would first look at home ; and have been so answered by Englishmen. ' How can you blame the Captain-General,' they have said, ' when the same thing is done by the French and English consuls through the islands ?' That the French and English consuls do take bribes to wink at the importation of slaves, I cannot and do not believe. But Cæsar's wife should not even be suspected.

I found it difficult to learn what is exactly the present population of Cuba. I believe it to be about 1,300,000, and of this number about 600,000 are slaves. There are many Chinese now in the island, employed as household servants, or on railways, or about the sugar-works. Many are also kept at work on the cane-pieces, though it seems that for this labour they have hardly sufficient strength. These unfortunate deluded creatures receive, I fear, very little better treatment than the slaves.

My best wish for the island is that it may speedily be reckoned among the annexations of the United States.

CHAPTER XI.

THE PASSAGE OF THE WINDWARD ISLANDS.

In the good old days, when men called things by their proper names, those islands which run down in a string from north to south, from the Virgin Islands, to the mouth of the Orinoco River, were called the Windward Islands—the Windward or Caribbean Islands. They were also called the Lesser Antilles. The Leeward Islands were, and properly speaking are, another cluster lying across the coast of Venezuela, of which Curaçoa is the chief. Oruba and Margarita also belong to this lot, among which, England, I believe, never owned any. *

But now-a-days we Britishers are not content to let the Dutch and others keep a separate name for themselves; we have, therefore, divided the Lesser Antilles, of which the greater number belong to ourselves, and call the northern portion of these the Leeward Islands. Among them Antigua is the chief, and is the residence of a governor supreme in this division.

After leaving St. Thomas the first island seen of any

* The greater Antilles are Cuba, Jamaica, Hayti, and Porto Rico, though I am not quite sure whether Porto Rico does not more properly belong to the Virgin Islands. The scattered assemblage to the north of the greater Antilles are the Bahamas, at one of the least considerable of which, San Salvador, Columbus first landed. Those now named, I believe, comprise all the West India Islands.

note is St. Christopher, commonly known as St. Kitts, and Nevis is close to it. Both these colonies are prospering fairly. Sugar is exported, now I am told in increasing, though still not in great quantities, and the appearance of the cultivation is good. Looking up the side of the hills, one sees the sugar-canes apparently in cleanly order, and they have an air of substantial comfort. Of course the times are not so bright as in the fine old days previous to emancipation; but nevertheless matters have been on the mend, and people are again beginning to get along. On the journey from Nevis to Antigua, Montserrat is sighted, and a singular island-rock called the Redonda is seen very plainly. Montserrat, I am told, is not prospering so well as St. Kitts or Nevis.

These islands are not so beautiful, not so greenly beautiful, as are those further south to which we shall soon come. The mountains of Nevis are certainly fine as they are seen from the sea, but they are not, or do not seem to be covered with that delicious tropical growth which is so lovely in Jamaica and Trinidad, and, indeed, in many of the smaller islands.

Antigua is the next, going southward. This was, and perhaps is, an island of some importance. It is said to have been the first of the West Indian colonies which itself advocated the abolition of slavery, and to have been the only one which adopted complete emancipation at once, without any intermediate system of apprenticeship. Antigua has its own bishop, whose diocese includes also such of the Virgin Islands as belong to us, and the adjacent islands of St. Kitts, Nevis, and Montserrat.

Neither is Antigua remarkable for its beauty. It is approached, however, by an excellent and picturesque harbour, called English Harbour, which in former days was much used by the British navy; indeed, I believe it was at one time the head-quarters of a naval station.

Premising, in the first place, that I know very little about harbours, I would say that nothing could be more secure than that. Whether or no it may be easy for sailing-vessels to get in and out with certain winds, that, indeed, may be doubtful.

St. John's, the capital of Antigua, is twelve miles from English Harbour. I was in the island only three or four hours, and did not visit it. I am told that it is a good town—or city, I should rather say, now that it has its own bishop.

In all these islands they have Queen, Lords, and Commons in one shape or another. It may, however, be hoped, and I believe trusted, that, for the benefit of the communities, matters chiefly rest in the hands of the first of the three powers. The other members of the legislature, if they have in them anything of wisdom to say, have doubtless an opportunity of saying it—perhaps also an opportunity when they have nothing of wisdom. Let us trust, however, that such opportunities are limited.

After leaving Antigua we come to the French island of Guadaloupe, and then passing Dominica—of which I will say a word just now—to Martinique, which is also French. And here we are among the rich green wild beauties of these thrice beautiful Caribbean islands. The mountain grouping of both is very fine, and the hills are covered up to their summits with growth of the greenest. At both these islands one is struck with the great superiority of the French West Indian towns to those which belong to us. That in Guadaloupe is called Basseterre, and the capital of Martinique is St. Pierre. These towns offer remarkable contrast to Roseau and Port Castries, the chief towns in the adjacent English islands of Dominica and St. Lucia. At the French ports one is landed at excellently contrived little piers, with proper apparatus for lighting, and well-kept steps. The quays are shaded by trees, the streets are neat and in good order, and the shops show that ordinary trade is thriving. There are water conduits with clear streams through the towns, and everything is ship-shape. I must tell a very different tale when I come to speak of Dominica and St. Lucia.

The reason for this is, I think, well given in a useful guide to the West Indies, published some years since, under the direction of the Royal Mail Steam-Packet Company. Speaking of St. Pierre, in Martinique, the author says: 'The streets are neat, regular, and cleanly. The houses are high, and have more the air of European houses than those of the English colonies. Some of the streets have an avenue of trees, which overshadow the footpath, and on either side are deep gutters, down which the water flows. There are five booksellers' houses, and the fashions are well displayed in other shops. The French colonists, whether Creoles * or French, consider the West Indies as their country. They cast no wistful looks towards France. They marry, educate, and build in and for the West Indies, and for the West Indies alone. In our colonies it is different. They are considered more as temporary lodging-places, to be deserted as soon as the occupiers have made money enough by molasses and sugar to return *home*.'

All this is quite true. There is something very cheering to an English heart in that sound, and reference to the word home—in that great disinclination to the idea of

---

* It should be understood that a Creole is a person born in the West Indies, of a race not indigenous to the islands. There may be white Creoles, coloured Creoles, or black Creoles. People talk of Creole horses and Creole poultry: those namely which have not been themselves imported, but which have been bred from imported stock. The meaning of the word Creole is, I think, sometimes misunderstood.

life-long banishment. But nevertheless, the effect as shown in these islands is not satisfactory to the *amour propre* of an Englishman. And it is not only in the outward appearance of things that the French islands excel those belonging to England which I have specially named. Dominica and St. Lucia export annually about 6,000 hogsheads of sugar each. Martinique exports about 60,000 hogsheads. Martinique is certainly rather larger than either of the other two, but size has little or nothing to do with it. It is anything rather than want of fitting soil which makes the produce of sugar so inconsiderable in Dominica and St. Lucia.

These French islands were first discovered by the Spaniards; but since that time they, as well as the 'two English islands above named, have passed backwards and forwards between the English and French, till it was settled in 1814 that Martinique and Guadaloupe should belong to France, and Dominica and St. Lucia, with some others, to England. It certainly seems that France knew how to take care of herself in the arrangement.

There is another little island belonging to France, at the back of Guadaloupe to the westward, called Marie-Galante; but I believe it is but of little value.

To my mind, Dominica, as seen from the sea, is by far the most picturesque of all these islands. Indeed, it would be difficult to beat it either in colour or grouping. It fills one with an ardent desire to be off and rambling among those green mountains—as if one could ramble through such wild, bush country, or ramble at all with the thermometer at 85. But when one has only to think of such things without any idea of doing them, neither the bushes nor the thermometer are considered.

One is landed at Dominica on a beach. If the water be quiet, one gets out dry-shod by means of a strong jump; if the surf be high, one wades through it; if it be very high, one is of course upset. The same things happen at Jacmel, in Hayti; but then Englishmen look on the Haytians as an uncivilized, barbarous race. Seeing that Dominica lies just between Martinique and Guadaloupe, the difference between the English beach and serf and the French piers is the more remarkable.

And then, the perils of the surf being passed, one walks into the town of Roseau. It is impossible to conceive a more distressing sight. Every house is in a state of decadence. There are no shops that can properly be so called; the people wander about chattering, idle and listless; the streets are covered with thick, rank grass; there is no sign either of money made or of money making. Everything seems to speak of desolation, apathy, and ruin. There is nothing, even in Jamaica, so sad to look at as the town of Roseau.

The greater part of the population are French in manner, religion, and language, and one would be so glad to attribute to that fact this wretched look of apathetic poverty—if it were only possible. But we cannot do that after visiting Martinique and Guadaloupe. It might be said that a French people will not thrive under British rule. But if so, what of Trinidad? This look of misery has been attributed to a great fire which occurred some eighty years since; but when due industry has been at work, great fires have usually produced improved towns. Now eighty years have afforded ample time for such improvement if it were forthcoming. Alas! it would seem that it is not forthcoming.

It must, however, be stated in fairness that Dominica produces more coffee than sugar, and that the coffee estates have latterly been the most thriving. Singularly enough, her best customer has been the neighbouring French island of Martinique, in which some disease has latterly attacked the coffee-plants.

We then reach St. Lucia, which is also very lovely as seen from the sea. This too is an island French in its language, manners, and religion; perhaps more entirely so than any other of the islands belonging to ourselves. The laws even are still French, and the people are, I believe, blessed with no Lords and Commons. If I understand the matter rightly, St. Lucia is held as a colony or possession conquered from the French, and is governed, therefore, by a quasi-military governor, with the aid of a council. It is, however, in some measure dependent on the Governor of Barbados, who is again one of your supreme governors. There has, I believe, been some recent change which I do not pretend to understand. If these changes be not completed, and if it would not be presumptuous in me to offer a word of advice, I would say that in the present state of the island, with a Negro-Gallic population who do little or nothing, it might be as well to have as much as possible of the Queen, and as little as possible of the Lords and Commons.

To the outward physical eye St. Lucia is not so triste as Dominica. There is good landing there, and the little town of Castries, though anything but prosperous in itself, is prosperous in appearance as compared with Roseau.

St. Lucia is peculiarly celebrated for its snakes. One cannot walk ten yards off the road—so one is told—without being bitten. And if one be bitten, death is certain— except by the interposition of a single individual of the island, who will cure the sufferer for a consideration. Such, at least, is the report made on this matter. The first question one should ask on going there is as to the whereabouts and usual terms of that worthy and useful practitioner. There is, I believe, a great deal that is remarkable to attract the visitor among the mountains and valleys of St. Lucia.

And then in the usual course, running down the island, one goes to that British advanced post, Barbados—Barbados, that lies out to windward, guarding the other islands as it were! Barbados, that is and ever was entirely British! Barbados, that makes money, and is in all respects so respectable a little island! King George need not have feared at all; nor yet need Queen Victoria. If anything goes wrong in England—Napoleon coming here, not to kiss Her Majesty this time, but to make himself less agreeable—let Her Majesty go to Barbados, and she will be safe! I have said that Jamaica never boasts, and have on that account complained of her. Let such complaint be far from me when I speak of Barbados. But shall I not write a distinct chapter as to this most respectable little island—an island that pays its way?

St. Vincent is the next in our course, and this, too, is green and pretty, and tempting to look at. Here also the French have been in possession, but comparatively for a short time. In settling this island, the chief difficulty the English had was with the old native Indians, who more than once endeavoured to turn out their British masters. The contest ended in their being effectually turned out by those British masters, who expelled them all bodily to the island of Ruatan, in the Bay of Honduras; where their descendants are now giving the Anglo-American diplomatists so much trouble in deciding whose subjects they truly are. May we not say that, having got rid of them out of St. Vincent, we can afford to get rid of them altogether?

Kingston is the capital here. It looks much better than either Roseau or Castries, though by no means equal to Basseterre or St. Pierre.

This island is said to be healthy, having in this respect a much better reputation than its neighbour St. Lucia, and as far as I could learn, it is progressing—progressing slowly, but progressing—in spite even of the burden of Queens, Lords, and Commons. The Lords and Commons are no doubt considerably modified by official influence.

And then the traveller runs down the Grenadines, a pretty cluster of islands lying between St. Vincent and Grenada, of which Becquia and Cariacou are the chief. They have no direct connection with the mail steamers, but are, I believe, under the Governor of Barbados. They are very pretty, though not, as a rule, very productive. Of one of them I was told that the population were all females. What a Paradise of Houris, if it were but possible to find a good Mahommedan in these degenerate days!

Grenada will be the last upon the list; for I did not visit or even see Tobago, and of Trinidad I have ventured to write a separate chapter, in spite of the shortness of my visit. Grenada is also very lovely, and is, I think, the head-quarters of the world for fruit. The finest mangoes I ever ate I found there; and I think the finest oranges and pine-apples.

The town of St. Georges, the capital, must at one time have been a place of considerable importance, and even now it has a very different appearance from some of those that I have just mentioned. It is more like a goodly English town than any other that I saw in any of the smaller British islands. It is well built, though built up and down steep hills, and contains large and comfortable houses. The market-place also looks like a market-place; and there are shops in it, in which trade is apparently carried on and money made.

Indeed, Grenada was once a prince among these smaller islands, having other islands under it, with a Governor supreme, instead of tributary. It was fertile also, and productive,—in every way of importance.

But now here, as in so many other spots among the West Indies, we are driven to exclaim, Ichabod! The glory of our Grenada has departed, as has the glory of its great namesake in the old world. The houses, though so goodly, are but as so many Alhambras, whose tenants now are by no means great in the world's esteem.

All the hotels in the West Indies are, as I have said, or shall say in some other place, kept by ladies of colour; in the most part by ladies who are no longer very young. They are generally called familiarly by their double name. Betsy Austen, for instance, or Caroline Lee. I went to the house of some such lady in St. George's, and she told me a woful tale of her miseries. She was Kitty something, I think—soon, apparently, to become Kitty of another world. 'An hotel,' she said. 'No; she kept no hotel now-a-days—what use was there for an hotel in St. Georges? She kept a lodging-house; though, for the matter of that, no lodgers ever came nigh her. That little granddaughter of hers sometimes sold a bottle of ginger beer; that was all.' It must be hard for living eyes to see one's trade die off in that way.

There is a feminine accomplishment so much in vogue among the ladies of the West Indies, one practised there with a success so specially brilliant, as to make it deserving of special notice. This art is one not wholly confined to ladies, although, as in the case with music, dancing, and cookery, it is to be looked for chiefly among the female sex. Men, indeed, do practise it in England, the West Indies, and elsewhere; and as Thalberg and Soyer are greatest among pianists and cooks, so perhaps are the greatest adepts in this art to be found among the male practitioners;—elsewhere, that is, than in the West Indies. There are to be found ladies never equalled in this art by any effort of manhood. I speak of the science of flirting.

And be it understood that here among these happy islands no idea of impropriety—perhaps remembering

some of our starched people at home, I should say of crimi-
nality—is attached to the pursuit. Young ladies flirt, as
they dance and play, or eat and drink, quite as a matter
of course. There is no undutiful, unfilial idea of waiting
till mamma's back be turned; no uncomfortable fear of
papa; no longing for secluded corners, so that the world
should not see. The doing of anything that one is ashamed
of is bad. But as regards flirting, there is no such doing
in the West Indies. Girls flirt not only with the utmost
skill, but with the utmost innocence also. Fanny Grey,
with her twelve admirers, required no retired corners, no
place apart from father, mother, brothers, or sisters. She
would perform with all the world around her as some
other girl would sing, conscious that in singing she would
neither disgrace herself nor her masters.

It may be said that the practice of this accomplishment
will often interfere with the course of true love. Perhaps so,
but I doubt whether it does not as often assist it. It
seemed to me that young ladies do not hang on hand in
the West Indies. Marriages are made up there with
apparently great satisfaction on both sides; and then the
flirting is laid aside—put by, at any rate, till the days of
widowhood, should such evil days come. The flirting is
as innocent as it is open, and is confined to ladies without
husbands.

It is confined to ladies without husbands, but the victims are not bachelors alone. No position, or age, or
state of health secures a man from being drawn, now into
one and now into another Circean circle, in which he is
whirled about, sometimes in a most ridiculous manner,
jostled amongst a dozen neighbours, left without power to
get out or to plunge further in, pulled back by a skirt at
any attempt to escape, repulsed in the front at every
struggle made to fight his way through.

Rolling about in these Charybdis pools are, perhaps,
oftenest to be seen certain wearers of red coats; wretches

girt with tight sashes, and with gilding on their legs and backs.   To and fro they go, bumping against each other without serious injury, but apparently in great discomfort. And then there are black-coated strugglers, with white neck-ties, very valiant in their first efforts, but often to be seen in deep grief, with heads thoroughly submersed. And you may see ¦gray-haired sufferers with short necks, making little useless puffs, puffs which would be so impotent were not Circe merciful to those short-necked gray-haired sufferers.

If there were, as perhaps there should be, a college in the West Indies, with fellowships and professorships, established with the view of rewarding proficiency in this science, Fanny Grey should certainly be elected warden, or principal, or provost of that college.   Her wondrous skill deserves more than mere praise, more than such slight glory as my ephemeral pages can give her.   Pretty, laughing, brilliant, clever Fanny Grey?   Whose cheeks ever were so pink, whose teeth so white, whose eyes so bright, whose curling locks so raven black!   And then who ever smiled as she smiled?   or frowned as she can frown?   Sharply go those brows together, and down beneath the gurgling pool sinks the head of the red-coated wretch, while with momentary joy up pops the head of another, who is received with a momentary smile.

Yes; oh my reader! it is too true, I also have been in that pool, making, indeed, no wilful struggles, attempting no Leander feat of swimming, sucked in as my steps unconsciously strayed too near the dangerous margin; sucked in and then buffeted about, not altogether unmercifully when my inaptitude for such struggling was discovered.   Yes; I have found myself choking in those Charybdis waters, —have glanced into the Circe cave.   I have been seen in my insane struggles.   But what shame of that?   All around me, from the old patriarch dean of the island to the last subaltern fresh from Chatham, were there as well as I.

CHAPTER XII.

BRITISH GUIANA.

WHEN I settle out of England, and take to the colonies for good and all, British Guiana shall be the land of my adoption. If I call it Demerara perhaps I shall be better understood. At home there are prejudices against it I know. They say that it is a low, swampy, muddy strip of alluvial soil, infested with rattlesnakes, gallinippers, and musquitoes as big as turkey-cocks; that yellow fever rages there perennially; that the heat is unendurable; that society there is as stagnant as its waters; that men always die as soon as they reach it; and when they live are such wretched creatures that life is a misfortune. Calumny reports it to have been ruined by the abolition of slavery; milk of human kindness would forbid the further exportation of Europeans to this white man's grave; and philanthropy, for the good of mankind, would wish to have it drowned beneath its own rivers. There never was a land so ill spoken of—and never one that deserved it so little. All the above calumnies I contradict; and as I lived there for a fortnight—would it could have been a month! —I expect to be believed.

If there were but a snug secretaryship vacant there— and these things in Demerara are very snug—how I would invoke the goddess of patronage; how I would nibble round the officials of the Colonial Office; how I

M

would stir up my friend's friends to write little notes to their friends! For Demerara is the Elysium of the tropics —the West Indian happy valley of Rasselas—the one true and actual Utopia of the Caribbean Seas—the Transatlantic Eden.

The men in Demerara are never angry, and the women are never cross. Life flows along on a perpetual stream of love, smiles, champagne, and small talk. Everybody has enough of everything. The only persons who do not thrive are the doctors; and for them, as the country affords them so little to do, the local government no doubt provides liberal pensions.

The form of government is a mild despotism, tempered by sugar. The Governor is the father of his people, and the Governor's wife the mother. The colony forms itself into a large family, which gathers itself together peaceably under parental wings. They have no noisy sessions of Parliament as in Jamaica, no money squabbles as in Barbados. A clean bill of health, a surplus in the colonial treasury, a rich soil, a thriving trade, and a happy people—these are the blessings which attend the fortunate man who has cast his lot on this prosperous shore. Such is Demerara as it is made to appear to a stranger.

That custom which prevails there, of sending to each new comer a deputation with invitations to dinner for the period of his sojourn, is an excellent institution. It saves a deal of trouble in letters of introduction, economizes one's time, and puts one at once on the most-favoured-nation footing. Some may fancy that they could do better as to the bestowal of their evenings by individual diplomacy; but the matter is so well arranged in Demerara that such people would certainly find themselves in the wrong.

If there be a deficiency in Georgetown—it is hardly necessary to explain that Georgetown is the capital of the province of Demerara, and that Demerara is the centre province in the colony of British Guiana; or that there are three provinces, Berbice, Demerara, and Essequibo, so called from the names of the three great rivers of the country—But if there be a deficiency in Georgetown, it is in respect to cabs. The town is extensive, as will by-and-by be explained; and though I would not so far militate against the feelings of the people as to say that the weather is ever hot—I should be ungrateful as well as incredulous were I to do so—nevertheless, about noonday one's inclination for walking becomes subdued. Cabs would certainly be an addition to the luxuries of the place. But even these are not so essential as might at the first sight appear, for an invitation to dinner always includes an offer of the host's carriage. Without a carriage no one dreams of dragging on existence in British Guiana. In England one would as soon think of living in a house without a fireplace, or sleeping in a bed without a blanket.

For those who wander abroad in quest of mountain scenery it must be admitted that this colony has not much attraction. The country certainly is flat. By this I mean to intimate, that go where you will, travel thereabouts as far as you may, the eye meets no rising ground. Everything stands on the same level. But then, what is the use of mountains? You can grow no sugar on them, even with ever so many Coolies. They are big, brown, valueless things, cumbering the face of the creation; very well for autumn idlers when they get to Switzerland, but utterly useless in a colony which has to count its prosperity by the number of its hogsheads. Jamaica has mountains, and look at Jamaica!

Yes; Demerara is flat; and Berbice is flat; and so is Essequibo. The whole of this land is formed by the mud which has been brought down by these great rivers and by others. The Corentyne is the most easterly, separating our colony from Dutch Guiana, or Surinam. Then comes the Berbice. The next, counting only the larger rivers, is the Demerara. Then, more to the west, the Essequibo, and running into that the Mazarony and the Cuyuni; and then, north-west along the coast, the Pomeroon; and lastly of our own rivers, the Guiana, though I doubt whether for absolute purposes of colonization we have ever gone so far as this. And beyond that are rolled in slow but turbid volume the huge waters of the Orinoco. On its shores we make no claim. Though the delta of the Orinoco is still called Guiana, it belongs to the republic of Venezuela.

These are our boundaries along the South American shore, which hereabouts, as all men know, looks northward, with an easterly slant towards the Atlantic. Between us and our Dutch friends on the right hand the limits are clear enough. On the left hand, matters are not quite so clear with the Venezuelians. But to the rear! To the rear there is an eternity of sugar capability in mud running back to unknown mountains, the wildernesses of Brazil, the river Negro, and the tributaries of the Amazon —an eternity of sugar capability, to which England's colony can lay claim if only she could manage so much as the surveying of it. 'Sugar!' said an enterprising Demerara planter to me. 'Are you talking of sugar? Give me my heart's desire in Coolies, and I will make you a million of hogsheads of sugar without stirring from the colony!' Now, the world's supply, some twelve years ago, was about a million hogsheads. It has since increased maybe by a tenth. What a land, then, is this of British Guiana, flowing with milk and honey—with sugar and rum! A million hogsheads can be made there, if we only had the Coolies. I state this on the credit of my excellent enterprising friend. But then the Coolies!

Guiana is an enormous extent of flat mud, the alluv

deposit of those mighty rivers which for so many years
have been scraping together earth in those wild unknown
upland countries, and bringing it down conveniently to
the sea-board, so that the world might have sugar to its
tea. I really think my friend was right. There is no
limit to the fertility and extent of this region. The only
limit is in labour. The present culture only skirts the
sea-board and the riversides. You will hardly find an
estate—I do not think that you can find one—that has
not a water frontage. This land formerly belonged to the
Dutch, and by them was divided out into portions which
on a map have about them a Euclidical appearance. Let
A B C D be a right-angled parallelogram, of which the
sides A B and C D are three times the length of the other
sides A C and B D. 'Tis thus you would describe a
Demerara property, and the Q. E. D. would have reference
to the relative quantities of sugar, molasses, and rum pro-
ducible therefrom.

But these strips of land, though they are thus marked
out on the maps with four exact lines, are presumed to
run back to any extent that the owner may choose to
occupy. He starts from the water, and is bounded on
each side ; but backwards ! Backwards he may cultivate
canes up to the very Andes, if only he could get Coolies.
Oh, ye soft-hearted, philanthropic gentry of the Anti-
Slavery Society, only think of that; a million hogsheads
of sugar—and you like cheap sugar yourselves—if you
will only be quiet, or talk on subjects that you understand !

The whole of this extent of mud, beyond the present
very limited sugar-growing limits, is covered by timber.
One is apt to think of an American forest as being as
magnificent in its individual trees as it is huge in its
extent of surface. But I doubt much whether this is
generally the case. There are forest giants no doubt ;

but indigenous primeval wood is, I take it, for the most part a disagreeable, scrubby, bushy, sloppy, unequal, inconvenient sort of affair, to walk through which a man should be either an alligator or a monkey, and to make much way he should have a touch of both. There be no forest glades there in which uncivilized Indian lovers walk at ease, with their arms round each other's naked waists; no soft grass beneath the well-trimmed trunk on which to lie and meditate poetical. But musquitoes abound there; and grass flies, which locate themselves beneath the toenails; and marabunters, a villanous species of wasp; and gallinippers, the grandfathers of musquitoes; and from thence up to the xagua and the boa constrictor all nature is against a cool comfortable ramble in the woods.

But I must say a word about Georgetown, and a word also about New Amsterdam, before I describe the peculiarities of a sugar estate in Guiana. A traveller's first thought is about his hotel; and I must confess, much as I love Georgetown—and I do love Georgetown—that I ought to have coupled the hotel with the cabs, and complained of a joint deficiency. The Clarendon—the name at any rate is good—is a poor affair; but poor as it is, it is the best.

It is a rickety, ruined, tumble-down, wooden house, into which at first one absolutely dreads to enter, lest the steps should fail and let one through into unutterable abysses below. All the houses in Georgetown are made of wood, and therefore require a good deal of repair and paint. And all the houses seem to receive this care except the hotel. Ah, Mrs. Lenny, Mrs. Lenny! before long you and your guests will fall prostrate, and be found buried beneath a pile of dust and a colony of cockroaches!

And yet it goes against my heart to abuse the inn, for the people were so very civil. I shall never forget that big black chambermaid; how she used to curtsy to me when she came into my room in the morning with a huge tub of water on her head! That such a weight should be put on her poor black skull—a weight which I could not lift —used to rend my heart with anguish. But that, so weighted, she should think that manners demanded a curtsy! Poor, courteous, overburdened maiden!

'Don't, Sally; don't. Don't curtsy,' I would cry. 'Yes, massa,' she would reply, and curtsy again, oh, so painfully! The tub of water was of such vast proportions! It was big enough—big enough for me to wash in!

This house, as I have said, was all in ruins, and among other ruined things was my bedroom-door lock. The door could not be closed within, except by the use of a bolt; and without the bolt would swing wide open to the winds, exposing my arrangements to the public, and disturbing the neighbourhood by its jarring. In spite of the inconvenient difficulty of ingress I was forced to bolt it.

At six every morning came Sally with the tub, knocking gently at the door—knocking gently at the door with that ponderous tub upon her skull! What could a man do when so appealed to but rush quickly from beneath his musquito curtains to her rescue? So it was always with me. But having loosed the bolt, time did not suffice to enable me to take my position again beneath the curtain. A jump into bed I might have managed—but then, the musquito curtain! So, under those circumstances, finding myself at the door in my deshabille, I could only open it, and then stand sheltered behind it, as behind a bulwark, while Sally deposited her burden.

But, no. She curtsied, first at the bed; and seeing that I was not there, turned her head and tub slowly round the room, till she perceived my whereabouts. Then gently, but firmly, drawing away the door till I stood before her plainly discovered in my night-dress, she curtsied again. She knew better than to enter a room without due saluta-

tion to the guest—even with a tub of water on her head.
Poor Sally! Was I not dressed from my chin downwards,
and was not that enough for her? 'Honi soit qui mal y
pense.'

After that, how can I say aught against the hotel?
And when I complained loudly of the holes in the curtain,
the musquitoes having driven me to very madness, did not
they set to work, Sunday as it was, and make me a new curtain? Certainly without avail—for they so hung it that
the musquitoes entered worse than ever. But the intention was no less good.

And that waiter, David; was he not for good-nature
the pink of waiters? 'David, this house will tumble
down! I know it will—before I leave it. The stairs
shook terribly as I came up.' 'Oh no, massa,' and David
laughed benignly. 'It no tumble down last week, and
derefore it no tumble down next.' It did last my time,
and therefore I will say no more.

Georgetown to my eyes is a prepossessing city, flat as
the country round it is, and deficient as it is—as are all
the West Indies—in anything like architectural pretension. The streets are wide and airy. The houses, all
built of wood, stand separately, each a little off the road;
and though much has not been done in the way of their
gardens—for till the great coming influx of Coolies all
labour is engaged in making sugar—yet there is generally
something green attached to each of them. Down the
centre of every street runs a wide dyke. Of these dykes
I must say something further when I come to speak again
of the sugar doings; for their importance in these provinces cannot well be overrated.

The houses themselves are generally without a hall.
By that I mean that you walk directly into some sitting-
room. This, indeed, is general through the West Indies;
and now that I bethink me of the fact, I may mention

that a friend of mine in Jamaica has no door whatsoever
to his house. All ingress and egress is by the windows.
My bedroom had no door, only a window that opened.
The sitting-rooms in Georgetown open through to each
other, so that the wind, let it come which way it will,
may blow through the whole house. For though it is
never absolutely hot in Guiana—as I have before mentioned—nevertheless, 'a current of air is comfortable. One
soon learns to know the difference of windward and leeward when living in British Guiana.

The houses are generally of three stories; but the two
upper only are used by the family. Outer steps lead up
from the little front garden, generally into a verandah,
and in this verandah a great portion of their life is led.
It is cooler than the inner rooms. Not that I mean to say
that any rooms in Demerara are ever hot.

We all know the fine burst with which Scott opens a
certain canto in one of his poems :

> Breathes there the man, with soul so dead,
> Who never to himself hath said,
>   This is my own, my native land?
>   *   *   *   *   *
> If such there breathe, go, mark him well.

At any rate, there breathes no such man in this pleasant
colony. A people so happily satisfied with their own
position I never saw elsewhere,—except at Barbados. And
how could they fail to be satisfied, looking at their advantages? A million hogsheads of sugar to be made when
the Coolies come !

They do not, the most of them, appeal to the land as
being that of their nativity, but they love it no less as
that of their adoption. ' Look at me,' says one; ' I have
been thirty years without leaving it, and have never had
a headache.' I look and see a remarkably hale man, of
forty I should say, but he says fifty. ' That's nothing,'

says another, who certainly may be somewhat stricken in
years : ' I have been here five-and-fifty years, and was
never ill but once, when I was foolish enough to go to
England. Ugh! I shall never forget it. Why, sir,
there was frost in October !' ' Yes,' I said, ' and snow in
May sometimes. It is not all sunshine with us, whatever
it may be with you.'

' Not that we have too much sunshine,' interposed a
lady. ' You don't think we have, do you ?'

' Not in the least. Who could ask more, madam, than
to bask in such sunshine as yours from year's end to year's
end ?'

' And is commerce tolerably flourishing ?' I asked of a
gentleman in trade.

' Flourishing, sir! If you want to make money, here's
your ground. Why, sir, here, in this wretched little
street, there has been more money turned in the last ten
years—than—than—' And he rummaged among the
half-crowns in his breeches-pocket for a simile, as though
not a few of the profits spoken of had found their way
thither.

' Do you ever find it dull here ?' I asked of a lady—
perhaps not with very good taste—for we Englishmen
have sometimes an idea that there is perhaps a little same-
ness about life in a small colony.

' Dull ! no. What should make us dull ? We have
a great deal more to amuse us than most of you have at
home.' This perhaps might be true of many of us.
' We have dances, and dinner-parties, and private the-
atricals. And then Mrs. ——!' Now Mrs. —— was
the Governor's wife, and all eulogiums on society in
Georgetown always ended with a eulogium upon her.

I went over the hospital with the doctor there; for
even in Demerara they require a hospital—for the negroes.
' And what is the prevailing disease of the colony ?' I

asked him. 'Dropsy with the black men,' he answered; 'and brandy with the white.'

'You don't think much of yellow fever?' I asked him.

'No; very little. It comes once in six or seven years; and like influenza or cholera at home, it requires its victims. What is that to consumption, whose visits with you are constant, who daily demands its hecatombs? We don't like yellow fever, certainly; but yellow fever is not half so bad a fellow as the brandy bottle.'

Should this meet the eye of any reader in this colony who needs medical advice, he may thus get it, of a very good quality, and without fee. On the subject of brandy I say nothing myself, seeing how wrong it is to kiss and tell.

Excepting as regards yellow fever, I do not imagine that Demerara is peculiarly unhealthy. And as regards yellow fever, I am inclined to think that his Satanic majesty has in this instance been painted too black. There are many at home—in England—who believe that yellow fever rages every year in some of these colonies, and that half the white population of the town is swept off by it every August. As far as I can learn it is hardly more fatal at one time of the year than at another. It returns at intervals, but by no means regularly or annually. Sometimes it will hang on for sixteen or eighteen months at a time, and then it will disappear for five or six years. Those seem to be most subject to it who have been out in the West Indies for a year or so: after that, persons are not so liable to it. Sailors, and men whose work keeps them about the sea-board and wharves, seem to be in the greatest danger. White soldiers also, when quartered in unhealthy places, have suffered greatly. They who are thoroughly acclimatized are seldom attacked; and there seems to be an idea that the white Creoles are nearly safe. I believe that there are instances in which coloured people and even negroes have been attacked by yellow fever. But such cases are very rare. Cholera is the negroes' scourge.

Nor do I think that this fever rages more furiously in Demerara than among the islands. It has been very bad in its bad times at Kingston Jamaica, at Trinidad, at Barbados, among the shipping at St. Thomas, and nowhere worse than at the Havana. The true secret of its fatality I take to be this:—that the medical world has not yet settled what is the proper mode of medical treatment. There are, I believe, still two systems, each directly opposite to the other; but in the West Indies they call them the French system and the English. In a few years, no doubt, the matter will be better understood.

From Georgetown Demerara, to New Amsterdam Berbice, men travel either by steamer along the coast, or by a mail phaeton. The former goes once a week to Berbice and back, and the latter three times. I went by the mail phaeton and returned by the steamer. And here, considering the prosperity of the colony, the well-being and comfort of all men and women in it, the go-ahead principles of the place, and the coming million hogsheads of sugar—the millennium of a West Indian colony—considering all these great existing characteristics of Guiana, I must say that I think the Governor ought to look to the mail phaeton. It was a woful affair, crumbling to pieces along the road in the saddest manner; very heart-rending to the poor fellow who had to drive it, and body-rending to some of the five passengers who were tossed to and fro as every fresh fragment deserted the parent vehicle with a jerk. And then, when we had to send the axle to be mended, that staying in the road for two hours and a half among the musquitoes! Ohe! ohe! Ugh! ugh!

It grieves me to mention this, seeing that rose colour was so clearly the prevailing tint in all matters belonging

to Guiana. And I would have forgiven it had the
phaeton simply broken down on the road. All sublunar
phaetons are subject to such accidents. Why else should
they have been named after him of the heavens who first
suffered from such mishaps? But this phaeton had broken
down before it commenced its journey. It started on a
system of ropes, bandages, and patches which were dis-
graceful to such a colony and such a Governor; and I
should intromit a clear duty, were I to allow it to escape
the gibbet.

But we did reach New Amsterdam not more than
five hours after time. I have but very little to say of the
road, except this; that there is ample scope for sugar and
ample room for Coolies.

Every now and then we came upon negro villages.
All villages in this country must be negro villages, one
would say, except the few poor remaining huts of the
Indians, which are not encountered on the white man's
path. True; but by a negro village I mean a site which
is now the freehold possession of negroes, having been
purchased by them since the days of emancipation, with
their own money, and for their own purposes; so that
they might be in all respects free; free to live in idleness, or to do such work as an estated man may choose to
do for himself, his wife, his children, and his property.

There are many such villages in Guiana, and I was
told that when the arrangements for the purchases were
made the dollars were subscribed by the negroes so
quickly and in such quantities that they were taken to
the banks in wheelbarrows. At any rate, the result has
been that tracts of ground have been bought by these
people and are now owned by them in fee simple.

It is grievous to me to find myself driven to differ on
such points as these from men with whose views I have
up to this period generally agreed. But I feel myself

bound to say that the freeholding negroes in Guiana do
not appear to me to answer. In the first place it seems
that they have found great difficulty in dividing the land
among themselves. In all such combined actions some
persons must be selected as trustworthy; and those who
have been so selected have not been worthy of the trust.
And then the combined action has ceased with the purchase of the land, whereas, to have produced good it
should have gone much further. Combined draining
would have been essential; combined working has been
all but necessary; combined building should have been
adopted. But the negroes, the purchase once made,
would combine no further. They could not understand
that unless they worked together at draining, each man's
own spot of ground would be a swamp. Each would
work a little for himself; but none would work for the
community. A negro village therefore is not a picturesque object.

They are very easily known. The cottages, or houses
—for some of them have aspired to strong, stable, two-
storied slated houses—stand in extreme disorder, one here
and another there, just as individual caprice may have
placed them. There seems to have been no attempt at
streets or lines of buildings, and certainly not at regu-
larity in building. Then there are no roads, and hardly
a path to each habitation. As the ground is not drained,
in wet weather the whole place is half drowned. Most of
the inhabitants will probably have made some sort of dyke
for the immediate preservation of their own dwellings;
but as those dykes are not cut with any common purpose,
they become little more than overflowing ponds, among
which the negro children crawl and scrape in the mud;
and are either drowned, or escape drowning, as Providence
may direct. The spaces between the buildings are covered
with no verdure: they are mere mud patches, and are

cracked in dry weather, wet, slippery, and filthy in the rainy seasons.

The plantation grounds of these people are outside the village, and afford, I am told, cause for constant quarrelling. They do, however, also afford means of support for the greater part of the year, so that the negroes can live, some without work and some by working one or two days in the week.

It may perhaps be difficult to explain why a man should be expected to work if he can live on his own property without working, and enjoy such comforts as he desires. And it may be equally difficult to explain why complaint should be made as to the wretchedness of any men who do not themselves feel that their own state is wretched. But, nevertheless, on seeing what there is here to be seen, it is impossible to withstand the instinctive conviction that a village of freeholding negroes is a failure ; and that the community has not been served by the process, either as regards themselves or as regards the country.

Late at night we did reach New Amsterdam, and crossed the broad Berbice after dark in a little ferry-boat which seemed to be perilously near the water. At ten o'clock I found myself at the hotel, and pronounce it, without hesitation, to be the best inn, not only in that colony, but in any of these Western colonies belonging to Great Britain. It is kept by a negro, one Mr. Paris Brittain, of whom I was informed that he was once a slave. ' O, si sic omnes!' But as regards my experience, he is merely the exception which proves the rule. I am glad, however, to say a good word for the energies and ambition of one of the race, and shall be glad if I can obtain for Mr. Paris Brittain an innkeeper's immortality.

His deserts are so much the greater in that his scope for displaying them is so very limited. No man can walk along the broad strand street of New Amsterdam, and then up into its parallel street, so back towards the starting point, and down again to the sea, without thinking of Knickerbocker and Rip van Winkle. The Dutchman who built New Amsterdam and made it once a thriving town must be still sleeping, as the New York Dutchman once slept, waiting the time when an irruption from Paramaribo and Surinam shall again restore the place to its old possessors.

At present life certainly stagnates at New Amsterdam. Three persons in the street constitute a crowd, and five collected for any purpose would form a goodly club. But the place is clean and orderly, and the houses are good and in good repair. They stand, as do the houses in Georgetown, separately, each surrounded by its own garden or yard, and are built with reference to the wished-for breeze from the west.

The estates up the Berbice river, and the Canje creek which runs into it, are, I believe, as productive as those on the coast, or on the Demerara or Essequibo rivers, and are as well cultivated; but their owners no longer ship their sugars from New Amsterdam. The bar across the Berbice river is objectionable, and the trade of Georgetown has absorbed the business of the colony. In olden times Berbice and Demerara were blessed each with its own Governor, and the two towns stood each on its own bottom as two capitals. But those halcyon days—halcyon for Berbice—are gone; and Rip van Winkle, with all his brethren, is asleep.

I should have said, in speaking of my journey from Demerara to Berbice, that the first fifteen miles were performed by railway. The colony would have fair ground of complaint against me were I to omit to notice that it has so far progressed in civilization as to own a railway. As far as I could learn, the shares do not at present stand at a high premium. From Berbice I returned in a coasting steamer. It was a sleepy, dull, hot journey, without subject of deep interest. I can only remember of it that they gave us an excellent luncheon on board, and luncheons at such times are very valuable in breaking the tedium of the day.

And now a word as to the million hogsheads of sugar and as to the necessary Coolies. Guiana has some reason to be proud, seeing that at present it beats all the neighbouring British colonies in the quantity of sugar produced. I believe that it also beats them all as to the quantity of rum, though Jamaica still stands first as to the quality. In round numbers the sugar exported from Guiana may be stated at seventy thousand hogsheads.

Barbados exports about fifty thousand, Trinidad and Jamaica under forty thousand. No other British West Indian colony gives fifteen thousand; but Guadaloupe and Martinique, two French islands, produce, one over fifty thousand and the other nearly seventy thousand hogsheads. In order to make this measurement intelligible, I may explain that a hogshead is generally said to contain a ton weight of sugar, but that, when reaching the market, it very rarely does come up to that weight. I do not give this information as statistically correct, but as being sufficiently so to guide the ideas of a man only ordinarily anxious to be acquainted in an ordinary manner with what is going on in the West Indies. I would not, therefore, recommend any Member of Parliament to quote the above figures in the House.

Some twelve years ago the whole produce of sugar in the West Indies, including Guiana and excluding the Spanish islands, was 275,000 hogsheads. The amount which I have above recapitulated, in which the smaller islands have been altogether omitted, exceeds 310,000. It may therefore bé taken as a fact that, on the whole, the evil days have come to their worst, and that the

N

tables are turned. It must however be admitted that the above figures tell more for French than for English prosperity

In these countries sugar and labour are almost synonymous; at any rate, they are convertible substances. In none of the colonies named, except Barbados, is the amount of sugar produced limited by any other law than the amount of labour to be obtained ; and in none of them, with that one exception, can any prosperity be hoped for, excepting by means of immigrating labour. What I mean to state is this : that the extent of native work which can be obtained by the planters and land-owners at terms which would enable them to grow their produce and bring it to the market does not in any of these colonies suffice for success. It can be worth no man's while to lay out his capital in Jamaica, in Trinidad, or in Guiana, unless he has reasonable hope that labouring men will be brought into those countries. The great West Indian question is now this : Is there reasonable ground for such hope?

The Anti-Slavery Society tells us that we ought to have no such hope —that it is simply hoping for a return of slavery ; that black or coloured labourers brought from other lands to the West Indies cannot be regarded as free men ; that labourers so brought will surely be illused ; and that the native negro labourer requires protection. As to that question of the return to slavery I have already said what few words I have to offer. In one sense, no dependent man working for wages can be free. He must abide by the terms of his contract. But in the usually accepted sense of the word freedom, the Coolie or Chinaman immigrating to the West Indies is free.

As to the charge of ill usage, it appears to me that these men could not be treated with more tenderness, unless they were put separately, each under his own glass case, with a piece of velvet on which to lie. In England

we know of no such treatment for field labourers. On their
arrival in Demerara they are distributed among the planters
by the Governor, to each planter according to his application, his means of providing for them, and his willingness
and ability to pay the cost of the immigration by yearly
instalments. They are sent to no estate till a government
officer shall have reported that there are houses for them
to occupy. There must be a hospital for them on the
estate, and a regular doctor with a sufficient salary. The
rate of their wages is stipulated, and their hours of work.
Though the contract is for five years, they can leave the
estate at the end of the first three, transferring their services to any other master, and at the end of the five years
they are entitled to a free passage home.

If there be no hardship in all this to the immigrating
Coolie, it may, perhaps, be thought that there is hardship
to the planter who receives him. He is placed very much
at the mercy of the Governor, who, having the power of
giving or refusing Coolies, becomes despotic. And then,
when this stranger from Hindostan has been taught something of his work, he can himself select another master,
so that one planter may bribe away the labourers of
another. This, however, is checked to a certain degree
by a regulation which requires the bribing interloper to
pay a portion of the expense of immigration.

As to the native negro requiring protection—protection,
that is, against competitive labour—the idea is too absurd
to require any argument to refute it. As it at present is,
the competition having been established, and being now in
existence to a certain small extent, these happy negro
gentlemen will not work on an average more than three
days a week, nor for above six hours a day. I saw a gang
of ten or twelve negro girls in a cane-piece, lying idle on
the ground, waiting to commence their week's labour. It
was Tuesday morning. On the Monday they had of

course not come near the field. On the morning of my
visit they were lying with their hoes beside them, medi-
tating whether or no they would measure out their work.
The planter was with me, and they instantly attacked
him. ' No, massa ; we no workey ; money no nuff,' said
one. ' Four bits no pay ! no pay at all !' said another.
' Five bits, massa, and we gin morrow 'arly.' It is hardly
necessary to say that the gentleman refused to bargain
with them. ' They'll measure their work to-morrow,' said
he ; ' on Thursday they will begin, and on Friday they
will finish for the week.' ' But will they not look elsewhere for other work ?' I asked. ' Of course they will,'
he said ; ' occupy a whole day in looking for it ; but
others cannot pay better than I do, and the end will be as
I tell you.' Poor young ladies ! It will certainly be cruel
to subject them to the evil of competition in their labour.

In Guiana the bull has been taken by the horns, as in
Jamaica it unfortunately has not ; and the first main
difficulties of immigration have, I think, been overcome.
For some years past, both from India and from China,
labourers have been brought in freely, and during the last
twelve months the number has been very considerable.
The women also are coming now as well as the men, and
they have learned to husband their means and put money
together.

Such an affair as this—the regular exodus, that is, of a
people to another land—has always progressed with great
rapidity when it has been once established. The difficulty
is to make a beginning. It is natural enough that men
should hesitate to trust themselves to a future of which
they know nothing ; and as natural that they should
hasten to do so when they have heard of the good things
which Providence has in store for them. It required
that some few should come out and prosper, and return
with signs of prosperity. This has now been done, and

as regards Guiana it will not, I imagine, be long before
negro labour is, if not displaced, made, at any rate, of
secondary consequence in the colony. As far as the workmen are concerned, the million hogsheads will, I think,
become a possibility, though not perhaps in the days of
my energetic hopeful friend.

Both the Coolies and the Chinamen have aptitude in
putting money together; and when a man has this aptitude he will work as long as good wages are to be earned.
'Crescit amor nummi quantum ipsa, &c.' We teach our
children this lesson, intending them to understand that
it is pretty nearly the worst of all 'amors,' and we go on
with the 'irritamenta malorum' till we come to the 'Spernere fortior.' It is all, however, of no use. 'Naturam
expellas furcâ;' but the result is still the same. Nature
knows what she is about. The love of money is a good
and useful love. What would the world now be without
it? Or is it even possible to conceive of a world progressing without such a love? Show me ten men without
it, and I will show you nine who lack zeal for improvement. Money, like other loved objects—women, for
instance—should be sought for with honour, won with a
clean conscience, and used with a free hand. Provided it
be so guided, the love of money is no ignoble passion.

The negroes, as a class, have not this aptitude, consequently they lie in the sun and eat yams, and give no
profitable assistance towards that saccharine millennium.
'Spernere fortior!' That big black woman would so say,
she who is not contented with four bits, if her education
had progressed so far. And as she said it, how she would
turn up her African nose, and what contempt she would
express with her broad eyes! Doubtless she does so express
herself among her negro friends in some nigger patois—
'Pernere furshaw!' If so, her philosophy does but little
to assist the world, or herself.

There is another race of men, and of women too, who
have been and now are of the greatest benefit to this
colony, and with them the ' Spernere fortior ' is by no
means a favourite doctrine. There are the Portuguese
who have come to Demerara from Madeira. I believe
that they are not to be found in any of the islands; but
here, in Guiana, they are in great numbers, and thrive
wonderfully. At almost every corner of two streets in
Georgetown is to be seen a small shop; and those shops
are, I think without exception, kept by Portuguese.
Nevertheless they all reached the Demerara river in
absolute poverty, intending to live on the wages of field
labour, and certainly prepared to do their work like men.
As a rule, they are a steady, industrious class, and have
proved themselves to be good citizens. In the future
amalgamation of races, which will take place here as elsewhere in the tropics, the Portugee-Madeira element will
not be the least efficient.

I saw the works on three or four sugar estates in
Demerara, and though I am neither a sugar grower nor
a mechanic, I am able to say that the machinery and
material of this colony much exceed anything I have seen
in any of our own West Indian islands; and in the point
of machinery, equals what I saw in Cuba. Everything is
done on a much larger scale, and in a more proficient
manner than at—Barbados, we will say. I instance
Barbados because the planters there play so excellent a
melody on their own trumpets. In that island not one
planter in five, not one I believe in fifteen, has any steam
appliance on his estate. They trust to the wind for their
motive power, as did their great-great-grandfathers. But
there is steam on every estate in Guiana. The vacuum
pan and the centrifugal machine for extracting the molasses
are known only by name in Barbados, whereas they are
common appliances in Demerara. There two hundred

hogsheads is a considerable produce for one planter. Here they make eight hundred hogsheads, a thousand, and twelve hundred. A Barbados man will reply to this that the thing to be looked to is the profit, or what he will call the clearance. The sugar-consuming world, however, will know nothing about this, will hear nothing of individual profits. But it will recognize the fact that the Demerara sugar is of a better quality than that which comes from Barbados, and will believe that the merchant or planter who does not use the latest appliances of science, whether it be in manufacture or agriculture, will before long go to the wall.

Looking over a sugar estate and sugar works is an exciting amusement certainly, but nevertheless it palls upon one at last. I got quite into the way of doing it; and used to taste the sugars and examine the crystals; make comparisons and pronounce, I must confess as regards Barbados, a good deal of adverse criticism. But this was merely to elicit the true tone of Barbadian eloquence, the long-drawn nasal fecundity of speech which comes forth so fluently when their old windmills are attacked.

But the amusement, as I have said, does pall upon one. In spite of the difference of the machinery, the filtering-bags and centrifugals in one, the Gadsden pans in another, and the simple oscillators in a third—(the Barbados estate stands for the third)—one does get weary of walking up to a sugar battery, and looking at the various heated caldrons, watching till even the inexperienced eye perceives that the dirty liquor has become brown sugar, as it runs down from a dipper into a cooling vat.

I wonder whether I could make the process in any simple way intelligible; or whether in doing so I should afford gratification to a single individual? Were I myself reading such a book of travels I should certainly skip such description. Reader, do thou do likewise. Nevertheless, it shall not exceed three or four pages.

The cane must first be cut. As regards a planted cane, that is the first crop from the plant—(for there are such things as ratoons, of which a word or two will be found elsewhere)—as regards the planted cane, the cutting, I believe, takes place after about fourteen months' growth. The next process is that of the mill; the juice, that is, has to be squeezed out of it. The cane should not lie above two days before it is squeezed. It is better to send it to the mill the day after it is cut, or the hour after; in fact, as soon indeed as may be. In Demerara they are brought to the mill by water always; in Barbados, by carts and mules; in Jamaica, by waggons and oxen; so also in Cuba. The mill consists of three rollers, which act upon each other like cogwheels. The canes are passed between two, an outside one, say, and a centre one; and the refuse stalk, or trash (so called in Jamaica), or magass (so called in Barbados and Demerara), comes out between the same centre one and the other outside roller. The juice meanwhile is strained down to a cistern or receptacle below. These rollers are quite close, so that it would seem to be impossible that the cane should go through; but it does go through with great ease, if the mill be good and powerful; but frequently with great difficulty, if the mill be bad and not powerful; for which latter alternative vide Barbados. The canes give from sixty to seventy per cent. of juice. Sometimes less than sixty, not often over seventy.

The juice, which is then of a dirty-yellow colour, and apparently about the substance of milk, is brought from the mill through a pipe into the first vat, in which it is tempered. This is done with lime, and the object is to remedy the natural acidity of the juice. In this first vat it is warmed, but not more than warmed. It then runs from these vats into boilers, or at any rate into receptacles in which it is boiled. These in Barbados are called taches. At each of these a man stands with a long skimmer, skimmering the juice as it were, and scraping off certain skum which comes to the top. There are from three to seven of these taches, and below them, last of all, is the boiler, the veritable receptacle in which the juice becomes sugar. In the taches, especially the first of them, the liquor becomes dark green in colour. As it gets nearer the boiler it is thicker and more clouded, and begins to assume its well-known tawny hue.

Over the last boiler stands the man who makes the sugar. It is for him to know what heat to apply and how long to apply it. The liquor now ceases to be juice and becomes sugar. This is evident to the eye and nose, for though the stuff in the boiler is of course still liquid, it looks like boiled melted sugar, and the savour is the savour of sugar. When the time has come, and the boiling is boiled, a machine suspended from on high, and called a dipper, is let down into the caldron. It nearly fits the caldron, being, as it were, in itself a smaller caldron going into the other. The sugar naturally runs over the side of this and fills it, some little ingenuity being exercised in the arrangement. The dipper, full of sugar, is then drawn up on high. At the bottom of it is a valve, so that on the pulling of a rope, the hot liquid runs out. This dipper is worked like a crane, and is made to swing itself from over the boiler to a position in which the sugar runs from it through a wooden trough to the flat open vats in which it is cooled.

But at this part of the manufacture there are various different methods. According to that which is least advanced, the sugar is simply cooled in the vat, then put into buckets in a half-solid state, and thrown out of the buckets into the hogsheads.

According to the more advanced method it runs from the dipper down through filtering bags, is then pumped into a huge vacuum pan, a utensil like a kettle-drum turned topsy-turvy, a kettle-drum that is large enough to hold six tons of sugar. Then it is reheated, and then put into open round boxes called centrifugals, the sides of which are made of metal pierced like gauze. These are whisked round and round by steam-power at an enormous rate, and the molasses flies out through the gauze, leaving the sugar dry and nearly white. It is then fit to go into the hogshead, and fit also to be shipped away.

But in the simpler process, the molasses drains from the sugar in the hogshead. To facilitate this, as the sugar is put into the cask, reeds are stuck through it, which communicate with holes at the bottom, so that there may be channels through which the molasses may run. The hogsheads stand upon beams lying a foot apart from each other, and below is a dark abyss into which the molasses falls. I never could divest myself of the idea that the negro children occasionally fall through also, and are then smothered and so distilled into rum.

There are various other processes, intermediate between the highly-civilized vacuum pan and the simple cooling, with which I will not trouble my reader. Nor will I go into the further mystery of rum-making. That the rum is made from the molasses every one knows; and from the negro children, as I suspect.

The process of sugarmaking is very rapid if the appliances be good. A planter in Demerara assured me that he had cut his canes in the morning, and had the sugar in Georgetown in the afternoon. Fudge! however, was the remark made by another planter to whom I repeated this. Whether it was fudge or not I do not know; but it was clearly possible that such should be the case. The manufacture is one which does not require any delay.

In Demerara an acre of canes will on an average give over a ton and a half of sugar. But an acre of cane ground will not give a crop once in twelve months. Two crops in three years may perhaps be the average. So much for the manufacture of sugar. I hope my account may not be criticised by those who are learned in the art, as it is only intended for those who are utterly unlearned.

But if looking over sugar works be at last fatiguing, what shall I say to that labour of 'going aback,' which Guiana planters exact from their visitors. Going aback in Guiana means walking from the house and manufactory back to the fields where the canes grow. I have described the shape of a Demerara estate. The house generally stands not far from the water frontage, so that the main growth of the sugar is behind. This going aback generally takes place before breakfast. But the breakfast is taken at eleven, and a Demerara sun is in all its glory for three hours before that. Remember, also, that there are no trees in these fields, no grass, no wild flowers, no meandering paths Everything is straight, and open, and ugly; and everything has a tendency to sugar, and no other tendency whatever, unless it be to rum. Sugar-canes is the only growth. So that a walk aback, except to a very close inquirer, is not delightful. It must however be confessed that the subsequent breakfast makes up for a deal of misery. There is no such breakfast going as that of a Guiana planter. Talk of Scotland! Pooh! But one has to think of that doctor's dictum—' The prevalent disease, sir? Brandy!' It seems, however, to me to show itself more generally in the shape of champagne.

There is one other peculiar characteristic of landed

property in this colony which I must mention. All the carriage is by water, not only from the works to the town, but from the fields to the works, and even from field to field. The whole country is intersected by drains, which are necessary to carry off the surface waters; there is no natural fall of water, or next to none, and but for its drains and sluices the land would be flooded in wet weather. Parallel to these drains are canals; there being, as nearly as I could learn, one canal between each two drains. These different dykes are to a stranger similar in appearance, but their uses are always kept distinct.

Nor do these canals run only between wide fields, or at a considerable distance from each other. They pierce every portion of land, so that the canes when cut have never to be carried above a few yards. The expense of keeping them in order is very great, but the labour of making them must have been immense. It was done by the Dutch. One may almost question whether any other race would have had the patience necessary for such a work.

I was told on one estate that there were no less than sixty-three miles of these cuttings to be kept in order. But the gentleman who told me was he to whom the other gentleman alluded, when he used our old friend Mr. Burchell's exclamation. There can be no doubt but that these Guiana planters know each other.

On the whole I must express my conviction that this is a fine colony, and will become of very great importance.

Our great Thunderer the other day spoke of the governance of a sugar island as a duty below a man's notice; as being almost worthy of contempt. We cannot all be gods and forge thunderbolts. But we all wish to consume sugar; and if we can do in one of our colonies without slaves what Cuba is doing with slaves, the work I think will not be contemptible, nor the land contemptible in which it is done. I do look to see our free Cuba in Guiana, and even have my hopes as to that million of hogsheads.

I have said, in speaking of Jamaica, that I thought the negro had hardly yet shown himself capable of understanding the teaching of the Christian religion. As regards Guiana, what I heard on this matter I heard chiefly from clergymen of the Church of England ; and though they would of course not agree with me—for it is not natural that a man should doubt the efficacy of his own teaching —nevertheless, what I gathered from them strengthens my former opinions.

I do think that the Guiana negro is in this respect somewhat superior to his brother in Jamaica. He is more intelligent, and comes nearer to our idea of a thoughtful being. But still even here it seems to me that he never connects his religion with his life ; never reflects that his religion should bear upon his conduct.

Here, as in the islands, the negroes much prefer to belong to a Baptist congregation, or to a so-called Wesleyan body. That excitement is there allowed to them which is denied in our church. They sing and hallo and scream, and have revivals. They talk of their ' dear brothers ' and ' dear sisters,' and in their ecstatic howlings get some fun for their money. I doubt also whether those disagreeable questions as to conduct are put by the Baptists which they usually have to undergo from our clergymen. ' So-called Wesleyans,' I say, because the practice of their worship here is widely removed from the sober gravity of the Wesleyan churches in England.

I have said that the form of government in Guiana was a mild despotism, tempered by sugar. The Governor, it must be understood, has not absolute authority. There is a combined house, with a power of voting, by whom he is controlled—at any rate in financial matters. But of those votes he commands many as Governor, and as long as he will supply Coolies quick enough—and Coolies mean sugar—he may command them all.

' We are not particular to a shade,' the planters wisely say to him, ' in what way we are governed. If you have any fads of your own about this or about that, by all means indulge them. Even if you want a little more money, in God's name take it. But the business of a man's life is sugar : there's the land ; the capital shall be forthcoming, whether begged, borrowed, or stolen ;—do you supply the labour. Give us Coolies enough, and we will stick at nothing. We are an ambitious colony. There looms before us a great future—a million hogsheads of sugar !'

The form of government here is somewhat singular. There are two Houses—Lords and Commons—but not acting separately as ours do. The upper House is the Court of Policy. This consists of five official members, whose votes may therefore be presumed to be at the service of the Governor, and of five elected members. The Governor himself, sitting in this court, has the casting vote. But he also has something to say to the election of the other five. They are chosen by a body of men called Kiezers—probably Dutch for choosers. There is a college of Kiezers, elected for life by the tax-payers, whose main privilege appears to be that of electing these members of the Court of Policy. But on every occasion they send up two names, and the Governor selects one ; so that he can always keep out any one man who may be peculiarly disagreeable to him. This Court of Policy acts, I think, when acting by itself, more as a privy council to the Governor than as a legislative body.

Then there are six Financial Representatives ; two from Berbice, one from town and one from country ; two from Demerara, one from town and one from country ; and two from Essequibo, both from the country, there

being no town. These are elected by the tax-payers.
They are assembled for purposes of taxation only, as far
as I understood; and even as regards this they are joined
with the Court of Policy, and thus form what is called the
Combined Court. The Crown, therefore, has very little
to tie its hands; and I think that I am justified in describing the government as a mild despotism, tempered by
sugar.

So much for British Guiana. I cannot end this crude
epitome of crude views respecting the colony without
saying that I never met a pleasanter set of people than
I found there, or ever passed my hours much more
joyously.

CHAPTER XIII.

BARBADOS.

BARBADOS is a very respectable little island, and it makes a great deal of sugar. It is not picturesquely beautiful, as are almost all the other Antilles, and therefore has but few attractions for strangers.

But this very absence of scenic beauty has saved it from the fate of its neighbours. A country that is broken into landscapes, that boasts of its mountains, woods, and waterfalls, that is regarded for its wild loveliness, is seldom propitious to agriculture. A portion of the surface in all such regions defies the improving farmer. But, beyond this, such ground under the tropics offers every inducement to the negro squatter. In Jamaica, Dominica, St. Lucia, and Grenada, the negro, when emancipated, could squat and make himself happy; but in Barbados there was not an inch for him.

When emancipation came there was no squatting ground for the poor Barbadian. He had still to work and make sugar—work quite as hard as he had done while yet a slave. He had to do that or to starve. Consequently, labour has been abundant in this island, and in this island only; and in all the West Indian troubles it has kept its head above water, and made sugar respectably—not, indeed, showing much sugar genius, or going ahead in the way of improvements, but paying twenty shillings in the pound, supporting itself, and earning its bread decently by the sweat of its brow. The pity is that the Barbadians themselves should think so much of their own achievements.

The story runs, that when Europe was convulsed by revolutions and wars—when continental sovereigns were flying hither and thither, and there was so strong a rumour that Napoleon was going to eat us—the great Napoleon I mean—that then, I say, the Barbadians sent word over to poor King George the Third, bidding him fear nothing. If England could not protect him, Barbados would. Let him come to them, if things looked really blue on his side of the Channel. It was a fine, spirited message, but perhaps a little self-glorious. That, I should say, is the character of the island in general.

As to its appearance, it is, as I have said, totally different from any of the other islands, and to an English eye much less attractive in its character. But for the heat its appearance would not strike with any surprise an Englishman accustomed to an ordinary but ugly agricultural country. It has not the thick tropical foliage which is so abundant in the other islands, nor the wild, grassy dells. Happily for the Barbadians every inch of it will produce canes; and, to the credit of the Barbadians, every inch of it does so. A Barbadian has a right to be proud of this, but it does not make the island interesting. It is the waste land of the world that makes it picturesque. But there is not a rood of waste land in Barbados. It certainly is not the country for a gipsy immigration. Indeed, I doubt whether there is even room for a picnic.

The island is something over twenty miles long, and something over twelve broad. The roads are excellent, but so white that they sadly hurt the eye of a stranger. The authorities have been very particular about their milestones, and the inhabitants talk much about their

o

journeys. I found myself constantly being impressed with ideas of distance, till I was impelled to suggest a rather extended system of railroads—a proposition which was taken in very good part. I was informed that the population was larger than that of China, but my informant of course meant by the square foot. He could hardly have counted by the square mile in Barbados.

And thus I was irresistibly made to think of the frog that would blow itself out and look as large as an ox.

Bridgetown, the metropolis of the island, is much like a second or third rate English town. It has none of the general peculiarities of the West Indies, except the heat. The streets are narrow, irregular, and crooked, so that at first a stranger is apt to miss his way. They all, however, converge at Trafalgar Square, a spot which, in Barbados, is presumed to compete with the open space at Charing Cross bearing the same name. They have this resemblance, that each contains a statue of Nelson. The Barbadian Trafalgar Square contains also a tree, which is more than can be said for its namesake. It can make also this boast, that no attempt has been made within it which has failed so grievously as our picture gallery. In saying this, however, I speak of the building only—by no means of the pictures.

There are good shops in Bridgetown—good, respectable, well-to-do shops, that sell everything from a candle down to a coffin, including wedding-rings, corals, and widows' caps. But they are hot, fusty, crowded places, as are such places in third-rate English towns. But then the question of heat here is of such vital moment! A purchase of a pair of gloves in Barbados drives one at once into the ice-house.

And here it may be well to explain this very peculiar, delightful, but too dangerous West Indian institution. By-the-by I do not know that there was any ice-house in

Kingston, Jamaica. If there be one there, my friends were peculiarly backward, for I certainly was not made acquainted with it. But everywhere else—at Demerara, Trinidad, Barbados, and St. Thomas—I was duly introduced to the ice-house.

There is something cool and mild in the name, which makes one fancy that ladies would delight to frequent it. But, alas! a West Indian ice-house is but a drinking-shop —a place where one goes to liquor, as the Americans call it, without the knowledge of the feminine creation. It is a drinking-shop, at which the draughts are all cool, are all iced, but at which, alas! they are also all strong. The brandy, I fear, is as essential as the ice. A man may, it is true, drink iced soda water without any concomitant, or he may simply have a few drops of raspberry vinegar to flavour it. No doubt many an easy-tempered wife so imagines. But if so, I fear that they are deceived. Now the ice-house in Bridgetown seemed to me to be peculiarly well attended. I look upon this as the effect of the white streets and the fusty shops.

Barbados claims, I believe—but then it claims everything—to have a lower thermometer than any other West Indian island—to be, in fact, cooler than any of her sisters. As far as the thermometer goes, it may be possible; but as regards the human body, it is not the fact. Let any man walk from his hotel to morning church and back, and then judge.

There is a mystery about hotels in the British West Indies. They are always kept by fat, middle-aged coloured ladies, who have no husbands. I never found an exception except at Berbice, where my friend Paris Brittain keeps open doors in the city of the sleepers. These ladies are generally called Miss So-and-So; Miss Jenny This, or Miss Jessy That; but they invariably seemed to have a knowledge of the world, especially of

o 2

the male hotel-frequenting world, hardly compatible with
a retiring maiden state of life. ·I only mention this. I
cannot solve the riddle. 'Davus sum, non Œdipus.'
But it did strike me as singular that the profession should
always be in the hands of these ladies, and that they should
never get husbands.

As a rule, there is not much to be said against these
hotels, though they will not come up to the ideas of a
traveller who has been used to the inns of Switzerland.
The table is always plentifully supplied, and the viands
generally good. Of that at Barbados I can make no
complaint, except this; that the people over the way kept
a gray parrot which never ceased screaming day or night.
I was deep in my Jamaica theory of races, and this
wretched bird nearly drove me wild.

'Can anything be done to stop it, James?'

'No, massa.'

'Nothing? Wouldn't they hang a cloth over it for a
shilling?'

'No, massa; him only make him scream de more to
speak to him.'

I took this as final, though whether the 'him' was the
man or the parrot, I did not know. But such a bird I
never heard before, and the street was no more than
twelve feet broad. He was, in fact, just under my
window. Thrice had I to put aside my theory of races.
Otherwise than on this score Miss Caroline Lee's hotel
at Barbados is very fair. And as for hot pickles—she is
the very queen of them.

Whether or no my informant was right in saying that
the population of Barbados is more dense than that of
China, I cannot say; but undoubtedly it is very great;
and hence, as the negroes cannot get their living without
working, has come the prosperity of the island. The inhabitants are, I believe, very nearly 150,000 in number.

This is a greater population than that of the whole of Guiana. The consequence is, that the cane-pieces are cultivated very closely, and that all is done that manual labour can do.

The negroes here differ much, I think, from those in the other islands, not only in manner, but even in form and physiognomy. They are of heavier build, broader in the face, and higher in the forehead. They are also certainly less good-humoured, and more inclined to insolence ; so that if anything be gained in intelligence it is lost in conduct. On the whole, I do think that the Barbados negroes are more intelligent than others that I have met. It is probable that this may come from more continual occupation.

But if the black people differ from their brethren of the other islands, so certainly do the white people. One soon learns to know a—Bim. That is the name in which they themselves delight, and therefore, though there is a sound of slang about it, I give it here. One certainly soon learns to know a Bim. The most peculiar distinction is in his voice. There is always a nasal twang about it, but quite distinct from the nasality of a Yankee. The Yankee's word rings sharp through his nose ; not so that of the first-class Bim. There is a soft drawl about it, and the sound is seldom completely formed. The effect on the ear is the same as that on the hand when a man gives you his to shake, and instead of shaking yours, holds his own still. When a man does so to me I always wish to kick him.

I had never any wish to kick the Barbadian, more especially as they are all stout men ; but I cannot but think that if he were well shaken a more perfect ring would come out of him.

The Bims, as I have said, are generally stout fellows. As a rule they are larger and fairer than other West

Indian Creoles, less delicate in their limbs, and more
clumsy in their gait. The male graces are not much
studied in Barbados. But it is not only by their form or
voice that you may know them—not only by the voice,
but by the words. No people ever praised themselves so
constantly: no set of men were ever so assured that they
and their occupations are the main pegs on which the
world hangs. Their general law to men would be this:
' Thou shalt make sugar in the sweat of thy brow, and
make it as it is made in Barbados.' Any deviation from
that law would be a deviation from the highest duty of
man.

Of many of his sister colonies a Barbadian can speak
with temper. When Jamaica is mentioned philanthropic
compassion lights up his face, and he tells you how much
he feels for the poor wretches there who call themselves
planters. St. Lucia also he pities, and Grenada; and of
St. Vincent he has some hope. Their little efforts he
says are praiseworthy; only, alas! they are so little! He
does not think much of Antigua; and turns up his nose
at Nevis and St. Kitts, which in a small way are doing a
fair stroke of business. The French islands he does not
love, but that is probably patriotism: as the French
islands are successful sugar growers such patriotism is
natural. But do not speak to him of Trinidad; that
subject is very sore. And as for Guiana ——! One
knows what to expect if one holds a red rag up to a bull.
Praise Guiana sugar-making in Bridgetown, and you will
be holding up a red rag to a dozen bulls, no one of which
will refuse the challenge. And thus you may always
know a Bim.

When I have met four or five together, I have not
dared to try this experiment, for they are wrathy men,
and have rough sides to their tongues; but I have so
encountered two at a time.

'Yes,' I have said; 'the superiority of Barbados cannot be doubted. We all grant that. But which colony is second in the race?'

'It is impossible to say,' said A. 'They are none of them well circumstanced.'

'None of them have got any labour,' said B.

'They can't make returns,' said A.

'Just look at their clearances,' said B; 'and then look at ours.'

'Jamaica sugar is paying now,' I remarked.

'Jamaica, sir, has been destroyed root and branch,' said A, well pleased; for they delight to talk of Jamaica.

'And no one can lament it more than I do,' said B. 'Jamaica is a fine island, only utterly ruined.'

'Magnificent! such scenery!' I replied.

'But it can't make sugar,' said B.

'What of Trinidad?' I asked.

'Trinidad, sir, is a fine wild island; and perhaps some day we may get our coal there.'

'But Demerara makes a little sugar,' I ventured to remark.

'It makes deuced little money, I know,' said A.

'Every inch of it is mortgaged,' said B.

'But their steam-engines,' said I.

'Look at their clearances,' said A.

'They have none,' said B.

'At any rate, they have got beyond windmills,' I remarked, with considerable courage.

'Because they have got no wind,' said A.

'A low bank of mud below the sea-level,' said B.

'But a fine country for sugar,' said I.

'They don't know what sugar is,' said A.

'Look at their vacuum pans,' said I.

'All my eye,' said B.

'And their filtering-bags,' said I.

'Filtering-bags be d—,' said A.

'Centrifugal machines,' said I, now nearly exhausted.

'We've tried them, and abandoned them long ago,' said B, only now coming well on to the fight.

'Their sugar is nearly white,' said I ; 'and yours is a dirty brown.'

'Their sugar don't pay,' said A, 'and ours does.'

'Look at the price of our land,' said B.

'Yes, and the extent of it,' said I.

'Our clearances, sir ! The clearances, sir, are the thing,' said A.

'The year's income,' said B.

'A hogshead to the acre,' said I ; 'and that only got from guano.'

This was my last shot at them. They both came at me open-mouthed together, and I confess that I retired, vanquished, from the field.

It is certainly the fact that they do make their sugar in a very old-fashioned way in Barbados, using windmills instead of steam, and that you see less here of the improved machinery for the manufacture than in Demerara, or Cuba, or Trinidad, or even in Jamaica. The great answer given to objections is that the old system pays best. It may perhaps do so for the present moment, though I should doubt even that. But I am certain that it cannot continue to do so. No trade, and no agriculture can afford to dispense with the improvements of science.

I found some here who acknowledged that the mere produce of the cane from the land had been pressed too far by means of guano. A great crop is thus procured, but it appears that the soil is injured, and that the sugar is injured also. The canes, moreover, will not ratoon as they used to do, and as they still do in other parts of the West Indies. The cane is planted, and when ripe is cut. If allowed, another cane will grow from the same plant, and that is a ratoon; and again a third will grow, giving a third crop from the same plant; and in many soils a fourth; and in some few many more; and one hears of canes ratooning for twenty years.

If the same amount and quality of sugar be produced, of course the system of ratooning must be by far the cheapest and most profitable. In I believe most of our colonies the second crop is as good as the first, and I understand that it used to be so in Barbados. But it is not so now. The ratoon almost always looks poor, and the second ratoons appear to be hardly worth cutting. I believe that this is so much the case that many Barbados planters now look to get but one crop only from each planting. This falling off in the real fertility of the soil is I think owing to the use of artificial manure, such as guano.

There is a system all through these sugar growing countries of burning the magass, or trash; that is the stalk of the cane, or remnant of the stalk after it comes through the mill. What would be said of an English agriculturist who burnt his straw? It is I believe one of the soundest laws of agriculture that the refuse of the crop should return to the ground which gave it.

To this it will be answered that the English agriculturist is not called on by the necessity of his position to burn his straw. He has not to boil his wheat, nor yet his beef and mutton; whereas the Barbados farmer is obliged to boil his crop. At the present moment the Barbados farmer is under this obligation; but he is not obliged to do it with the refuse produce of his fields. He cannot perhaps use coals immediately under his boilers, but he can heat them with steam which comes pretty much to the same thing.

All this applies not to Barbados only, but to Guiana, Jamaica, and the other islands also. At all of them the magass or trash is burnt. But at none of them is manure so much needed as at Barbados. They cannot there take into cultivation new fresh virgin soil when they wish it, as they can in Guiana.

And then one is tempted to ask the question, whether every owner of land is obliged to undertake all the complete duties which now are joined together at a sugar estate? It certainly is the case, that no single individual could successfully set himself against the system. But I do not see why a collection of individuals should not do so.

A farmer in England does not grow the wheat, then grind it, and then make the bread. The growing is enough for him. Then comes the miller, and the baker. But on a sugar estate, one and the same man grows the cane, makes the sugar, and distils the rum; thus altogether opposing the salutary principle of the division of labour. I cannot see why the grower should not sell his canes to a sugar manufacturer. There can, I believe, be no doubt of this, that sugar can be made better and cheaper in large quantities than in small.

But the clearance, sir; that is the question. How would this affect the clearance? The sugar manufacturer would want his profit. Of course he would, as do the miller and the baker.

They complain greatly at Barbados, as they do indeed elsewhere, that they are compelled to make bad sugar by the differential duty. The duty on good sugar is so much higher than that on bad sugar, that the bad or coarse sugar pays them best. This is the excuse they give for not making a finer article, and I believe that the excuse is true.

I made one or two excursions in the island, and was allowed the privilege of attending an agricultural breakfast, at which there were some twenty or thirty planters. It seems that a certain number of gentlemen living in the same locality had formed themselves into a society, with the object of inspecting each other's estates. A committee of three was named in each case by the president; and this committee, after surveying the estate in question, and looking at the works and stock, drew up a paper, either laudatory or the reverse, which paper was afterwards read to the society. These readings took place after the breakfast, and the breakfast was held monthly. To the planter probably the reading of the documents was the main object. It may not be surprising that I gave the preference to the breakfast, which of its kind was good.

But this was not the only breakfast of the sort at which I was allowed to be a guest. The society has always its one great monthly breakfast; but the absolute inspection gives occasions for further breakfasts. I was also at one of these, and assisted in inspecting the estate. There were, however, too many Barbadians present to permit of my producing my individual views respecting the Guiana improvements.

The report is made at the time of the inspection, but it is read in public at the monthly meeting. The effect no doubt is good, and the publicity of the approval or disapproval stimulates the planter. But I was amused with the true Barbadian firmness with which the gentlemen criticised declared that they would not the less take their own way, and declined to follow the advice offered to them in the report. I heard two such reports read, and in both cases this occurred.

All this took place at Hookleton cliff, which the Barbadians regard as the finest point for scenery in the island. The breakfast I own was good, and the discourse useful and argumentative. But as regards the scenery, there is little to be said for it, considering that I had seen Jamaica, and was going to see Trinidad.

Even in Barbados, numerous as are the negroes, they certainly live an easier life than that of an English labourer, earn their money with more facility, and are more independent of their masters. A gentleman having one hundred and fifty families living on his property would not expect to obtain from them the labour of above ninety men at the usual rate of pay, and that for not more than five days a week. They live in great comfort, and in some things are beyond measure extravagant.

'Do you observe,' said a lady to me, 'that the women when they walk never hold up their dresses?'

'I certainly have,' I answered. 'Probably they are but ill shod, and do not care to show their feet.'

'Not at all. Their feet have nothing to do with it. But they think it economical to hold up their petticoats. It betokens a stingy, saving disposition, and they prefer to show that they do not regard a few yards of muslin more or less.'

This is perfectly true of them. As the shopman in Jamaica said to me—In this part of the world we must never think of little economies. The very negroes are ashamed to do so.

Of the coloured people I saw nothing, except that the shops are generally attended by them. They seemed not to be so numerous as they are elsewhere, and are, I think, never met with in the society of white people. In no instance did I meet one, and I am told that in Barbados there is a very rigid adherence to this rule. Indeed, one never seems to have the alternative of seeing them; whereas in Jamaica one has not the alternative of avoiding them. As regards myself, I would much rather have been thrown among them.

I think that in all probability the white settlers in Barbados have kept themselves more distinct from the negro race, and have not at any time been themselves so burdened with coloured children as is the case elsewhere. If this be so, they certainly deserve credit for their prudence.

Here also there is a King, Lords, and Commons, or a governor, a council, and an assembly. The council consists of twelve, and are either chosen by the Crown, or enjoy their seat by virtue of office held by appointment from the Crown. The Governor in person sits in the council. The assembly consists of twenty-two, who are annually elected by the parishes. None but white men do vote at these elections, though no doubt a black man could vote, if a black man were allowed to obtain a freehold. Of course, therefore, none but white men can be elected. How it is decided whether a man be white or not, that I did not hear. The greater part of the legislative business of the island is done by committees, who are chosen from these bodies.

Here, as elsewhere through the West Indies, one meets with unbounded hospitality. A man who dines out on Monday will receive probably three invitations for Tuesday, and six for Wednesday. And they entertain very well. That haunch of mutton and turkey, which are now the bugbear of the English dinner-giver, do not seem to trouble the minds or haunt the tables of West Indian hosts.

And after all, Barbados—little England as it delights to call itself—is and should be respected among islands. It owes no man anything, pays its own way, and never makes a poor mouth. Let us say what we will self-respect is a fine quality, and the Barbadians certainly enjoy that. It is a very fine quality, and generally leads to respect from others. They who have nothing to say for themselves will seldom find others to say much for them. I therefore repeat what I said at first. Barbados is a very respectable little island, and, considering the limited extent of its acreage, it does make a great deal of sugar.

CHAPTER XIV.

TRINIDAD.

No scenery can be more picturesque than that afforded by the entrance to Port of Spain, the chief town in the island of Trinidad. Trinidad, as all men doubtless know, is the southernmost of the West Indian islands, and lies across the delta of the Orinoco river. The western portion of the island is so placed that it nearly reaches with two horns two different parts of the mainland of Venezuela, one of the South American republics. And thus a bay is formed closed in between the island and the mainland, somewhat as is the Gulf of Mexico by the island of Cuba; only that the proportions here are much less in size. This enclosed sea is called the Gulf of Paria.

The two chief towns, I believe I may say the two only towns in Trinidad, are situated on this bay. That which is the larger, and the seat of government, is called the Port of Spain, and lies near to the northern horn. San Fernando, the other, which is surrounded by the finest sugar districts of the island, and which therefore devotes its best energies to the export of that article, is on the other side of the bay and near the other horn.

The passages into the enclosed sea on either side are called the Bocas, or mouths. Those nearest to the delta of the Orinoco are the Serpent's mouths. The ordinary approach from England or the other islands is by the other or more northern entrance. Here there are three passages, of which the middle is the largest one, the Boca Grande. That between the mainland and a small island is used by the steamers in fine weather, and is by far the prettiest. Through this, the Boca di Mona, or Monkey's mouth, we approached Port of Spain. These northern entrances are called the Dragon's mouths. What may be the nautical difference between the mouth of a dragon and that of a serpent I did not learn.

On the mainland, that is the land of the main island, the coast is precipitous, but clothed to the very top with the thickest and most magnificent foliage. With an opera-glass one can distinctly see the trees coming forth from the sides of the rocks as though no soil were necessary for them, and not even a shelf of stone needed for their support. And these are not shrubs, but forest trees, with grand spreading branches, huge trunks, and brilliant coloured foliage. The small island on the other side is almost equally wooded, but is less precipitous. Here, however, there are open glades, and grassy enclosures, which tempt one to wish that it was one's lot to lie there in the green shade and eat bananas and mangoes. This little island in the good old days, regretted by not a few, when planters where planters and slaves were slaves, produced cotton up to its very hill-tops. Now I believe it yields nothing but the grass for a few cattle.

Our steamer as she got well into the boca drew near to the shore of the large island, and as we passed along we had a succession of lovely scenes. Soft-green smiling nooks made themselves visible below the rocks, the very spots for picnics. One could not but long to be there with straw hats and crinoline, pigeon pies and champagne baskets. There was one narrow shady valley, into which a creek of the sea ran up, that must have been made for such purposes, either for that, or for the less noisy joys of some Paul of Trinidad with his creole Virginia.

As we steamed on a little further we came to a whaling establishment. Ideas of whaling establishments naturally connect themselves with icebergs and the North Pole. But it seems that there are races of whales as there are of men, proper to the tropics as well as to the poles; and some of the former here render up their oily tributes. From the look of the place I should not say that the trade was flourishing. The whaling huts are very picturesque, but do not say much for the commercial enterprise of the proprietors.

From them we went on through many smaller islands to Port of Spain. This is a large town, excellently well laid out, with the streets running all at right angles to each other, as is now so common in new towns. The spaces have been prepared for a much larger population than that now existing, so that it is at present straggling, unfilled, and full of gaps. But the time will come, and that before long, when it will be the best town in the British West Indies. There is at present in Port of Spain a degree of commercial enterprise quite unlike the sleepiness of Jamaica or the apathy of the smaller islands.

I have now before me at the present moment of writing a debate which took place in the House of Commons the other day—it is only the other day as I now write—on a motion made by Mr. Buxton for a committee to inquire into the British West Indies; and though somewhat afraid of being tedious on the subject of immigration to these parts, I will say a few words as to this motion in as far as it affects not only Trinidad, but all those colonies. Of all subjects this is the one that is of real importance to the West Indies; and it may be expected that the sugar colonies will or will not prosper, as that subject is or is not understood by its rulers.

I think I may assume that the intended purport of Mr. Buxton's motion was to throw impediments in the way of the immigration of Coolies into Jamaica, and that in making it he was acting as the parliamentary mouthpiece of the Anti-Slavery Society. The legislature of Jamaica has at length passed a law with the object of promoting this immigration, as it has been promoted at the Mauritius, and in a lesser degree in British Guiana and Trinidad; but the Anti-Slavery Society have wished to induce the Crown to use its authority and abstain from sanctioning this law, urging that it will be injurious to the interests of the negro labourers.

The 'peculiar institution' of slavery is, I imagine, quite as little likely to find friends in England now as it was when the question of its abolition was so hotly pressed some thirty years since. And God forbid that I should use either the strength or the weakness of my pen in saying a word in favour of a system so abhorrent to the feelings of a Christian Englishman. But may we not say that that giant has been killed? Is it not the case that the Anti-Slavery Society has done its work?—has done its work at any rate as regards the British West Indies? What should we have said of the Anti-Corn-Law League, had it chosen to sit in permanence after the repeal of the obnoxious tax, with the view of regulating the fixed price of bread?

Such is the attempt now being made by the Anti-Slavery Society with reference to the West Indian negroes. If any men are free, these men are so. They have been left without the slightest constraint or bond over them. In the sense in which they are free, no English labourer is free. In England a man cannot select whether he will work or whether he will let it alone. He, the poor Englishman, has that freedom which God seems to have intended as good for man; but work he must. If he do not do so willingly, compulsion is in some sort brought to bear upon him. He is not free to be idle; and I presume that no English philanthropists will go so far as to wish to endow him with that freedom.

But that is the freedom which the negro has in Jamaica, which he still has in many parts of Trinidad, and which the Anti-Slavery Society is so anxious to secure for him. It—but no; I will give the Society no monopoly of such honour. We, we Englishmen, have made our negroes free. If by further efforts we can do anything towards making other black men free—if we can assist in driving slavery from the earth, in God's name let us still be doing. Here may be scope enough for an Anti-Slavery Society. But I maintain that these men are going beyond their mark—that they are minding other than their own business, in attempting to interfere with the labour of the West Indian colonies. Gentlemen in the West Indies see at once that the Society is discussing matters which it has not studied, and that interests of the utmost import-ance to them are being played with in the dark.

Mr. Buxton grounded his motion on these two pleas:— Firstly, That the distress of the West Indian planters had been brought about by their own apathy and indiscretion. And secondly, That that distress was in course of relief, —would quickly be relieved without any further special measures for its mitigation. I think that he was sub-stantially wrong in both these allegations.

That there were apathetic and indiscreet planters— that there were absentees whose property was not suffi-cient to entitle them to the luxury of living away from it, may doubtless have been true. But the tremendous distress which came upon these colonies fell on them in too sure a manner, with too sudden a blow, to leave any doubt as to its cause. Slavery was first abolished, and the protective duty on slave-grown sugar was then withdrawn. The second measure brought down almost to nothing the property of the most industrious as well as that of the most idle of the planters. Except in Barbados, where the nature of the soil made labour compulsory, where the negro could no more be idle and exist than the poor man can do in England, it became impossible to produce sugar with a profit on which the grower could live. It was not only the small men who fell, or they who may be supposed to have been hitherto living on an income raised to an unjustly high pitch. Ask the Gladstone family what proceeds have come from their Jamaica property since the protective duty was abolished. Let Lord Howard de Walden say how he has fared.

Mr. Buxton has drawn a parallel between the state of Ireland at and after the famine and that of the West Indies at and after the fall in the price of sugar, of which I can by no means admit the truth. In the one case, that of Ireland, the blow instantly effected the remedy. A tribe of pauper landlords had grown up by slow degrees who, by their poverty, their numbers, their rapacity, and their idleness, had eaten up and laid waste the fairest parts of the country. Then came the potato rot, bringing after it pestilence, famine, and the Encumbered Estates Court; and lo! in three years the air was cleared, the cloud had passed away, and Ireland was again prosperous. Land bought at fifteen pounds the acre was worth thirty before three crops had been taken from it. The absentees to whom Mr. Buxton alludes were comparatively little affected. They were rich men whose backs were broad enough to bear the burden for a while, and they stood their ground. It is not their property which as a rule has changed hands, but that of the small, grasping, profit-rent landlords whose lives had been passed in exacting the last farthing of rent from the cottiers. When no farthing

of rent could any longer be exacted, they went to the wall
at once.

There was nothing like this in the case of the West
Indies. Indiscretion and extravagance there may have
been. These are vices which will always be more or less
found among men living with the thermometer at eighty
in the shade. But in these colonies, long and painful
efforts were made, year after year, to bear against the
weight which had fallen on them. In the West Indies
the blow came from man, and it was withstood on the
whole manfully. In Ireland the blow came from God,
and submission to it was instantaneous.

Mr. Buxton then argues that everything in the West
Indies is already righting itself, and that therefore nothing
further need be done. The facts of the case exactly
refute this allegation. The four chief of these colonies
are Barbados, British Guiana, Trinidad, and Jamaica.
In Barbados, as has been explained, there was no distress,
and of course no relief has been necessary. In British
Guiana and Trinidad very special measures have been taken.
Immigration of Coolies to a great extent has been
brought about—to so great an extent that the tide of
human beings across the two oceans will now run on in
an increasing current. But in Jamaica little or nothing
has yet been done. And in Jamaica, the fairest, the
most extensive, the most attractive of them all; in
Jamaica, of all the islands on God's earth the one most
favoured by beauty, fertility, and natural gifts; in
Jamaica the earth can hardly be made to yield its natural
produce.

All this was excellently answered by Sir Edward Lyt-
ton, who, whatever may have been his general merits as
a Secretary of State, seems at any rate to have understood
this matter. He disposed altogether of the absurdly
erroneous allegations which had been made as to the

mortality of these immigrants on their passage. As is too usual in such cases arguments had been drawn from one or two specially unhealthy trips. Ninety-nine ships ride safe to port, while the hundredth unfortunately comes to grief. But we cannot on that account afford to dispense with the navigation of the seas. Sir Edward showed that the Coolies themselves—for the Anti-Slavery Society is as anxious to prevent this immigration on behalf of the Coolies, who in their own country can hardly earn two-pence a day, as it is on the part of the negroes, who could with ease, though they won't, earn two shillings a day—he showed that these Coolies, after having lived for a few years on plenty in these colonies, return to their own country with that which is for them great wealth. And he showed also that the present system—present as regards Trinidad, and proposed as regards Jamaica—of indenturing the immigrant on his first arrival is the only one to which we can safely trust for the good usage of the labourer. For the present this is clearly the case. When the Coolies are as numerous in these islands as the negroes—and that time will come—such rules and restrictions will no doubt be withdrawn. And when these different people have learned to mix their blood—which in time will also come—then mankind will hear no more of a lack of labour, and the fertility of these islands will cease to be their greatest curse.

I feel that I owe an apology to my reader for introducing him to an old, forgotten, and perhaps dull debate. In England the question is one not generally of great interest. But here, in the West Indies, it is vital. The negro will never work unless compelled to do so; that is, the negro who can boast of pure unmixed African blood. He is as strong as a bull, hardy as a mule, docile as a dog when conscious of a master—a salamander as regards heat. He can work without pain and without

annoyance. But he will never work as long as he can
eat and sleep without it. Place the Coolie or Chinaman
alongside of him, and he must work in his own defence.
If he do not, he will gradually cease to have an existence.

We are now speaking more especially of Trinidad. It
is a large island, great portions of which are but very
imperfectly known; of which but comparatively a very
small part has been cultivated. During the last eight
or ten years, ten or twelve thousand immigrants, chiefly
Coolies from Madras and Calcutta, have been brought
into Trinidad, forming now above an eighth part of its
entire population; and the consequence has been that
in two years, from 1855, namely, to 1857, its imports
were increased by one-third, and its exports by two-
thirds! The difference is of course that between
absolute distress and absolute prosperity. Such having
hitherto been the result of immigration into Trinidad,
such also having been the result in British Guiana, it
does appear singular that men should congregate in
Exeter Hall with the view of preventing similar immigration into Jamaica!

This would be altogether unintelligible were it not
that similar causes have produced similar effects in so many
other cases. Men cannot have enough of a good thing.

Exactly the same process has taken place with reference to criminals in England. Some few years since
we ill used them, stowed them away in unwholesome holes,
gave them bad food for their bodies and none for their
minds, and did our best to send them devilwards rather
than Godwards. Philanthropists have now remedied this,
and we are very much obliged to them. But the philanthropists will not be content unless they be allowed to
pack all their criminals up in lavender. They must be
treated not only as men, but much better than men of their
own class who are not criminal.

In this matter of the negroes, the good thing is negro-protection, and our friends cannot have enough of that. The negroes in being slaves were ill used; and now it is not enough that they should all be made free, but each should be put upon his own soft couch, with rose-leaves on which to lie. Now your Sybarite negro, when closely looked at, is not a pleasing object. Distance may doubtless lend enchantment to the view.

As my sojourn in Trinidad did not amount to two entire days, I do not feel myself qualified to give a detailed description of the whole island. Very few, I imagine, are so qualified, for much of it is unknown; there is a great want of roads, and a large proportion of it has, I believe, never been properly surveyed.

Immediately round Port of Spain the country is magnificent, and the views from the town itself are very lovely. Exactly behind the town, presuming the sea to be the front, is the Savanah, a large enclosed, park-like piece of common, the race-course and Hyde Park of Trinidad. I was told that the drive round it was three English miles in length; but if it be so much, the little pony which took me that drive in a hired buggy must have been a fast trotter.

On the further side of this lives the Governor of the island, immediately under the hills. When I was there the Governor's real house was being repaired, and the great man was living in a cottage hard by. Were I that great man I should be tempted to wish that my great house might always be under repair, for I never saw a more perfect specimen of a pretty spacious cottage, opening as a cottage should do on all sides and in every direction, with a great complexity as to doors and windows, and a delicious facility of losing one's way. And then the necessary freedom from boredom, etiquette, and Governor's grandeur, so hated by Governors themselves, which must necessarily be brought about by such a residence! I could almost wish to be a Governor myself, if I might be allowed to live in such a cottage.

On the other side of the Savanah nearest to the town, and directly opposite to those lovely hills, are a lot of villa residences, and it would be impossible, I imagine, to find a more lovely site in which to fix one's house. With the Savanah for a foreground, the rising gardens behind the Governor's house in the middle distance, and a panorama of magnificent hills in the back of the picture, it is hardly within the compass of a man's eye and imagination to add anything to the scene. I had promised to call on Major ——, who was then, and perhaps is still, in command of the detachment of white troops in Trinidad, and I found him and his young wife living in this spot.

'And yet you abuse Trinidad,' I said, pointing to the view.

'Oh! people can't live altogether upon views,' she answered; 'and besides, we have to go back to the barracks. The yellow fever is over now.'

The only place at which I came across any vestiges of the yellow fever was at Trinidad. There it had been making dreadful havoc, and chiefly among the white soldiers. My visit was in March, and the virulence of the disease was then just over. It had been raging, therefore, not in the summer but during the winter months. Indeed, as far as I could learn, summer and winter had very little to do with the matter. The yellow fever pays its visit in some sort periodically, though its periods are by no means understood. But it pays them at any time of the year that may suit itself.

At this time a part of the Savanah was covered with tents, to which the soldiers had been moved out of their barracks. The barracks are lower down, near the shore, at a place called St. James, and the locality is said to be wretchedly unhealthy. At any rate, the men were stricken with fever there, and the proportion of them that died was very great. I believe, indeed, that hardly any recovered of those on whom the fever fell with any violence. They were then removed into these tents, and matters began to mend. They were now about to return to their barracks, and were, I was told, as unwilling to do so as my fair friend was to leave her pretty house.

If it be necessary to send white troops to the West Indies—and I take it for granted that it is necessary—care at any rate should be taken to select for their barracks sites as healthy as may be found. It certainly seems that this has not been done at Trinidad. They are placed very low, and with hills immediately around them. The good effect produced by removing them to the Savanah—a very inconsiderable distance; not, as I think, much exceeding a mile—proves what may be done by choosing a healthy situation. But why should not the men be taken up to the mountains, as has been done with the white soldiers in Jamaica? There they are placed in barracks some three or four thousand feet above the sea, and are perfectly healthy. This cannot be done in Barbados, for there are no mountains to which to take them. But in Trinidad it may be done, quite as easily, and indeed at a lesser distance, and therefore with less cost for conveyance, than in Jamaica.

At the first glance one would be inclined to say that white troops would not be necessary in the West Indies, as we have regiments of black soldiers, negroes dressed in Zouave costume, specially trained for the service; but it seems that there is great difficulty in getting these regiments filled. Why should a negro enlist any more than work? Are there not white men enough—men and brothers—to do the somewhat disagreeable work of soldiering for him? Consequently, except in Barbados, it is difficult to get recruits. Some men have been procured from the coast of Africa, but our philanthropy is interfering even with this supply. Then the recruiting officers enlisted Coolies, and these men made excellent soldiers; but when interfered with or punished, they had a nasty habit of committing suicide, a habit which it was quite possible the negro soldier might himself assume; and therefore no more Coolies are to be enlisted.

Under such circumstances white men must, I presume, do the work. A shilling a day is an object to them, and they are slow to blow out their own brains; but they should not be barracked in swamps, or made to live in an air more pestilential than necessary.

My hostess, the lady to whom I have alluded, had been attacked most virulently by the yellow fever, and I had heard in the other islands that she was dead. Her case had indeed been given up as hopeless.

On the morning after my arrival I took a ride of some sixteen miles through the country before breakfast, and the same lady accompanied me. 'We must start very early,' she said, 'so as to avoid the heat. I will have coffee at half-past four, and we will be on horseback at five.'

I have had something to say as to early hours in the West Indies before, and hardly credited this. A morning start at five usually means half-past seven, and six o'clock is a generic term for moving before nine. So I meekly asked whether half-past four meant half-past four. 'No,' said the husband. 'Yes,' said the wife. So I went away declaring that I would present myself at the house at any rate not after five.

And so I did, according to my own very excellent watch, which had been set the day before by the ship's chronometer. I rode up to the door two minutes before five, perfectly certain that I should have the pleasure of watching the sun's early manœuvres for at least an hour. But, alas! my friend had been waiting for me in her riding-habit for more than that time. Our watches were frightfully at variance. It was perfectly clear to me that the Trinidadians do not take the sun for their guide as to time. But in such a plight as was then mine, a man cannot go into his evidence and his justification. My only plea was for mercy; and I hereby take it on myself to say that I do not know that I ever kept any lady waiting before—except my wife.

At five to the moment—by my watch—we started, and I certainly never rode for three hours through more lovely scenery. At first, also, it was deliciously cool, and as our road lay entirely through woods, it was in every way delightful. We went back into the hills, and returned again towards the sea-shore over a break in one of the spurs of the mountain called the Saddle; from whence we had a distant view into the island, as fine as any view I ever saw without the adjunct of water.

I should imagine that a tour through the whole of Trinidad would richly repay the trouble, though, indeed, it would be troublesome. The tourist must take his own provisions, unless, indeed, he provided himself by means of his gun, and must take also his bed. The musquitoes, too, are very vexatious in Trinidad, though I hardly think that they come up in venom to their brethren in British Guiana.

The first portion of our ride was delightful; but on our return we came down upon a hot, dusty road, and then the loss of that hour in the morning was deeply felt. I think that up to that time I had never encountered such heat, and certainly had never met with a more disagreeable, troublesome amount of dust, all which would have been avoided had I inquired over-night into the circum-

stances of the Trinidad watches. But the lady said never
a word, and so heaped coals of fire on my head in addition
to the consuming flames of that ever-to-be-remembered
sun.

As Trinidad is an English colony, one's first idea is
that the people speak English; and one's second idea,
when that other one as to the English has fallen to the
ground, is that they should speak Spanish, seeing that the
name of the place is Spanish. But the fact is that they
all speak French; and, out of the town, but few of the
natives speak anything else. Whether a Parisian would
admit this may be doubted; but he would have to acknowledge that it was a French patois.

And the religion is Roman Catholic. The island of
course did belong to France, and in manners, habits,
language, and religion is still French. There is a
Roman Catholic archbishop resident in Trinidad, who
is, I believe, at present an Italian. We pay him, I have
been told, some salary, which he declines to take for his
own use, but applies to purposes of charity. There is a
Roman Catholic cathedral in Port of Spain, and a very
ugly building it is.

The form of government also is different from that, or
rather those, which have been adopted in the other West
Indian colonies, such as Jamaica, Barbados, and British
Guiana. As this was a conquered colony, the people of the
island are not allowed to have so potent a voice in their
own management. They have no House of Commons
or Legislative Assembly, but take such rules or laws as
may be necessary for their guidance direct from the
Crown. The Governor, however, is assisted by a council,
in which sit the chief executive officers in the island.
That the fact of the colony having been conquered need
preclude it from the benefit (?) of self-government, one
does not clearly see. But one does see clearly enough,

that as they are French in language and habits, and
Roman Catholic in religion, they would make even a
worse hash of it than the Jamaicans do in Jamaica.

And it is devoutly to be hoped, for the island's sake,
that it may be long before it is endowed with a constitution. It would be impossible now-a-days to commence
a legislature in the system of electing which all but
white men should be excluded from voting. Nor would
there be white men enough to carry on an election. And
may Providence defend my friends there from such an
assembly as would be returned by French negroes and
hybrid mulattoes!

A scientific survey has just been completed of this
island, with reference to its mineral productions, and the
result has been to show that it contains a very large
quantity of coal. I was fortunate enough to meet one of
the gentlemen by whom this was done, and he was kind
enough to put into my hand a paper showing the exact
result of their investigation. But, unfortunately, the
paper was so learned, and I was so ignorant, that I could
not understand one word of it. The whole matter also
was explained to me verbally, but not in language adapted
to my child-like simplicity. So I am not able to say
whether the coal be good or bad—whether it would make
a nice, hot, crackling, Christmas fire, or fly away in slaty
flakes and dirty dust. It is a pity that science cannot be
made to recognise the depth of unscientific ignorance.

There is also here in Trinidad a great pitch lake, of
which all the world has heard, and out of which that in-
defatigable old hero, Lord Dundonald, tried hard to make
wax candles and oil for burning. The oil and candles,
indeed, he did make, but not, I fear, the money which
should have been consequent upon their fabrication. I
have no doubt, however, that in time we shall all have
our wax candles from thence; for Lord Dundonald is one

of those men who are born to do great deeds of which others shall reap the advantages. One of these days his name will be duly honoured, for his conquests as well as for his candles.

And so I speedily took my departure, and threaded my way back again through the Bocas, in that most horrid of all steam-vessels, the ' Prince.'

CHAPTER XV.

ST. THOMAS.

ALL persons travelling in the West Indies have so much
to do with the island of St. Thomas, that I must devote a
short chapter to it. My circumstances with reference to
it were such that I was compelled to remain there a longer
time, putting all my visits together, than in any other of the
islands except Jamaica.

The place belongs to the Danes, who possess also the
larger and much more valuable island of Santa Cruz, as
they do also the small island of St. Martin. These all
lie among the Virgin Islands, and are considered as belonging to that thick cluster. As St. Thomas at present
exists, it is of considerable importance. It is an emporium, not only for many of the islands, but for many also
of the places on the coast of South and Central America.
Guiana, Venezuela, and New Granada, deal there largely.
It is a depôt for cigars, light dresses, brandy, boots, and
Eau de Cologne. Many men therefore of many nations
go thither to make money, and they do make it. These
are men, generally not of the tenderest class, or who have
probably been nursed in much early refinement. Few men
will select St. Thomas as a place of residence from mere
unbiassed choice and love of the locale. A wine merchant
in London, doing a good trade there, would hardly give
up that business with the object of personally opening an

establishment in this island : nor would a well-to-do milli-
ner leave Paris with the same object. Men who settle
at St. Thomas have most probably roughed it elsewhere
unsuccessfully.

These St. Thomas tradesmen do make money I believe,
and it is certainly due to them that they should do so.
Things ought not, if possible, to be all bad with any man ;
and I cannot imagine what good can accrue to a man at
St. Thomas if it be not the good of amassing money.
It is one of the hottest and one of the most unhealthy
spots among all these hot and unhealthy regions. I do
not know whether I should not be justified in saying
that of all such spots it is the most hot and the most
unhealthy.

I have said in a previous chapter that the people one
meets there may be described as an Hispano-Dano-Niggery-
Yankee-doodle population. In this I referred not only
to the settlers, but to those also who are constantly passing
through it. In the shops and stores, and at the hotels, one
meets the same mixture. The Spanish element is of course
strong, for Venezuela, New Granada, Central America, and
Mexico are all Spanish, as also is Cuba. The people of
these lands speak Spanish, and hereabouts are called
Spaniards. To the Danes the island belongs. The soldiers, officials, and custom-house people are Danes. They
do not, however, mix much with their customers. They
affect, I believe, to say that the island is overrun and
destroyed by these strange comers, and that they would as
lief be without such visitors. If they are altogether indifferent to money making, such may be the case. The
labouring people are all black—if these blacks can be called
a labouring people. They do coal the vessels at about a
dollar a day each—that is when they are so circumstanced
as to require a dollar. As to the American element, that
is by no means the slightest or most retiring. Dollars are

going there, and therefore it is of course natural that
Americans should be going also. I saw the other day a
map, 'The United States as they now are, and in pro-
spective;' and it included all these places—Mexico,
Central America, Cuba, St. Domingo, and even poor
Jamaica. It may be that the man who made the map
understood the destiny of his country; at any rate he
understood the tastes of his countrymen.

All these people are assembled together at St. Thomas,
because St. Thomas is the meeting-place and central
depôt of the West Indian steam-packets. That reason
can be given easily enough; but why St. Thomas should
be the meeting-place of these packets,—I do not know
who can give me the reason for that arrangement. Tor-
tola and Virgin Gorda, two of the Virgin islands, both
belong to ourselves, and are situated equally well for the
required purpose as is St. Thomas. I am told also, that
at any rate one, probably at both, good harbour accommodation is to be found. It is certain that in other respects
they are preferable. They are not unhealthy, as is St.
Thomas; and, as I have said above, they belong to ourselves. My own opinion is that Jamaica should be the
head-quarters of these packets; but the question is one
which will not probably be interesting to the reader of
these pages.

'They cannot understand at home why we dislike the
inter-colonial work so much,' said the captain of one of
the steam-ships to me. By inter-colonial work he meant
the different branch services from St. Thomas. 'They
do not comprehend at home what it is for a man to be
burying one young officer after another; to have them
sent out, and then to see them mown down in that ac-
cursed hole of a harbour by yellow fever. Such a work
is not a very pleasant one.'

Indeed this was true. The life cannot be a very pleasant one. These captains themselves and their senior officers are doubtless acclimated. The yellow fever may reach them, but their chance of escape is tolerably good; but the young lads who join the service, and who do so at an early age, have at the first commencement of their career to make St. Thomas their residence, as far as they have any residence. They live of course on board their ships; but the peculiarity of St. Thomas is this, that the harbour is ten times more fatal than the town. It is that hole, up by the coaling wharves, which sends so many English lads to the grave. If this be so, this alone, I think, constitutes a strong reason why St. Thomas should not be so favoured. These vessels now form a considerable fleet, and some of them spend nearly a third of their time at this place. The number of Englishmen so collected and endangered is sufficient to warrant us in regarding this as a great drawback on any utility which the island may have—if such utility there be.

But we must give even the devil his due. Seen from the water St. Thomas is very pretty. It is not so much the scenery of the island that pleases as the aspect of the town itself. It stands on three hills or mounts, with higher hills, green to their summit, rising behind them. Each mount is topped by a pleasant, cleanly edifice, and pretty-looking houses stretch down the sides to the water's edge. The buildings do look pretty and nice, and as though chance had arranged them from a picture. Indeed, as seen from the harbour, the town looks like a panorama exquisitely painted. The air is thin and transparent, and every line shows itself clearly. As so seen the town of St. Thomas is certainly attractive. But it is like the Dead Sea fruit; all the charm is gone when it is tasted. Land there, and the beauty vanishes.

The hotel at St. Thomas is quite a thing of itself. There is no fair ground for complaint as regards the accommodation, considering where one is, and that people do not visit St. Thomas for pleasure; but the people that one meets there form as strange a collection as may perhaps be found anywhere. In the first place, all languages seem alike to them. One hears English, French, German, and Spanish spoken around one, and apparently it is indifferent which. The waiters seem to speak them all.

The most of these guests I take it—certainly a large proportion of them—are residents of the place, who board at the inn. I have been there for a week at a time, and it seemed that all then around me were so. There were ladies among them, who always came punctually to their meals, and went through the long course of breakfast and long course of dinner with admirable perseverance. I never saw eating to equal that eating. When I was there the house was always full; but the landlord told me that he found it very hard to make money, and I can believe it.

A hot climate, it is generally thought, interferes with the appetite, affects the gastric juices with lassitude, gives to the stomach some of the apathy of the body, and lessens at any rate the consumption of animal food. That charge cannot be made against the air of St. Thomas. To whatever sudden changes the health may be subject, no lingering disinclination for food affects it. Men eat there as though it were the only solace of their life, and women also. Probably it is so.

They never talk at meals. A man and his wife may interchange a word or two as to the dishes; or men coming from the same store may whisper a syllable as to their culinary desires; but in an ordinary way there is no talking. I myself generally am not a mute person at my meals; and having dined at sundry tables d'hôte have got over in a great degree that disinclination to speak to my neighbour which is attributed—I believe wrongly—to Englishmen. But at St. Thomas I took it into my head

to wait till I was spoken to, and for a week I sat, twice
daily, between the same persons without receiving or speaking a single word.

I shall not soon forget the stout lady who sat opposite to
me, and who was married to a little hooked-nosed Jew,
who always accompanied her.　Soup, fish, and then meat
is the ordinary rule at such banquets; but here the fashion
is for the guests, having curried favour with the waiters,
to get their plates of food brought in and put round before
them in little circles; so that a man while taking his soup
may contemplate his fish and his roast beef, his wing of
fowl, his allotment of salad, his peas and potatoes, his
pudding, pie, and custard, and whatever other good things
a benevolent and well-fee'd waiter may be able to collect
for him.　This somewhat crowds the table, and occasionally
it becomes necessary for the guest to guard his treasures
with an eagle's eye;—hers also with an eagle's eye, and
sometimes with an eagle's talon.

This stout lady was great on such occasions.　'A bit of
that,' she would exclaim, with head half turned round, as
a man would pass behind her with a dish, while she was
in the very act of unloading within her throat a whole
knifeful charged to the hilt.　The efforts which at first
affected me as almost ridiculous advanced to the sublime
as dinner went on.　There was no shirking, no half measures, no slackened pace as the breath became short.　The
work was daily done to the final half-pound of cheese.

Cheese and jelly, guava jelly, were always eaten
together.　This I found to be the general fashion of St.
Thomas.　Some men dipped their cheese in jelly; some
ate a bit of jelly and then a bit of cheese; some topped
up with jelly and some topped up with cheese, all having
it on their plates together.　But this lady—she must
have spent years in acquiring the exercise—had a knack
of involving her cheese in jelly, covering up by a rapid

twirl of her knife a bit about an inch thick, so that no cheesy surface should touch her palate, and then depositing the parcel, oh, ever so far down, without dropping above a globule or two of the covering on her bosom.

Her lord, the Israelite, used to fight hard too; but the battle was always over with him long before the lady showed even a sign of distress. He was one of those flashy weedy animals that make good running for a few yards and are then choked off. She was game up to the winning-post. There were many animals running at those races, but she might have given all the others the odds of a pound of solid food, and yet have beaten them.

But then, to see her rise from the table! Well; pace and extra weight together will distress the best horse that ever was shod!

Over and above this I found nothing of any general interest at St. Thomas.

CHAPTER XVI.

NEW GRANADA, AND THE ISTHMUS OF PANAMÁ.

IT is probably known to all that New Granada is the most northern of the republics of South America; or it should rather be said that it is the state nearest to the isthmus, of which indeed it comprehends a considerable portion; the territory of the Gulf of Darien and the district of Panamá all being within the limits of New Granada.

It was, however, but the other day that New Granada formed only a part of the republic of Columbia, the republic of which Bolivar was the hero. As the inhabitants of Central America found it necessary to break up their state into different republics, so also did the people of Columbia. The heroes and patriots of Caracas and Quito could not consent to be governed from Bogotá; and therefore three states were formed out of one. They are New Granada, with its capital of Bogotá; Venezuela, with its capital of Caracas, lying exactly to the east of New Granada; and Ecuador—the state, that is, of Equator—lying to the south of New Granada, having its seaport at Guayaquil on the Pacific, with Quito, its chief city, exactly on the line.

The district of Columbia was one of the grandest appanages of the Spanish throne when the appanages of the Spanish throne were grand indeed. The town and port of Cartagena, on the Atlantic, were admirably fortified, as was also Panamá on the Pacific. Its interior cities were populous, flourishing, and, for that age, fairly civilized. Now the whole country has received the boon of Utopian freedom; and the mind loses itself in contemplating to what lowest pitch of human degradation the people will gradually fall.

Civilization here is retrograding. Men are becoming more ignorant than their fathers, are learning to read less, to know less, to have fewer aspirations of a high order; to care less for truth and justice, to have more and more of the contentment of a brute,—that contentment which comes from a full belly and untaxed sinews; or even from an empty belly, so long as the sinews be left idle.

To what this will tend a prophet in these days can hardly see; or rather none less than a prophet can pretend to see. That those lands which the Spaniards have occupied, and to a great extent made Spanish, should have no higher destiny than that which they have already accomplished, I can hardly bring myself to think. That their unlimited fertility and magnificent rivers should be given for nothing; that their power of producing all that man wants should be intended for no use, I cannot believe. At present, however, it would seem that Providence has abandoned it. It is making no progress. Land that was cultivated is receding from cultivation; cities that were populous are falling into ruins; and men are going back into animals, under the influence of unlimited liberty and universal suffrage.

In 1851 emancipation from slavery was finally established in New Granada; and so far, doubtless, a good deed was done. But it was established at the same time that every man, emancipated slave or other, let him be an industrial occupier of land, or idle occupier of nothing, should have an equal vote in electing presidents and members of the Federal Congress, and members of the Congress of the different states; that, in short, all men should be equal for all state purposes. And the result, as may be supposed, is not gratifying. As far as I am able to judge, a negro has not generally those gifts of God which enable one man to exercise rule and masterdom over his fellow-men. I myself should object strongly to be represented, say in the city of London, by any black man that I ever saw. 'The unfortunate nigger gone masterless,' whom Carlyle so tenderly commiserates, has not strong ideas of the duties even of self-government, much less of the government of others. Universal suffrage in such hands can hardly lead to .good results. Let him at any rate have first saved some sixty pounds in a savings bank, or made himself undoubted owner—an easy thing in New Granada—of a forty-shilling freehold!

Not that pure-blooded negroes are common through the whole of New Granada. At Panamá and the adjacent districts they are so; but in the other parts of the republic they are, I believe, few in number. At Santa Martha, where I first landed, I saw few, if any. And yet the trace of the negroes, the woolly hair and flat nose, were common enough, mixed always with Indian blood, and of course to a great extent with Spanish blood also.

This Santa Martha is a wretched village—a city it is there called—at which we, with intense cruelty, maintain a British Consul, and a British post-office. There is a cathedral there of the old Spanish order, with the choir removed from the altar down towards the western door; and there is, I was informed, a bishop. But neither bishop nor cathedral were in any way remarkable. There is there a governor of the province, some small tradesman, who seemed to exercise very few governing functions. It may almost be said that no trade exists in the place, which seemed indeed to be nearly dead. A few black or nearly black children run about the streets in a state almost of nudity; and there are shops, from the extremities of which, as I was told, crinoline and hats laden with bugles may be extracted.

'Every one of my predecessors here died of fever,' said the Consul to me, in a tone of triumph. What could a man say to him on so terribly mortal a subject? 'And my wife has been down in fever thirteen times!' Heavens, what a life! That is, as long as it is life.

I rode some four or five miles into the country to visit the house in which Bolivar died. It is a deserted little country villa or chateau, called San Pedro, standing in a farm-yard, and now containing no other furniture than a marble bust of the Dictator, with a few wretchedly coloured French prints with cracked glass plates. The bust is not a bad one, and seems to have a solemn and sad meaning in its melancholy face, standing there in its solitary niche in the very room in which the would-be liberator died.

For Bolivar had grand ideas of freedom, though doubtless he had grand ideas also of personal power and pre-eminence; as has been the case with most of those who have moved or professed to move in the vanguard of liberty. To free mankind from all injurious thraldom is the aspiration of such men; but who ever thought that obedience to himself was a thraldom that could be injurious?

And here in this house, on the 17th December, 1830, Bolivar died, broken-hearted, owing his shelter to charity, and relieved in his last wants by the hands of strangers to his country. When the breath was out of him and he was well dead, so that on such a matter he himself could probably have no strong wish in any direction, they took away his body, of course with all honour, to the district that gave him birth, and that could afford to be proud of him now that he was dead,—into Venezuela, and reburied him at Caracas. But dying poverty and funeral honours have been the fate of great men in other countries besides Columbia.

'And why did you come to visit such a region as this?' asked Bolivar, when dying, of a Frenchman to whom in his last days he was indebted for much. 'For freedom,' said the Frenchman. 'For freedom!' said Bolivar. 'Then let me tell you that you have missed your mark altogether; you could hardly have turned in a worse direction.'

Our ride from Santa Martha to the house had been altogether between bushes, among which we saw but small signs of cultivation. Round the house I saw none. On my return I learnt that the place was the property of a rich man who possessed a large estate in its vicinity. 'But will nothing grow there?' I asked. 'Grow there! yes; anything would grow there. Some years since the whole district was covered with sugar-canes.' But since the emancipation in 1851 it had become impossible to procure labour; men could not be got to work; and so bush had grown up, and the earth gave none of her increase; except indeed where half-caste Indians squatted here and there, and made provision grounds.

I then went on to Cartagena. This is a much better town than Santa Martha, though even this is in its decadence. It was once a flourishing city, great in commerce and strong in war. It was taken by the English, not however without signal reverses on our part, and by the special valour—so the story goes—of certain sailors who dragged a single gun to the summit of a high abrupt hill called the 'Papa,' which commands the town. If the thermometer stood in those days as high at Cartagena as it does now, pretty nearly through the whole of the year, hose sailors ought to have had the Victoria cross. But

these deeds were done long years ago, in the time of
Drake and his followers; and Victoria crosses were then
chiefly kept for the officers.

The harbour at Cartagena is singularly circumstanced.
There are two entrances to it, one some ten miles from the
city and the other close to it. This nearer aperture was
blocked up by the Spaniards, who sank ships across the
mouth; and it has never been used or usable since. The
present entrance is very strongly fortified. The fortifications are still there, bristling down to the water's edge;
or they would bristle, were it not that all the guns have
been sold for the value of the brass metal.

Cartagena was hotter even than Santa Martha; but the
place is by no means so desolate and death-like. The
shops there are open to the streets, as shops are in other
towns. Men and women may occasionally be seen about
the square; and there is a trade,—in poultry if in nothing
else.

There is a cathedral here also, and I presume a bishop.
The former is built after the Spanish fashion, and boasts
a so-called handsome, large, marble pulpit. That it is
large and marble, I confess; but I venture to question its
claims to the other epithet. There are pictures also in
the cathedral; of spirits in a state of torture certainly;
and if I rightly remember of beatified spirits also. But in
such pictures the agonies of the damned always excite more
attention and a keener remembrance than the ecstasies
of the blest. I cannot say that the artist had come up
either to the spirit of Fra Angelico, or to the strength of
Orcagna.

At Cartagena I encountered a family of native ladies
and gentlemen, who were journeying from Bogotá to
Peru. Looking at the map, one would say that the route
from Bogotá to Buena-ventura on the Pacific was both easy
and short. The distance as the crow flies—the condor I

should perhaps more properly say—would not be much over two hundred miles. And yet this family, of whom one was an old woman, had come down to Cartagena, having been twenty days on the road, having from thence a long sea journey to the isthmus, thence the passage over it to Panamá, and then the journey down the Pacific! The fact of course is that there are no means of transit in the country except on certain tracks, very few in number; and that even on these all motion is very difficult. Bogotá is about three hundred and seventy miles from Cartagena, and the journey can hardly be made in less than fourteen days.

From Cartagena I went on to the isthmus; the Isthmus of Panamá, as it is called by all the world, though the American town of Aspinwall will gradually become the name best known in connexion with the passage between the two oceans.

This passage is now made by a railway which has been opened by an American company between the town of Aspinwall, or Colon, as it is called in England, and the city of Panamá. Colon is the local name for this place, which also bears the denomination of Navy Bay in the language of sailors. But our friends from Yankee-land like to carry things with a high hand, and to have a nomenclature of their own. Here, as their energy and their money and their habits are undoubtedly in the ascendant, they will probably be successful; and the place will be called Aspinwall in spite of the disgust of the New Granadians, and the propriety of the English, who choose to adhere to the names of the existing government of the country.

A rose by any other name would smell as sweet, and Colon or Aspinwall will be equally vile however you may call it. It is a wretched, unhealthy, miserably situated but thriving little American town, created by and for the railway and the passenger traffic which comes here both from Southampton and New York. That from New York is of course immensely the greatest, for this is at present the main route to San Francisco and California.

I visited the place three times, for I passed over the isthmus on my way to Costa Rica, and on my return from that country I went again to Panamá, and of course back to Colon. I can say nothing in its favour. My only dealing there was with a washerwoman, and I wish I could place before my readers a picture of my linen in the condition in which it came back from that artiste's hands. I confess that I sat down and shed bitter tears. In these localities there are but two luxuries of life, iced soda water and clean shirts. And now I was debarred from any true enjoyment of the latter for more than a fortnight.

The Panamá railway is certainly a great fact, as men now-a-days say when anything of importance is accomplished. The necessity of some means of passing the isthmus, and the question as to the best means, has been debated since, I may say, the days of Cortes. Men have foreseen that it would become a necessity to the world that there should be some such transit, and every conceivable point of the isthmus has, at some period or by some nation, been selected as the best for the purpose. This railway is certainly the first that can be regarded as a properly organized means of travelling ; and it may be doubted whether it will not remain as the best, if not the only permanent mode of transit.

Very great difficulty was experienced in erecting this line. In the first place it was necessary that terms should be made with the government of the country through which the line should pass, and to effect this it was expedient to hold out great inducements. Among the chief of these is an understanding that the whole line shall become the absolute property of the New Granadian government when it shall have been opened for forty-nine years. But who can tell what government will prevail in New Granada in forty-nine years? It is not impossible that the whole district may then be an outlying territory belonging to the United States. At any rate I should imagine that it is very far from the intention of the American company to adhere with rigid strictness to this part of the bargain. Who knows what may occur between this and the end of the century?

And when these terms were made there was great difficulty in obtaining labour. The road had to be cut through one continuous forest, and for the greater part of the way along the course of the Chagres river. Nothing could be more unhealthy than such work, and in consequence the men died very rapidly. The high rate of wages enticed many Irishmen here, but most of them found their graves amidst the works. Chinese were tried, but they were quite inefficacious for such labour, and when distressed had a habit of hanging themselves. The most useful men were to be got from the coast round Cartagena, but they were enticed thither only by very high pay.

The whole road lies through trees and bushes of thick tropical growth, and is in this way pretty and interesting. But there is nothing wonderful in the scenery, unless to one who has never before witnessed tropical forest scenery. The growth here is so quick that the strip of ground closely adjacent to the line, some twenty yards perhaps on each side, has to be cleared of timber and foliage every six months. If left for twelve months the whole would be covered with thick bushes, twelve feet high. At intervals of four and a half miles there are large wooden houses— pretty-looking houses they are, built with much taste,— in each of which a superintendent with a certain number of labourers resides. These men are supplied with provisions and all necessaries by the company. For there

are no villages here in which workmen can live, no shops
from which they can supply themselves, no labour which
can be hired as it may be wanted.

From this it may be imagined that the line is maintained at a great cost. But, nevertheless, it already pays
a dividend of twelve and a half per cent. So much at
least is acknowledged; but those who pretend to understand the matter declare that the real profit accruing to
the shareholders is hardly less than five-and-twenty per
cent. The sum charged for the passage is extremely high,
being twenty-five dollars, or five pounds for a single ticket.
The distance is under fifty miles. And there is no class
but the one. Everybody passing over the isthmus, if he
pay his fare, must pay twenty-five dollars. Steerage passengers from New York to San Francisco are at present
booked through for fifty dollars. This includes their food
on the two sea voyages, which are on an average of about
eleven days each. And yet out of this fifty dollars twenty-
five are paid to the railway for this conveyance over fifty
miles! The charge for luggage, too, is commensurately
high. The ordinary kit of a travelling Englishman—a
portmanteau, bag, desk, and hat-box—would cost two
pounds ten shillings over and above his own fare.

But at the same time nothing can be more liberal than
the general management of the line. On passengers journeying from New York to California, or from Southampton
to Chili and Peru, their demand no doubt is very high.
But to men of all classes, merely travelling from Aspinwall
to Panamá for pleasure—or, apparently, on business, if
travelling only between those two places,—free tickets
are given almost without restriction. One train goes each
way daily, and as a rule most of the passengers are carried
free, except on those days when packets have arrived at
either terminus. On my first passage over I paid my
fare, for I went across with other passengers out of the

mail packet. But on my return the superintendent not only gave me a ticket, but asked me whether I wanted others for any friends. The line is a single line throughout.

Panamá has doubtless become a place of importance to Englishmen and Americans, and its name is very familiar to our ears. But nevertheless it is a place whose glory has passed away. It was a large Spanish town, strongly fortified, with some thirty thousand inhabitants. Now its fortifications are mostly gone, its churches are tumbling to the ground, its old houses have so tumbled, and its old Spanish population has vanished. It is still the chief city of a State, and a congress sits there. There is a governor and a judge, and there are elections; but were it not for the passengers of the isthmus there would soon be but little left of the city of Panamá.

Here the negro race abounds, and among the common people the negro traits are stronger and more marked than those either of the Indians or Spaniards. Of Spanish blood among the natives of the surrounding country there seems to be but little. The negroes here are of course free, free to vote for their own governors, and make their own laws; and consequently they are often very troublesome, the country people attacking those in the town, and so on. 'And is justice ultimately done on the offenders?' I asked. 'Well, sir, perhaps not justice. But some notice is taken, and the matter is smoothed over.' Such was the answer.

There is a Spanish cathedral here also, in which I heard a very sweet-toned organ, and one magnificent tenor voice. The old church buildings still standing here are not without pretence, and are interesting from the dark tawny colour of the stone, if from no other cause. I should guess them to be some two centuries old. Their style in many respects resembles that which is so generally odious to an Englishman's eye and ear, under the title of Renaissance. It is probably an offshoot of that which is called Plateresque in the south of Spain.

During the whole time that I was at Panamá the thermometer stood at something above ninety. In Calcutta I believe it is often as high as one hundred and ten, so that I have no right to speak of the extreme heat. But, nevertheless, Panamá is supposed to be one of the hottest places in the western world; and I was assured, while there, that weather so continuously hot for the twenty-four hours had not been known during the last nine years. The rainy season should have commenced by this time—the early part of May. But it had not done so; and it appeared that when the rain is late, that is the hottest period of the whole year.

The heat made me uncomfortable, but never made me ill. I lost all pleasure in eating, and indeed in everything else. I used to feel a craving for my food, but no appetite when it came. I was lethargic, as though from repletion, when I did eat, and was always glad when my watch would allow me to go to bed. But yet I was never ill.

The country round the town is pretty and very well adapted for riding. There are large open savanahs which stretch away for miles and miles, and which are kept as grazing-farms for cattle. These are not flat and plain, but are broken into undulations, and covered here and there with forest bushes. The horses here are taught to pace, that is, move with the two off legs together and then with the two near legs. The motion is exceedingly gentle, and well fitted for this hot climate, in which the rougher work of trotting would be almost too much for the energies of debilitated mankind. The same pace is common in Cuba, Costa Rica, and other Spanish countries in the west.

R

Off from Panamá, a few miles distant in the western ocean, there are various picturesque islands. On two of these are the depôts of two great steam-packet companies, that belonging to the Americans, which carries on the trade to California, and an English company whose vessels run down the Pacific to Peru and Chili. I visited Toboga, in which are the head-quarters of the latter. Here I found a small English maritime colony, with a little town of their own, composed of captains, doctors, engineers, officers, artificers, and sailors, living together on the company's wages, and as regards the upper classes, at tables provided by the company. But I saw there no women of any description. I beg therefore to suggest to the company that their servants would probably be much more comfortable if the institution partook less of the monastic order.

If, as is probable, this becomes one of the high-roads to Australia, then another large ship company will have to fix its quarters here.

CHAPTER XVII.

CENTRAL AMERICA—PANAMÁ TO SAN JOSÉ.

I HAD intended to embark at Panamá in the American steam-ship 'Columbus' for the coast of Central America. In that case I should have gone to San Juan del Sur, a port in Nicaragua, and made my way from thence across the lake, down the river San Juan to San Juan del Norte, now called Greytown, on the Atlantic. But I learnt that the means of transit through Nicaragua had been so utterly destroyed—as I shall by-and-by explain—that I should encounter great delay in getting across the lake ; and as I found that one of our men-of-war steamers, the 'Vixen,' was immediately about to start from Panamá to Punta-arenas, on the coast of Costa Rica, I changed my mind, and resolved on riding through Costa Rica to Greytown. And accordingly I did ride through Costa Rica.

My first work was to make petition for a passage in the 'Vixen,' which was accorded to me without difficulty. But even had I failed here I should have adhered to the same plan. The more I heard of Costa Rica, the more I was convinced that that republic was better worth a visit than Nicaragua. At this time I had in my hands a pamphlet written by M. Belly, a Frenchman, who is, or says that he is, going to make a ship canal from the Atlantic to the Pacific. According to him the only Para-

dise now left on earth is in this republic of Costa Rica.
So I shipped myself on board the ' Vixen.'

I had never before been on the waters of the Pacific.
Now when one premeditates one's travels, sitting by the
domestic fireside, one is apt to think that all those advancing steps into new worlds will be taken with some
little awe, some feeling of amazement at finding oneself in
very truth so far distant from Hyde Park Corner. The
Pacific! I was absolutely there, on the ocean in which
lie the Sandwich Islands, Queen Pomare, and the Canni-
bals! But no; I had no such feeling. My only solicitude
was whether my clean shirts would last me on to the
capital of Costa Rica.

And in travelling these are the things which really
occupy the mind. Where shall I sleep? Is there anything to eat? Can I have my clothes washed? At
Panamá I did have my clothes washed in a very short
space of time; but I had to pay a shilling apiece for them
all round. In all these ports, in New Granada, Central
America, and even throughout the West Indies, the
luxury which is the most expensive in proportion to its
cost in Europe is the washing of clothes—the most expensive, as it is also the most essential.

But I must not omit to say that before shipping myself
in the ' Vixen' I called on the officers on board the United
States frigate ' Merrimac,' and was shown over that vessel.
I am not a very good judge of ships, and can only say
that the officers were extremely civil, the sherry very
good, and the guns very large. They were coaling, the
captain told me, and he professed to be very much ashamed
of the dirt. Had I not been told so I should not have
known that the ship was dirty.

The ' Merrimac,' though rated only as a frigate, having
guns on one covered deck only, is one of their largest
men-of-war, and has been regarded by them, and by us,

as a show vessel. But according to their own account, she fails altogether as a steamer. The greatest pace her engines will give is seven knots an hour; and this is felt to be so insufficient for the wants of the present time, that it is intended to take them out of her and replace them by a new set as soon as an opportunity will allow. This will be done, although the vessel and the engines are new. I mention this, not as reflecting in any way disgracefully on the dockyard from whence she came; but to show that our Admiralty is not the only one which may have to chop and change its vessels after they are built. We hear much—too much perhaps—of the misfortunes which attend our own navy; but of the misfortunes of other navies we hear very little. It is a pity that we cannot have some record of all the blunders committed at Cherbourg.

The 'Merrimac' carries the flag of Flag-officer Long, on whom also we called. He is a fine old gentleman, with a magnificent head and forehead, looking I should say much more like an English nobleman than a Yankee sailor. Flag-officer Long! Who will explain to us why the Americans of the United States should persist in calling their senior naval officers by so awkward an appellation, seeing that the well-known and well-sounding title of admiral is very much at their disposal?

When I returned to the shore from the 'Merrimac,' I had half an hour to pack before I again started for the 'Vixen.' As it would be necessary that I should return to Panamá, and as whatever luggage I now took with me would have to be carried through the whole of Costa Rica on mules' backs, it became expedient that I should leave the greater part of my kit behind me. Then came the painful task of selection, to be carried out with the thermometer at ninety, and to be completed in thirty minutes! To go or not to go had to be asked and answered as to every shirt and pair of trousers. Oh, those weary clothes!

If a man could travel as a dog, how delightful it would be to keep moving from year's end to year's end!

We steamed up the coast for two days quietly, placidly, and steadily. I cannot say that the trip was a pleasant one, remembering how intense was the heat. On one occasion we stopped for practice-shooting, and it behoved me of course to mount the paddle-box and see what was going on. This was at eleven in the morning, and though it did not last for above an hour, I was brought almost to fainting by the power of the sun.

Punta-arenas—Sandy Point—is a small town and harbour situated in Costa Rica, near the top of the Bay of Nicoya. The sail up the bay is very pretty, through almost endless woods stretching away from the shores to the hills. There is, however, nothing majestic or grand about the scenery here. There are no Andes in sight, no stupendous mountains such as one might expect to see after coming so far to see them. It is all pretty, quiet, and ordinary; and on the whole perhaps superior to the views from the sea at Herne Bay.

The captain of the 'Vixen' had decided on going up to San José with me, as at the last moment did also the master, San José being the capital of Costa Rica. Our first object therefore was to hire a guide and mules, which, with the assistance of the acting English consul, we soon found. For even at Punta-arenas the English flag flies, and a distressed British subject can claim protection.

It is a small village lying along a creek of the sea, inside the sandy point from whence it is named. Considerable business is done here in the exportation of coffee, which is the staple produce of Costa Rica. It is sent chiefly to England; but it seemed to me that the money-making inhabitants of Punta-arenas were mostly Americans; men who either had been to California or who had got so far on their road thither and then changed their minds. It is a hot, dusty, unattractive spot, with a Yankee inn, at which men may 'liquor,' and a tram railroad running for twelve miles into the country. It abounds in oysters and beer, on which we dined before we started on our journey.

I was thus for the first time in Central America. This continent, if it may be so called, comprises the five republics of Guatemala, Honduras, San Salvador, Nicaragua, and Costa Rica. When this country first broke away from Spanish rule in 1821, it was for a while content to exist as one state, under the name of the Republic of Guatemala; as it had been known for nearly three hundred years as a Spanish province under the same denomination —that of Guatemala. After a hard tussle with Mexico, which endeavoured to devour it, and which forty years ago was more prone to annex than to be annexed, this republic sat itself fairly going, with the city of Guatemala for its capital. But the energies and ambition of the different races comprised among the two million inhabitants of Central America would not allow them to be governed except each in its own province. Some ten years since, therefore, the five States broke asunder. Each claimed to be sovereign and independent. Each chose its own president and had its own capital; and consequently, as might be expected, no part of the district in question has been able to enjoy those natural advantages with which Providence has certainly endowed it. To these States must be added, in counting up the countries of Central America, British Honduras, consisting of Belize and the adjacent district, and the Mosquito coast which so lately was under British protection; and which is ——. But here I must be silent, or I may possibly trench upon diplomatic subjects still unsettled.

My visit was solely to Costa Rica, which has in some respects done better than its neighbours. But this has been owing to the circumstances of its soil and climate rather than to those of its government, which seems to me to be as bad as any can be which deserves that name. In Costa Rica there certainly is a government, and a very despotic one it is.

I am not much given to the sins of dandyism, but I must own I was not a little proud of my costume as I left Punta-arenas. We had been told that according to the weather our ride would be either dusty or muddy in no ordinary degree, and that any clothes which we might wear during the journey would be utterly useless as soon as the journey was over. Consequently we purchased for ourselves, in an American store, short canvas smock-frocks which would not come below the saddle, and coarse holland trousers. What class of men may usually wear these garments in Costa Rica I cannot say; but in England I have seen navvies look exactly as my naval friends looked; and I flatter myself that my appearance was quite equal to theirs. I had procured at Panamá a light straw hat, with an amazing brim, and had covered the whole with white calico. I have before said that my beard had become 'poblada,' so that on the whole I was rather gratified than otherwise when I was assured by the storekeeper that we should certainly be taken for three filibusters. Now the name of filibuster means something serious in those localities, as I shall in a few pages have to explain.

We started on our journey by railroad, for there is a tramway that runs for twelve miles through the forest. We were dragged along on this by an excellent mule till our course was suddenly impeded by a tree which had fallen across the road. But in course of time this was removed, and in something less than three hours we found ourselves at a saw-mill in the middle of the forest.

The first thing that met my view on stepping out of the truck was a solitary Englishman seated on a half-sawn log of wood. Those who remember Hood's Whims and Oddities may bear in mind a heartrending picture of the last man. Only that the times do not agree, I·should have said that this poor fellow must have sat for the picture. He was undeniably an English labourer. No man of any other nation would have had that face, or worn those clothes, or kicked his feet about in that same awkward, melancholy humour.

He was, he said, in charge of the saw-mill, having been induced to come out into that country for three years. According to him, it was a wretched, miserable place. ' No man,' he said, ' ever found himself in worse diggings.' He earned a dollar and a half a day, and with that he could hardly buy shoes and have his clothes washed. ' Why did he not go home ?' I asked. ' Oh, he had come for three years, and he'd stay his three years out—if so be he didn't die.' The saw-mill was not paying, he said ; and never would pay. So that on the whole his account of Costa Rica was not encouraging.

We had been recommended to stay the first night at a place called Esparza, where there is a decent inn. But before we left Punta-arenas we learnt that Don Juan Rafael Mora, the President of the Republic, was coming down the same road with a large retinue of followers to inaugurate the commencement of the works of the canal. He would be on his way to meet his brother-president of the next republic, Nicaragua, at San Juan del Sur ; and at a spot some little distance from thence this great work was to be begun at once. He and his party were to sleep at Esparza. Therefore we decided on going on further before we halted ; and in truth at that place we did meet Don Juan and his retinue.

As both Costa Rica and Nicaragua are chiefly of importance to the eastern and western worlds, as being the district in which the isthmus between the two Americas may be most advantageously pierced by a canal—if it be ever so pierced—this subject naturally intrudes itself into all matters concerning these countries. Till the opening of the Panamá railway the transit of passengers through Nicaragua was immense. At present the railway has it all its own way. But the subject, connected as it has been with that of filibustering, mingles itself so completely with all interests in Costa Rica, that nothing of its present doings or politics can be well understood till something is understood on this canal subject. Sooner or later I must write a chapter on it; and it would almost be well if the reader would be pleased to take it out of its turn and get through it at once. The chapter, however, cannot well be brought in till these, recording my travels in Costa Rica, are completed.

Don Juan Mora and his retinue had arrived some hours before us, and had nearly filled the little hotel. This was kept by a Frenchman, and as far as provisions and beer were concerned seemed to be well kept. Our requirements did not go beyond these. On entering the public sitting-room a melodiously rich Irish brogue at once greeted my ears, and I saw seated at the table, joyous in a semi-military uniform, The O'Gorman Mahon, great as in bygone unemancipated days, when with head erect and stentorian voice he would make himself audible to half the County Clare. The head was still as erect, and the brogue as unexceptionable.

He speedily introduced us to a brother-workman in the same mission, the Prince Polignac. With the President himself I had not the honour of making acquaintance, for he speaks only Spanish, and my tether in that language is unfortunately very short. But the captain of the 'Vixen' was presented to him. He seemed to be a courteous little gentleman, though rather flustered by the magnitude of the work on which he was engaged.

There was something singular in the amalgamation of
the three men who had thus got themselves together in
this place to do honour to the coming canal. The President of the Republic, Prince Polignac, and The O'Gorman Mahon! I could not but think of the heterogeneous
heroes of the ' Groves of Blarney.'

'There were Nicodemus, and Polyphemus,
Oliver Cromwell, and Leslie Foster.'*

'And now, boys, ate a bit of what's going, and take a
dhrop of dhrink,' said The O'Gorman, patting us on the
shoulders with kind patronage. We did as we were bid,
ate and drank, paid the bill, and went our way rejoicing.
That night, or the next morning rather, at about 2 A.M.,
we reached a wayside inn called San Mateo, and there
rested for five or six hours. That we should obtain any
such accommodation along the road astonished me, and of
such as we got we were very glad. But it must not be
supposed that it was of a very excellent quality. We
found three bedsteads in the front room into which the
door of the house opened. On these were no mattresses,
not even a palliasse. They consisted of flat boards sloping
away a little towards the feet, with some hard substance
prepared for a pillow. In the morning we got a cup of
coffee without milk. For these luxuries and for pastur-
age for the mules we paid about ten shillings a head.
Indeed, everything of this kind in Costa Rica is exces-
sively dear.

Our next day's journey was a very long one, and to
my companions very fatiguing, for they had not latterly
been so much on horseback as had been the case with
myself. Our first stage before breakfast was of some five
hours' duration, and from the never-ending questions put

---

* I am not quoting the words rightly, I fear; but the selection in
the true song is miscellaneous in the same degree.

to the guide as to the number of remaining leagues, it seemed to be eternal. The weather also was hot, for we had not yet got into the high lands ; and a continued seat of five hours on a mule, under a burning sun, is not refreshing to a man who is not accustomed to such exercise ; and especially is not so when he is unaccustomed to the half-trotting, half-pacing steps of the beast. The Spaniard sits in the saddle without moving, and generally has his saddle well stuffed and padded, and then covered with a pillion. An Englishman disdains so soft a seat, and endeavours to rise in his stirrup at every step of the mule, as he would on a trotting horse at home. In these Hispano-American countries this always provokes the ridicule of the guide, who does not hesitate to tell the poor wretch who is suffering in his pillory that he does not know how to ride.

With some of us the pillory was very bad, and I feared for a time that we should hardly have been able to mount again after breakfast. The place at which we were is called Atenas, and I must say in praise of this modern Athens, and of the three modern Athenian girls who waited on us, that their coffee, eggs, and grilled fowl were very good. The houses of these people are exceedingly dirty, their modes of living comfortless and slovenly in the extreme. But there seems to be no lack of food, and the food is by no means of a bad description. Along this road from Punta-arenas to San José we found it always supplied in large quantities and fairly cooked. The prices demanded for it were generally high. But then all prices are high ; and it seems that, even among the poorer classes, small sums of money are not valued as with us. There is no copper coin. Half a rial, equal to about threepence, is the smallest piece in use. A handful of rials hardly seems to go further, or to be thought more of, than a handful of pence with us ; and a dollar, eight rials, ranks hardly higher in estimation than a shilling does in England.

At last, by the gradual use of the coffee and eggs, and by the application, external and internal, of a limited amount of brandy, the outward and the inward men were recruited; and we once more found ourselves on the backs of our mules, prepared for another stage of equal duration. These evils always lessen as we become more accustomed to them, so that when we reached a place called Assumption, at which we were to rest for the night, we all gallantly informed the muleteer that we were prepared to do another stage. 'Not so the mules,' said the muleteer; and as his words were law, we prepared to spend the night at Assumption.

Our road hitherto had been rising nearly the whole way, and had been generally through a picturesque country. We ascended one long severe hill, severe that is as a road, though to a professed climber of mountains it would be as nothing. From the summit of this hill we had a magnificent view down to the Pacific. Again, at a sort of fortress through which we passed, and which must have been first placed there by the old Spaniards to guard the hill-passes, we found a very lovely landscape looking down into the valley. Here some show of a demand was made for passports; but we had none to exhibit, and no opposition was made to our progress. Except at these two places, the scenery, which was always more or less pretty, was never remarkable. And even at the two points named there was nothing to equal the mountain scenery of many countries in Europe.

What struck me most was the constant traffic on the road or track over which we passed. I believe I may call it a road, for the produce of the country is brought down over it in bullock carts; and I think that in South Wales I have taken a gig over one very much of the same

description. But it is extremely rude ; and only fit for
solid wooden wheels—circles, in fact, of timber—such as
are used, and for the patient, slow step of the bullocks.

But during the morning and evening hours the strings
of these bullock carts were incessant. They travel from
four till ten, then rest till three or four, and again proceed
for four or five hours in the cool of the evening. They
are all laden with coffee, and the idea they give is, that
the growth of that article in Costa Rica must be much
more than sufficient to supply the whole world. For
miles and miles we met them, almost without any interval.
Coffee, coffee, coffee ; coffee, coffee, coffee ! It is grown
in large quantities, I believe, only in the high lands of
San José ; and all that is exported is sent down to Punta-
arenas, though by travelling this route it must either pass
across the isthmus railway at a vast cost, or else be carried
round the Horn. At present half goes one way and half
the other. But not a grain is carried, as it should all be
carried, direct to the Atlantic. When I come to speak of
the road from San José to Greytown, their post on the
Atlantic, the reason for this will be understood.

The bivouacs made on the roadside by the bullock
drivers for their night and noon accommodation are very
picturesque when seen filled by the animals. A piece of
flat ground is selected by the roadside, about half an acre
in size, and close to a river or some running water. Into
this one or two hundred bullocks are taken, and then
released from their carts. But they are kept yoked
together to prevent their straying. Here they are fed
exclusively on sugar-canes, which the men carry with
them, and buy along the road. The drovers patiently cut
the canes up with their knives, and the beasts patiently
munch them. Neither the men nor the animals roar, as
they would with us, or squabble for the use of the watercourse, or curse their own ill luck or the good luck of

their neighbours. Drivers and driven are alike orderly, patient, and slow, spending their lives in taking coffee down to Punta-arenas, and in cutting and munching thousands of sugar-canes.

We passed some of those establishments by moonlight, and they looked like large crowded fairs full of low small booths. The men, however, do not put up tents, but sleep out in their carts.

They told me that the soil in Costa Rica was very favourable to the sugar-cane, and I looked out to see some sugar among the coffee. But not a hogshead came that way. We saw patches of the cane growing by the roadside; but no more was produced than what sufficed for the use of the proprietor himself, and for such sale as the traffic on the road afforded. Indeed, I found that they do not make sugar, so called, in Costa Rica, but import what they use. The article fabricated is called by them 'dulce.' It comes from their hands in ugly round brown lumps, of the consistency of brick, looking, in truth, much more like a large brickbat than any possible saccharine arrangement. Nevertheless, the canes are fairly good, and the juice as sweet as that produced in first-rate sugar-growing soils.

It seemed that the only use made of this 'dulce,' excepting that of sweetening the coffee of the peasants, is for distillation. A spirit is made from it at San José, called by the generic name of aguardiente; and this doubtless would give considerable impulse to the growth of sugar-canes but for a little law made on the subject by the present President of the republic. The President himself is a cane-grower, and by this law it is enacted that the only person in Costa Rica entitled to supply the distillery with dulce shall be Don Juan Mora. Now, Don Juan Mora is the President.

Before I left the country I came across an American

who was desirous of settling there with the view of producing cocoa. 'Well,' said I, 'and what do you think
of it?'

'Why, I like the diggings,' said he; 'and guess I
could make things fix well enough. But suppose the
President should choose to grow all the cocoa as well as
all the gin! Where would my cacao-plants be then?'
At a discount, undoubtedly. These are the effects on a
country of despotism in a small way.

On my way into San José I got off my mule to look
at an old peasant making dulce, or in other words grind-
ing his sugar-canes by the roadside. It was done in
the most primitive manner. One bullock turned the
mill, which consisted of three vertical wooden rollers. The
juice trickled into a little cistern; and as soon as the old
man found that he had enough, he baled it out and boiled
it down. And yet I imagine that as good sugar may be
made in Costa Rica as in British Guiana. But who will
put his capital into a country in which the President
can pass any law he pleases on his own behalf?

In the neighbourhood of San José we began to come
across the coffee plantations. They certainly give the
best existing proof of the fertility and progress of the
country. I had seen coffee plantations in Jamaica, but
there they are beautifully picturesque, placed like hanging gardens on the steep mountain-sides. Some of these
seem to be almost inaccessible, and the plant always has
the appearance of being a hardy mountain shrub. But
here in Costa Rica it is grown on the plain. The secret,
I presume, is that a certain temperature is necessary,
and that this is afforded by a certain altitude from the
sea. In Jamaica this altitude is only to be found among
the mountains, but it is attained in Costa Rica on the high
plains of the interior.

And then we jogged slowly into San José on the third

day after our departure from Punta-arenas. Slowly,
sorely, and with minds much preoccupied, we jogged
into San José. On leaving the saw-mill at the end of the
tramway my two friends had galloped gallantly away
into the forest, as though a brave heart and a sharp pair
of spurs would have sufficed to carry them right through
to their journey's end. But the muleteer with his pony
and the baggage-mule then lingered far behind. His
heart was not so brave, nor were his spurs apparently so
sharp. The luggage, too, was slipping every ten minutes,
for I unfortunately had a portmanteau of which no muleteer could ever make anything. It has been condemned
in Holy Land, in Jamaica, in Costa Rica, wherever it has
had to be fixed upon any animal's back. On this occasion it nearly broke both the heart of the muleteer and
the back of the mule.

But things were changed as we crept into San José.
The muleteer was all life, and led the way, driving before
him the pack-mule, now at length reconciled to his load.
And then, at straggling intervals, our jibes all silenced,
our showy canters all done, rising wearily in our stirrups
at every step, shifting from side to side to ease the galls
'That patient merit of the unworthy takes '—for our
merit had been very patient, and our saddles very unworthy—we jogged into San José.

CHAPTER XVIII.

CENTRAL AMERICA. COSTA RICA—SAN JOSÉ.

ALL travellers when entering unknown towns for the first time have felt that intense interest on the subject of hotel accommodation which pervaded our hearts as we followed our guide through the streets. We had been told that there were two inns in the town, and that we were to go to the Hotel San José. And accordingly we went to it.

It was quite evident that the landlord at first had some little doubt as to the propriety of admitting us; and but for our guide, whom he knew, we should have had to explain at some length who we were. But under his auspices we were taken in without much question.

The Spaniards themselves are not in their own country at all famous for their inns. No European nation has probably advanced so slowly towards civilization in this respect as Spain has done. And therefore, as these Costa Ricans are Spanish by descent and language, and as the country itself is so far removed from European civilization, we did not expect much. Had we fallen into the hands of Spaniards we should probably have received less than we expected. But as it was we found ourselves in a comfortable second-class little German inn. It was German in everything; its light-haired landlord, frequently to be seen with a beer tankard in hand; its tidy landlady, tidy at any rate in the evening, if not always so in the morning; its early hours, its cookery, its drink, and I think I may fairly add, its prices.

On entering the first town I had visited in Central America, I had of course looked about me for strange sights. That men should be found with their heads under their shoulders, or even living in holes burrowed in the ground, I had not ventured to hope. But when a man has travelled all the way to Costa Rica, he does expect something strange. He does not look to find everything as tame and flat and uninteresting as though he were riding into a sleepy little borough town in Wiltshire.

We cannot cross from Dover to Ostend without finding at once that we are among a set of people foreign to ourselves. The first glance of the eye shows this in the architecture of the houses, and the costume of the people. We find the same cause for excitement in France, Switzerland, and Italy; and when we get as far as the Tyrol, we come upon a genus of mankind so essentially differing from our own as to make us feel that we have travelled indeed.

But there is little more interest to be found in entering San José than in driving through the little Wiltshire town to which I have above alluded. The houses are comfortable enough. They are built with very ordinary doors and windows, of one or two stories according to the wealth of the owners, and are decently clean outside, though apparently rather dirty within. The streets are broad and straight, being all at right angles to each other, and though not very well paved, are not rough enough to elicit admiration. There is a square, the pláza, in which stand the cathedral, the barracks, and a few of the best houses in the town. There is a large and tolerably well-

arranged market-place.   There is a really handsome set of
public buildings, and there are two moderately good hotels.
What more can a man rationally want if he travel for
business?   And if he travel for pleasure how can he
possibly find less?

It so happened that at the time of my visit to Costa
Rica Sir William Ouseley was staying at San José with
his family.   He had been sent, as all the world that
knows anything doubtless knows very well, as minister
extraordinary from our Court to the governments of
Central America, with the view of settling some of those
tough diplomatic questions as to the rights of transit and
occupation of territory, respecting which such world-
famous Clayton-Bulwer treaties and Cass-Yrrisari treaties
have been made and talked of.   He had been in Nicaragua, making no doubt an equally famous Ouseley-Some-
thing treaty, and was now engaged on similar business
in the capital of Costa Rica.

Of the nature of this august work,—for such work must
be very august,—I know nothing.   I only hope that he
may have at least as much success as those who went
before him.   But to me it was a great stroke of luck
to find so pleasant and hospitable a family in so outlandish
a place as San José.   And indeed, though I have given
praise to the hotel, I have given it with very little
personal warrant as regards my knowledge either of the
kitchen or cellar.   My kitchen and cellar were beneath
the British flag at the corner of the pláza, and I had
reason to be satisfied with them in every respect.

And I had abundant reason to be greatly gratified.
For not only was there at San José a minister extraordinary, but also, attached to the mission, there was an
extra-ordinary secretary of legation, a very prince of good
fellows.   At home he would be a denizen of the Foreign
Office, and denizens of the Foreign Office are swells at

home. But at San José, where he rode on a mule, and
wore a straw hat, and slept in a linendraper's shop, he
was as pleasant a companion as a man would wish to
meet on the western, or indeed on any other side of the
Atlantic.

I shall never forget the hours I spent in that linendraper's shop. The rooms over the shop, over that shop
and over two or three others, were occupied by Sir
W. Ouseley and his family. There was a chemist's
establishment there, and another in the possession, I
think, of a hatter. They had been left to pursue their
business in peace; but my friend the secretary, finding
no rooms sufficiently secluded for himself in the upper
mansion, had managed to expel the haberdasher, and had
located himself, not altogether uncomfortably, among the
counters.

Those who have spent two or three weeks in some
foreign town in which they have no ordinary pursuits,
know what it is to have—or perhaps, more unlucky,
know what it is to be without—some pleasant accustomed
haunt, in which they can pretend to read, while in truth
the hours are passed in talking, with some few short
intervals devoted to contemplation and tobacco. Such
to me was the shop of the expelled linendraper at San
José. In it, judiciously suspended among the counters,
hung a Panamá grass hammock, in which it was the
custom of my diplomatic friend to lie at length and
meditate his despatches. Such at least had been his
custom before my arrival. What became of his despatches
during the period of my stay, it pains me to think; for
in that hammock I had soon located myself, and I fear
that my presence was not found to be a salutary incen-
tive to composition.

The scenery round San José is certainly striking, but
not sufficiently so to enable one to rave about it. I

cannot justly go into an ecstasy and sing of Pelion or Ossa; nor can I talk of deep ravines to which the Via Mala is as nothing. There is a range of hills, respectably broken into prettiness, running nearly round the town, though much closer to it on the southern than on the other sides. Two little rivers run by it, which here and there fall into romantic pools, or pools which would be romantic if they were not so very distant from home; —if having travelled so far one did not expect so very much. There are nice walks too, and pretty rides; only the mules do not like fast trotting when the weight upon them is heavy. About a mile and a half from the town, there is a Savanah, so-called, or large square park, the Hyde Park of San José; and it would be difficult to imagine a more pleasant place for a gallop. It is quite large enough for a race-course, and is open to everybody. Some part of the mountain range as seen from here is really beautiful.

The valley of San José, as it is called, is four thousand five hundred feet above the sea; and consequently, though within the tropics, and only ten degrees north of the line, the climate is good, and the heat, I believe, never excessive. I was there in April, and at that time, except for a few hours in the middle of the day, and that only on some days, there was nothing like tropical heat. Within ten days of my leaving San José I heard natives at Panamá complaining of the heat as being altogether unendurable. But up there, on that high plateau, the sun had no strength that was inconvenient even to an Englishman.

Indeed, no climate can, I imagine, be more favourable to fertility and to man's comfort at the same time than that of the interior of Costa Rica. The sugar-cane comes to maturity much quicker than in Demerara or Cuba. There it should be cut in about thirteen or fourteen

months from the time it is planted; in Nicaragua and
Costa Rica it comes to perfection in nine or ten. The
ground without manure will afford two crops of corn in
a year. Coffee grows in great perfection, and gives a
very heavy crop. The soil is all volcanic, or, I should
perhaps more properly say, has been the produce of vol-
canoes, and is indescribably fertile. And all this has
been given without that intensity of heat which in those
southern regions generally accompanies tropical fertility,
and which makes hard work fatal to a white man; while
it creates lethargy and idleness, and neutralizes gifts
which would otherwise be regarded as the fairest which
God has bestowed on his creatures. In speaking thus,
I refer to the central parts of Costa Rica only,—to those
which lie some thousand feet above the level of the sea.
Along the sea-shores, both of the Atlantic and Pacific,
the heat is as great, and the climate as unwholesome as
in New Granada or the West Indies. It would be difficult to find a place worse circumstanced in this respect
than Punta-arenas.

But though the valley or plateau of San José, and the
interior of the country generally is thus favourably situated, I cannot say that the nation is prosperous. It seems
to be God's will that highly-fertile countries should not
really prosper. Man's energy is brought to its highest
point by the presence of obstacles to be overcome, by the
existence of difficulties which are all but insuperable.
And therefore a Scotch farm will give a greater value
in produce than an equal amount of land in Costa Rica.
When nature does so much, man will do next to nothing!

Those who seem to do best in this country, both in
trade and agriculture, are Germans. Most of those who
are carrying on business on a large scale are foreigners,—
that is, not Spanish by descent. There are English here,
and Americans, and French, but I think the Germans are

the most wedded to the country. The finest coffee properties are in the hands of foreigners, as also are the plantations of canes, and saw-mills for the preparation of timber. But they have a very uphill task. Labour is extremely scarce, and very dear. The people are not idle as the negroes are, and they love to earn and put by money; but they are very few in number; they have land of their own, and are materially well off. In the neighbourhood of San José a man's labour is worth a dollar a day, and even at that price it is not always to be had.

It seems to be the fact that in all countries in which slavery has existed and has been abolished this subject of labour offers the great difficulty in the way of improvement. Labour becomes unpopular, and is regarded as being in some sort degrading. Men will not reconcile it with their idea of freedom. They wish to work on their own land if they work at all; and to be their own masters; to grow their own crops, be they ever so small; and to sit beneath their own vine, be the shade ever so limited. There are those who will delight to think that such has been the effect of emancipation; who will argue, —and they have strong arguments on their side,—that God's will with reference to his creatures is best carried out by such an order of things. I can only say that the material result has not hitherto been good. As far as we at present see, the struggle has produced idleness and sensuality, rather than prosperity and civilization.

It is hardly fair to preach this doctrine, especially with regard to Costa Rica, for the people are not idle. That, at least, is not specially their character. They are a humdrum, contented, quiet, orderly race of men; fond of money, but by no means fond of risking it; living well as regards sufficiency of food and raiment, but still living very close; anxious to effect small savings, and politically contented if the security of those savings

can be insured to them. They seem to be little desirous,
even among the upper classes, or what we would call the
tradespeople, of education, either religious or profane;
they have no enthusiasm, no ardent desires, no aspirations.
If only they could be allowed to sell their dulce to the
maker of aguardiente,—if they might be permitted to get
their little profit out of the manufacture of gin! That,
at present, is the one grievance that affects them, but even
that they bear easily.

It will perhaps be considered my duty to express an
opinion whether or no they are an honest people. In one
respect, certainly. They steal nothing; at any rate, make
no great thefts. No one is attacked on the roads; no life
is in danger from violence; houses are not broken open.
Nay, a traveller's purse left upon a table is, I believe,
safe; nor will his open portmanteau be rifled. But when
you come to deal with them, the matter is different.
Then their conscience becomes elastic; and as the trial
is a fair one between man and man, they will do their
best to cheat you. If they lie to you, cannot you lie to
them? And is it not reasonable to suppose that you
do so? If they, by the aid of law, can get to the windy
side of you, is not that merely their success in opposition
to your attempt—for of course you do attempt—to get to
the windy side of them? And then bribes are in great
vogue. Justice is generally to be bought; and when that
is in the market, trade in other respects is not generally
conducted in the most honest manner.

Thus, on the whole, I cannot take upon myself to say
that they are altogether an honest people. But they have
that kind of honesty which is most essential to the man
who travels in a wild country. They do not knock out
the traveller's brains, or cut his throat for the sake of what
he has in his pocket.

Generally speaking the inhabitants of Costa Rica are

of course Spanish by descent, but here, as in all these
countries, the blood is very much mixed: pure Spanish
blood is now, I take it, quite an exception. This is
seen more in the physiognomy than in the colour, and
is specially to be noticed in the hair. There is a mixture
of three races, the Spanish, the native Indian, and the
Negro; but the traces of the latter are comparatively
light and few. Negroes, men and women, absolutely
black, and of African birth or descent, are very rare;
and though traces of the thick lip and the woolly hair
are to be seen—to be seen in the streets and market-
places—they do not by any means form the staple of the
existing race.

The mixture is of Spanish and of Indian blood, in
which the Spanish no doubt much preponderates. The
general colour is that of a white man, but of one who is
very swarthy. Occasionally this becomes so marked that
the observer at once pronounces the man or woman to be
coloured. But it is the colouring of the Indian, and not
of the negro; the hue is rich, and to a certain extent
bright, and the lines of the face are not flattened and
blunted. The hair also is altogether human, and in no
wise sheepish.

I do not think that the inhabitants of Costa Rica have
much to boast of in the way of personal beauty. Indeed,
the descendant of the Spaniard, out of his own country,
seems to lose both the manly dignity and the female grace
for which old Spain is still so noted. Some pretty girls I
did see, but they could boast only the ordinary prettiness
which is common to all young girls, and which our friends
in France describe as being the special gift of the devil.
I saw no fine, flaming, flashing eyes; no brilliant figures,
such as one sees in Seville around the altar-rails in the
churches: no profiles opening upon me struck me with
mute astonishment.

The women were humdrum in their appearance, as the men are in their pursuits. They are addicted to crinoline, as is the nature of women in these ages; but so long as their petticoats stuck out, that seemed to be everything. In the churches they squat down on the ground, in lieu of kneeling, with their dresses and petticoats arranged around them, looking like huge turnips with cropped heads—like turnips that, by their persevering growth, had got half their roots above the ground. Now women looking like turnips are not specially attractive.

I was at San José during Passion Week, and had therefore an opportunity of seeing the processions which are customary in Roman Catholic countries at that period. I certainly should not say that the Costa Ricans are especially a religious people. They are humdrum in this as in other respects, and have no enthusiasm either for or against the priesthood. Free-thinking is not the national sin; nor is fanaticism. They are all Roman Catholics, most probably without an exception. Their fathers and mothers were so before them, and it is a thing of course.

There used to be a bishop of Costa Rica; indeed, they never were without one till the other day. But not long since the father of their church in some manner displeased the President: he had, I believe, taken it into his sacred head that he, as bishop, might make a second party in the state, and organize an opposition to the existing government; whereupon the President banished him, as the President can do to any one by his mere word, and since that time there has been no bishop. ' And will they not get another?' I asked. ' No; probably not; they don't want one. It will be so much money saved.' Looking at the matter in this light, there is often much to be said for the expediency of reducing one's establishment. ' And who manages the church?' 'It does not require much management. It goes on in the old way. When they want priests they get them from Guatemala.' If we could save all our bishoping, and get our priests as we want them from Guatemala, or any other factory, how excellent would be the economy !

The cathedral of San José is a long, low building, with side aisles formed by very rickety-looking wooden pillars —in substance they are hardly more than poles—running from the ground to the roof. The building itself is mean enough, but the internal decorations are not badly arranged, and the general appearance is neat, orderly, and cool. We all know the usual manner in which wooden and waxen virgins are dressed and ornamented in such churches. There is as much of this here as elsewhere ; but I have seen it done in worse taste both in France and Italy. The façade of the church, fronting the pláza, is hardly to be called a portion of the church ; but is an adjunct to it, or rather the church has been fixed on to the façade, which is not without some architectural pretension.

In New Granada—Columbia that was—the cathedrals are arranged as they are in old Spain. The choir is not situated round the altar, or immediately in front of it, as is the custom in Christian churches in, I believe, all other countries, but is erected far down the centre aisle, near the western entrance. This, however, was not the case in any church that I saw in Costa Rica.

During the whole of Passion Week there was a considerable amount of religious activity in the way of preaching and processions, which reached its acme on Good Friday. On that day the whole town was processioning from morning—which means four o'clock—till evening—which means two hours after sunset. They had three figures, or rather three characters,—for two of them appeared in more than one guise and form,—each larger than life ; those, namely, of our Saviour, the Virgin, and St. John. These figures are made of wax, and the faces of some of them were excellently moulded. These are manufactured in Guatemala—as the priests are ; and the people there pride themselves on their manufacture, not without reason.

The figures of our Saviour and the Virgin were in different dresses and attitudes, according to the period of the day which it was intended to represent ; but the St. John was always represented in the dress of a bishop of the present age. The figures were supported on men's shoulders, and were carried backwards and forwards through every portion of the town, till at last, having been brought forth in the morning from the cathedral, they were allowed at night to rest in a rival, and certainly better built, though smaller church.

I must notice one particularity in the church-going population of this country. The women occupy the nave and centre aisle, squatting on the ground, and looking, as I have said, like turnips ; whereas the men never advance beyond the side aisles. The women of the higher classes —all those, indeed, who make any pretence to dress and finery—bring with them little bits of carpet, on which they squat ; but there are none of those chairs with which churches on the Continent are so commonly filled.

It seemed that there is nothing that can be called society among the people of San José. They do not go out to each other's homes, nor meet in public ; they have neither tea-parties, nor dinner-parties, nor dancing-parties, nor card-parties. I was even assured—though I cannot say that the assurance reached my belief—that they never flirt ! Occasionally, on Sundays, for instance, and on holidays, they put on their best clothes and call on each other. But even then there is no conversation among them ; they sit stiffly on each other's sofas, and make remarks at intervals, like minute guns, about the weather.

'But what *do* they do ?' I asked. 'The men scrape

money together, and when they have enough they build a house, big or little according to the amount that they have scraped : that satisfies the ambition of a Costa Rican. When he wishes to amuse himself, he goes to a cock-fight.' ' And the women ?' ' They get married early if their fathers can give them a few ounces '—the ounce is the old doubloon, worth here about three pounds eight shillings sterling—' and then they cook, and have children.' ' And if the ounces be wanting, and they don't get married ?' ' Then they cook all the same, but do not have the children, —as a general rule.' And so people vegetate in Costa Rica.

And now I must say a word or two about the form of government in this country. It is a republic, of course, arranged on the model plan. A president is elected for a term of years,—in this case six. He has ministers who assist him in his government, and whom he appoints ; and there is a House of Congress, elected of course by the people, who make the laws. The President merely carries them out, and so Utopia is realized.

Utopia might perhaps be realized in such republics, or at any rate the realization might not be so very distant as it is at present, were it not that in all of them the practice, by some accident, runs so far away from the theory.

In Costa Rica, Don Juan Rafael Mora, familiarly called Juanito, is now the president, having been not long since re-elected (?) for the third time. ' We read in the " Gazette " on Tuesday morning that the election had been carried on Saturday, and that was all we knew about it.' It is thus they elect a president in Costa Rica ; no one knows anything of the affair, or troubles his head with the matter. If any one suggested a rival president, he would be banished. But such a thing is not thought of ; no note is taken as to five years or six years. At some period that pleases him the President says that he has been re-elected, and he is re-elected. Who cares? Why not Juanito as well as any one else? Only it is a pity he will not let us sell our dulce to the distillers!

The President's salary is three thousand dollars a year; an income which for so high a position is moderate enough. But then a further sum of six thousand dollars is added to this for official entertainment. The official entertainments, however, are not numerous. I was informed that he usually gives one party every year. He himself still lives in his private house, and still keeps a shop, as he did before he was president. It must be remembered that there is no aristocracy in this country above the aristocracy of the shop-keepers.

As far as I could learn, the Congress is altogether a farce. There is a congress or collection of men sent up from different parts of the country, some ten or dozen of whom sit occasionally round a table in the great hall; but they neither debate, vote, nor offer opinions. Some one man, duly instructed by the President, lets them know what law is to be made or altered, and the law is made or altered. Should any member of Congress make himself disagreeable, he would, as a matter of course, be banished; taken, that is, to Punta-arenas, and there told to shift for himself. Now this enforced journey to Punta-arenas does not seem to be more popular among the Costa Ricans than a journey to Siberia is among the Russians.

Such is the model republic of Central America,—admitted, I am told, to be the best administered of the cluster of republics there established. This, at any rate, may certainly be said for it—that life and property are safe. They are safe for the present, and will probably remain so, unless the filibusters make their way into the neighbouring state of Nicaragua in greater numbers and with better leaders than they have hitherto had.

And it must be told to the credit of the Costa Ricans,

that it was by them and their efforts that the invasion of
Walker and the filibusters into Central America was
stopped and repelled. These enterprising gentlemen, the
filibusters, landed on the coast of Nicaragua, having come
down from California. Here they succeeded in getting
possession of a large portion of the country, that portion
being the most thickly populated and the richest; many
of the towns they utterly destroyed, and among them
Granada, the capital. It seems that at this time the
whole state of Nicaragua was paralyzed, and unable to
strike any blow in its own defence.

Having laid waste the upper or more northern country,
Walker came down south as far as Rivas, a town still in
Nicaragua but not far removed from the borders of Costa
Rica. His intention, doubtless, was to take possession of
Costa Rica, so that he might command the whole transit
across the isthmus.

But at Rivas he was attacked by the soldiery of Costa
Rica, under the command of a brother of Don Juan Mora.
This was in 1856, and it seems that some three thousand
Costa Ricans were taken as far as Rivas. But few of
them returned. They were attacked by cholera, and
what with that, and want, and the intense heat, to which
of course must be added what injuries the filibusters could
do them, they were destroyed, and a remnant only came
back.

But in 1857 the different states of Central America
joined themselves in a league, with the object of expelling
these filibusters. I do not know that either of the three
northern states sent any men to Rivas, and the weight of
the struggle again fell upon Costa Rica. The Costa
Ricans and Nicaraguans together invested Rivas, in which
five hundred filibusters under Walker for some time
maintained themselves. These men were reduced to
great straits, and might no doubt have been taken bodily.

But the Central Americans also had their difficulties to contend with. They did not agree very well together, and they had but slender means of supporting themselves. It ended in a capitulation, under which Walker and his associates were to walk out with their arms and all the honours of war; and by which, moreover, it was stipulated that the five hundred were to be sent back to America at the expense of the Central American States. The States, thinking no doubt that it was good economy to build a golden bridge for a flying enemy, did so send them back; and in this manner for a while Central America was freed from the locusts.

Such was the capitulation of Rivas; a subject on which all Costa Ricans now take much pride to themselves. And indeed honour is due to them in this matter, for they evinced a spirit in the business when their neighbours of Nicaragua failed to do so. They soon determined that the filibusters would do them no good;—could indeed by no possibility do them anything but harm; consequently, they resolved to have the first blow, and they struck it manfully, though not so successfully as might have been wished.

The total population of Central America is, I believe, about two millions, while that of Costa Rica does not exceed two hundred thousand. Of the five states, Guatemala has by far the largest number of inhabitants; and indeed the town of Guatemala may still be regarded as the capital of all the isthmus territories. They fabricate there not only priests and wax images, but doctors and lawyers, and all those expensive luxuries for the production of which the air of a capital is generally considered necessary. The President of Guatemala is, they say, an Indian, nearly of pure descent; his name is Carrera.

I have spoken of the army of Costa Rica. In point of accoutrement and outward show, they are on ordinary

T

days somewhat like the troops that were not fit to march through Coventry. They wear no regimentals, and are only to be known when on duty by a very rusty-looking gun. On Sundays, however, and holidays they do wear a sort of uniform, consisting of a neat cap, and a little braiding upon their best clothes. This dress, such as it is, they are obliged to find for themselves. The clothing department, therefore, is not troublesome.

These men are enrolled after the manner of our militia. The full number should be nine thousand, and is generally somewhat above six thousand. Of this number five hundred are kept in barracks, the men taking it by turns, month by month. When in barracks they receive about one shilling and sixpence a day; at other times they have no pay.

I cannot close my notice of San José without speaking somewhat more specially of the range of public buildings. I am told that it was built by a German, or rather by two Germans; the basement and the upper story being the work of different persons. Be this as it may, it is a handsome building, and would not disgrace any European capital. There is in it a throne-room—in England, at least, we should call it a throne; on this the President sits when he receives ambassadors from foreign countries. The velvet and gilding were quite unexceptionable, and the whole is very imposing. The sitting of Congress is held in the same chamber; but that, as I have explained, is not imposing.

The chief produce of Costa Rica is coffee. Those who love statistics may perhaps care to know that the average yearly export is something under a hundred thousand quintals; now a quintal weighs a hundred pounds, or rather, I believe, ninety-nine pounds exact.

CHAPTER XIX.

CENTRAL AMERICA.　COSTA RICA—MOUNT IRAZU.

In the neighbourhood of San José there is a volcanic
mountain, the name of which is Irazu. I was informed
that it still smoked, though it had discontinued for the
present the ejection of flames and lava. Indeed, the
whole country is full of such mountains. There is one,
the Monte Blanco, the summit of which has never yet
been reached—so rumour says in Costa Rica—far distant,
enveloped among other mountains, and to be reached
only through dense aboriginal forests, which still emits,
and is always emitting fire and burning floods of molten
stones.

Different excursions have been made with the object
of ascending the Monte Blanco, but hitherto in vain.
Not long since it was attempted by a French baron, but
he and his guide were for twenty days in the woods, and
then returned, their provisions failing them.

'You should ascend the Monte Blanco,' said Sir
William Ouseley to me. 'You are a man at large, with
nothing to do. It is just the work for you.' This was Sir
William's satire on the lightness of my ordinary occupations. Light as they might be, however, I had neither
time nor courage for an undertaking such as that; so I
determined to satisfy myself with the Irazu.

It happened, rather unfortunately for me, that at the

moment of my arrival at San José, a large party, consisting of Sir William's family and others, were in the very
act of visiting the mountain. Those, therefore, who were
anxious to see the sight, and willing to undergo the
labour, thus had their opportunity; and it became impossible for me to make up a second party. One hope I had.
The Secretary of Legation had not gone. Official occupation, joined to a dislike of mud and rough stones, had
kept him at home. Perhaps I might prevail. The
intensity of that work might give way before a week's
unremitting labour, and that Sybarite propensity might
be overcome.

But all my eloquence was of no avail. An absence of
a day and a half only was required; and three were spent
in proving that this could not be effected. The stones
and mud too were becoming worse and worse, for the
rainy season had commenced. In fact, the Secretary of
Legation would not budge. 'Le jeu ne vaut pas la
chandelle,' said the Secretary of Legation; whereupon he
lighted another cigar, and took a turn in the grass hammock. Now in my mind it must be a very bad game
indeed that is not worth the candle; and almost any game
is better than no game at all.

I was thus in deep trouble, making up my mind to go
alone, or rather alone with my guide;—for the due appreciation of which state of loneliness it must be borne in
mind that, as I do not speak a word of Spanish, I should
have no possible means of communication with the guide,
—when a low and mild voice fell upon my ear, offering
me its proprietor as my companion.

'I went up with Sir William last week,' said the mild
voice; 'and if you will permit me, I shall be happy to go
with you. I should like to see it twice; and I live at
Cartago on the way.'

It was quite clear that the owner of the voice was

sacrificing himself, and offering to repeat this troublesome journey merely out of good nature; but the service which he proposed to render me was too essential, and I could not afford to reject the offer. He lived in the country, and spoke Spanish, and was, moreover, a mild, kind-hearted little gentleman, very suitable as a companion, and not given too pertinaciously to a will of his own. Now the Secretary of Legation would have driven me mad half a score of times during the journey. He would have deafened me with politics, and with such politics too! So that on the whole I knew myself to be well off with the mild voice.

'You must go through Cartago,' said the mild voice, 'and I live there. We will dine there at the inn to-morrow, and then do a portion of our work the same evening.' It was so arranged. I was to be with him the next day at three, with a guide and two mules.

On the next morning it rained provokingly. I ought to have started at twelve; but at that time it was pouring, and neither the guide nor the mule showed themselves. 'You will never get there,' said the Secretary of Legation, looking up to the murky clouds with a gleam of delight. 'The game is never worth such a candle as that.' 'I shall get there most assuredly,' said I, rather sulkily, 'let the candle cost what it may.' But still the mules did not come.

Men have no idea of time in any country that is or has been connected with Spain. 'Yes, señor; you said twelve, and it is now only two! Well, three. The day is long, señor; there is plenty of time. Vaminos? Since you are in such a hurry, shall we make a start of it?'

At half-past two o'clock so spoke—not my guide, for, as will be seen by-and-by, he never spoke at all—but my guide's owner, who came accompanying the mules. In huge hurry, with sundry mute exclamations, uttered by my countenance since my tongue was unintelligible, and with appeals to my watch which should have broken the man's heart as I thrust it into his face, I clomb into my saddle. And then a poor-looking, shoeless creature, with a small straw hat tied on to his head by a handkerchief, with difficulty poised himself on the other beast. 'Vamos,' I exclaimed, and trotted down the street; for I knew that in that direction lay the road to Cartago. 'God be with you,' said the Secretary of Legation. 'The rainy season has set in permanently, I know; but perhaps you may have half an hour of sunshine now and again. I hope you will enjoy yourself.'

It was not raining when I started, and in fact did not rain again the whole afternoon. I trotted valiantly down the street, knowing my way so far; but at the bottom of the town the roads divided, and I waited for my guide. 'Go on first,' said I, pointing along the road. But he did not understand me, and stood still. 'Go on,' said I, getting behind his mule as though to drive him. But he merely stared, and shuffled himself to the other side of the road. 'Cartago,' I shouted, meaning that he was to show me the way there. 'Si, señor,' he replied; and backed himself into the ditch out of my way. He was certainly the stupidest man I ever met in my life, and I believe the Secretary of Legation had selected him on purpose.

I was obliged to choose my own road out of two, and luckily chose the right one. Had I gone wrong, I doubt whether the man would have had wit enough to put me right. I again trotted on; but in a quarter of an hour was obliged to wait, for my attendant was behind me, out of sight, and I felt myself bound to look after my traps, which were fastened to his mule. 'Come on,' I shouted in good broad English as soon as I saw him. 'Why the mischief don't you come on?' And my voice was so pitched, that on this occasion I think he did understand something of what I meant.

'Co-o-ome along,' I repeated, as he gently drew up to me. And I hit his mule sharply on the crupper with my stick. 'Spur him,' I said; and I explained what I meant by sticking my own rowels into my own beast. Whereupon the guide showed me that he had no spurs.

Now if there be one rule of life more strictly kept in Costa Rica than another, it is this, that no man ever mounts horse or mule without spurs. A man in England would as soon think of hunting without breeches. No muleteer was ever seen without them. And when a mule is hired, if the hirer have no saddle, he may chance to have to ride without one; but if he have no spurs, he will always be supplied.

I took off one of my own, which, by-the-by, I had borrowed out of the Secretary of Legation's establishment, and offered it to the man, remembering the well-known doctrine of Hudibras. He then showed me that one of his hands was tied up, and that he could not put the spur on. Consequently I was driven to dismount, myself, and to act equerry to this knight. Thrice on the road I had to do so, for twice the spur slipped from off his naked foot. Even with this I could not bring him on. It is four leagues, or about sixteen miles, from San José to Cartago, and with all my hastening we were three hours on the road.

The way lay through a rich and finely-cultivated country. The whole of this is now called the valley of San José, and consists, in truth, of a broad plateau, diversified by moderate hills and valleys, but all being at a considerable height; that is, from three to four thousand feet above the sea. The road also is fairly good; so good that a species of omnibus runs on it daily, there being some considerable traffic between the places; for Cartago is the second town in the republic.

Cartago is now the second town, but not long since it was the first. It was, however, destroyed by an earthquake; and though it has been rebuilt, it has never again taken its former position. Its present population is said to be ten thousand; but this includes not only the suburbs, but the adjacent villages. The town covers a large tract of ground, which is divided into long, broad, parallel streets, with a large pláza in the middle; as though it had been expected that a fine Utopian city would have sprung up. Alas! there is nothing fine about it, and very little that is Utopian.

Lingering near the hotel door, almost now in a state of despair, I met him of the mild voice. 'Yes; he had been waiting for three hours, certainly,' he mildly said, as I spurred my beast up to the door. 'Now that I was come it was all right; and on the whole he rather liked waiting—that is, when it did not result in waiting for nothing.' And then we sat down to dinner at the Cartago hotel.

This also was kept by a German, who after a little hesitation confessed that he had come to the country as a filibuster. 'You have fallen on your legs pretty well,' said I; for he had a comfortable house, and gave us a decent dinner. 'Yes,' said he, rather dubiously; 'but when I came to Costa Rica I intended to do better than this.' He might, however, remember that not one in five hundred of them had done so well.

And then another guide had to be found, for it was clear that the one that I had brought with me was useless. And I had a visit to make; for my friend lived with a widow lady, who would be grieved he said, if I passed through without seeing her. So I did call on her. I saw her again on my return through Cartago, as I shall specify.

With all these delays it was dark when we started. Our plan was to ride up to an upland pasture farm at which visitors to the mountain generally stop, to sleep there for a few hours, and then to start between three and four so as to reach the top of the mountain by sunrise. Now I perfectly well remember what I said with reference to sunrises from mountain-tops on the occasion of that disastrous visit to the Blue Mountain Peak in Jamaica; how I then swore that I would never do another mountain sunrise, having always failed lamentably in such attempts. I remember, and did remember this; and as far as the sunrise was concerned would certainly have had nothing to do with the Irazu at five o'clock, A.M.

But the volcano and the crater made the matter very different. They were my attractions; and as the mild voice suggested an early hour, it would not have become me to have hesitated. 'Start at four?' 'Certainly,' I said. 'The beds at the potrero'—such was the name they gave the place at which we stopped—'will not be soft enough to keep us sleeping.' 'No,' said the mild voice, 'they are not soft.' And so we proceeded.

Our road was very rough, and very steep; and the night was very dark. It was rough at first, and then it became slippery, which was worse. I had no idea that earth could be so slippery. My mule, which was a very fine one, fell under me repeatedly, being altogether unable to keep her footing. On these occasions she usually scrambled up, with me still on her back. Once, however, near the beginning of my difficulties, I thought to relieve her; and to do so I got off her. I soon found my mistake. I immediately slipped down on my hands and knees, and found it impossible to stand on my feet. I did not sink into the mud, but slipped off it—down, down, down, as if I were going back to Cartago, all alone in the dark. It was with difficulty that I again mounted my beast; but when there, there I remained, let her fall as she would. At eleven o'clock we reached the potrero.

The house here was little more than a rancho or hut; one of those log farm buildings which settlers make when they first clear the timber from a part of their selected lots, intending to replace them in a year or two by such tidy little houses; but so rarely fulfilling their intentions. All through Costa Rica such esablishments are common. On the coffee plantations and in the more highly-cultivated part of the country, round the towns for instance, and along the road to Punta-arenas, the farmers have a better class of residence. They inhabit long, low-built houses, with tiled roofs and a ground floor only, not at all unlike farmers' houses in Ireland, only that there they are thatched or slated. Away from such patches of cultivation, one seldom finds any better accommodation than a rancho with a log-built hut.

But the rancho had a door, and that door was fastened; so we knocked and hallooed—'Dito,' cried the guide; such being, I presume, the familiar sobriquet of his friend within. 'Dito,' sang out my mild friend with all his small energy of voice. 'Dito,' shouted I; and I think that my voice was the one which wakened the sleepers within.

We were soon admitted into the hut, and found that we were by no means the first comers. As soon as a candle was lighted we saw that there were four bedsteads in the room, and that two of them were occupied. There were, however, two left for my friend and myself. And it appeared also that the occupiers were friends of my friend. They were German savants, one by profession an architect and the other a doctor, who had come up into the woods looking for birds, beasts, and botanical treasures, and had already been there some three or four days. They were amply supplied with provisions, and immediately offered us supper. The architect sat up in bed to welcome us, and the doctor got up to clear the two spare beds of his trappings.

There is a luck in these things. I remember once clambering to the top of Scafell-Pike, in Cumberland—if it chance to be in Westmoreland I beg the county's pardon. I expected nothing more than men generally look for on the tops of mountains; but to my great surprise I found a tent. I ventured to look in, and there I saw two officers of the Engineers, friends of my own, sharpening their knives preparatory to the dissection of a roast goose. And beside the goose stood a bottle of brandy. Now I always looked on that as a direct dispensation of Providence. Walking down the mountain that same evening to Whitehaven, I stopped at a small public-house on the side of Enerdale, and called for some whisky and water. The article produced was not good, and so I said, appealing to an elderly gentleman in black, who sat by the hobside, very contemplative. 'Ah,' said he; 'you can't get good drink in these parts, sir; I know that so well that I generally bring a bottle of my own.' I immediately opened a warm conversation with that gentleman. He ws a clergyman of a neighbouring parish; and in a few minutes a magnum of port had made its appearance out of a neighbouring cupboard. That I thought was another dispensation of Providence. It was odd that they should have come together; but the facts are as I state them.

I did venture on a glass of brandy and water and a slight morsel of bread and meat, and then I prepared to throw myself on the bed immediately opposite to the doctor's. As I did 'so I saw something move inside the doctor's bed. 'My wife is there,' said the doctor, seeing the direction of my eyes. 'Oh!' said I; and I at once became very moderate in the slight change which I made in my toilet.

We were to start at four, and at four precisely I woke. As my friend had said, there was little to tempt me to sleep. The great drawback to the comfort of these ranchos is the quantity of dirt which continually falls out of the roof into one's eyes. Then the boards are hard of course, and of course also they are infested with vermin. They tell you indeed of scorpions and centipedes, of preternatural wasps, and musquitos as big as young ostriches; but I found none of these large-looming beasts of prey. Of beasts of a smaller size I did find more than plenty.

At four I was up, but my friend was very unwilling to stir. It was long before I could induce the mild voice to make itself heard in any way. At that time it was fine, but it was long before I could get the muleteer. When I had done so, and he had thrown their grass to the beasts, it began to rain—of course. 'It rains like the d—' said I, very crossly. 'Does it?' said the mild voice from the bed. 'I am so sorry;' and in half a second he was again in the land of dreams. The doctor snored; but from the furthest remote corner I could see the eye of the doctor's wife looking out at me.

It was between six and seven when we started. At that time it was not raining, but the clouds looked as like rain as the Secretary of Legation could have desired. And the two Germans were anything but consolatory in their prophecies. 'You'll not see a stick or a stone,' said the architect; 'you'd better stop and breakfast with us.' 'It is very dangerous to be wet in the mountains, very dangerous,' said the doctor. 'It is a bad morning, certainly,' pleaded the mild voice piteously. The doctor's wife said nothing, but I could see her eyes looking out at the weather. How on earth was she to get herself dressed, it occurred to me then, if we should postpone our journey and remain there?

It ended in our starting just two hours after the prescribed time. The road up from the potrero is very steep almost the whole way to the summit, but it was not so muddy as that we had passed over on the preceding evening. For some little way there were patches of cultivation, the ground bearing sweet potatoes and Indian corn. Then we came into a tract of beautiful forest scenery. The land, though steep, was broken, and only partially covered with trees. The grass in patches was as good as in an English park, and the views through the open bits of the forest were very lovely. In four or five different places we found the ground sufficiently open for all the requirements of a picturesque country house, and no prettier site for such a house could well be found. This was by far the finest scenery that I had hitherto seen in Costa Rica ; but even here there was a want of water. In ascending the mountain we saw some magnificent forest trees, generally of the kind called cotton-trees in Jamaica. There were oaks also—so called there—very nearly approaching our holm-oak in colour and foliage, but much larger than that tree is with us. They were all more or less covered with parasite plants, and those parasites certainly add greatly to the beauty of the supporting trunk.

By degrees we got into thick forest—forest I mean so thick that it affords no views. You see and feel the trees that are close to you, but see nothing else. And here the path became so steep that we were obliged to dismount and let the beasts clamber up by themselves ; and the mist became very thick, so much so that we could hardly trace our path : and then the guide said that he thought he had lost his way.

' People often do come out and go back again without ever reaching the crater at all, don't they ?' said the mild voice.

' Very often,' said the guide.

' But we won't be such people,' said I.

' Oh no !' said the mild voice. ' Not if we can help it.'

' And we will help it. Allons ; andiamos ; vamos.'

The first word which an Englishman learns in any

language is that which signifies a determination to proceed.

And we did proceed, turning now hither and now thither, groping about in the mist, till at last the wood was all left behind us, and we were out among long grass on a mountain-side. 'And now,' said the guide, 'unless the mist clears I can't say which way we ought to go.'

The words were hardly out of his mouth when the mist did clear itself away altogether from one side of us. Looking down to the left, we could see far away into the valleys beneath, over large forests, and across a lower range of hills, till the eye could reach the cultivated plateau below. But on the other side, looking up to a mountain higher still than that on which we stood, all was not only misty, but perfectly dark and inscrutable.

The guide however now knew the spot. We were near the summit of Irazu, and a further ride of a quarter of an hour took us there; and indeed here there was no difficulty in riding. The side of the hill was covered with grass, and not over steep. 'There,' said the mild voice, pointing to a broad, bushy, stumpy tree, ' there is the place where Lady Ouseley breakfasted.' And he looked at our modest havresack. 'And we will breakfast there too,' I answered. 'But we will go down the crater first.'

'Oh, yes; certainly,' said the mild voice. 'But perhaps —I don't know—I am not sure I can go exactly down into the crater.'

The crater of the volcano is not at the top of the mountain, or rather it is not at what is now the top of the mountain; so that at first one has to look down upon it. I doubt even whether the volcano has ever effected the absolute summit. I may as well state here that the height of the mountain on which we were now standing is supposed to be 11,500 feet above the sea-level.

Luckily for us, though the mist reached to us where we stood, everything to the left of us was clear, and we could look down, down into the crater as into a basin. Everything was clear, so that we could count the different orifices, eight in number, of which two, however, had almost run themselves into one; and see, as far as it was possible to see, how the present formation of the volcano had been brought about.

It was as though a very large excavation had been made on the side of a hill, commencing, indeed, not quite from the summit, but very near it, and leaving a vast hole —not deep in proportion to its surface—sloping down the mountain-side. This huge excavation, which I take to be the extent of the crater, for it has evidently been all formed by the irruption of volcanic matter, is divided into two parts, a broken fragment of a mountain now lying between them; and the smaller of these two has lost all volcanic appearance. It is a good deal covered with bush and scrubby forest trees, and seems to have no remaining connection with sulphur and brimstone.

The other part, in which the crater now absolutely in use is situated, is a large hollow in the mountain-side, which might perhaps contain a farm of six hundred acres. Not having been able to measure it, I know no other way of describing what appeared to me to be its size. But a great portion of this again has lost all its volcanic appendages; except, indeed, that lumps of lava are scattered over the whole of it, as they are, though more sparingly, over the mountain beyond. There is a ledge of rock running round the interior of this division of the excavation, half-way down it, like a row of seats in a Roman amphitheatre, or an excrescence, if one can fancy such, half-way down a teacup. The ground above this ledge is of course more extensive than that below, as the hollow narrows towards the bottom. The present working mouth of the volcanic, and all those that have been working for many a long year — the eight in number of which I have spoken—lie at the bottom of this lowest hollow. This I should say might contain a farm of about two hundred acres.

Such was the form of the land on which we looked down. The descent from the top to the ledge was easy enough, and was made by myself and my friend with considerable rapidity. I started at a pace which convinced him that I should break my neck, and he followed, gallantly resolving to die with me. 'You'll surely kill yourself, Mr. Trollope; you surely will,' said the mild voice. And yet he never deserted me.

'Sir William got as far as this,' said he, when we were on the ledge, but he got no further. 'We will do better than Sir William,' said I. 'We will go down into that hole where we see the sulphur.' 'Into the very hole?' 'Yes. If we get to windward, I think we can get into the very hole. Look at the huge column of white smoke; how it comes all in this direction! On the other side of the crater we should not feel it.'

The descent below the ledge into my smaller farm was not made so easily. It must be understood that our guide was left above with the mules. We should have brought two men, whereas we had only brought one; and had therefore to perform our climbing unassisted. I at first attempted it in a direct line, down from where we stood; but I soon found this to be impracticable, and was forced to reascend. The earth was so friable that it broke away from me at every motion that I made; and after having gone down a few feet I was glad enough to find myself again on the ledge.

We then walked round considerably to the right, probably for more than a quarter of a mile, and there a little spur in the hillside—a buttress as it were to the ledge of which I have spoken—made the descent much easier, and I again tried.

'Do not you mind following me,' I said to my companion, for I saw that he looked much aghast. 'None of Sir William's party went down there,' he answered. 'Are you sure of that?' I asked. 'Quite sure,' said the mild voice. 'Then what a triumph we will have over Sir William!' and so saying I proceeded. 'I think I'll come too,' said the mild voice. 'If I do break my neck nobody'll be much the worse;' and he did follow me.

There was nothing very difficult in the clambering, but, unfortunately, just as we got to the bottom the mist came pouring down upon us, and I could not but bethink me that I should find it very difficult to make my way up again without seeing any of the landmarks. I could still see all below me, but I could see nothing that was above. It seemed as though the mist kept at our own level, and that we dragged it with us.

We were soon in one of the eight small craters or mouths of which I have spoken. Looking at them from above, they seemed to be nearly on a level, but it now appeared that one or two were considerably higher than the others. We were now in the one that was the highest on that side of the excavation. It was a shallow basin, or rather saucer, perhaps sixty yards in diameter, the bottom of which was composed of smooth light-coloured sandy clay. In dry weather it would partake almost of the nature of sand. Many many years had certainly rolled by since this mouth had been eloquent with brimstone.

The place at this time was very cold. My friend had brought a large shawl with him, with which over and over again he attempted to cover my shoulders. I, having meditated much on the matter, had left my cloak above. At the present moment I regretted it sorely: but, as

U

matters turned out, it would have half smothered me before our walk was over.

We had now nothing for it but to wait till the mist should go off. There was but one open mouth to this mountain—one veritable crater from which a column of smoke and sulphur did then actually issue, and this, though the smell of the brimstone was already oppressive, was at some little distance. Gradually the mist did go off, or rather it shifted itself continually, now ascending far above us, and soon returning to our feet. We then advanced between two other mouths, and came to that which was nearest to the existing crater.

Here the aperture was of a very different kind. Though no smoke issued from it, and though there was a small tree growing at the bottom of it,—showing, as I presume, that there had been no eruption from thence since the seed of that tree had fallen to the ground,—yet the sides of the crater were as sharp and steep as the walls of a house. Into those which we had hitherto visited we could walk easily; into this no one could descend even a single foot, unless, indeed, he descended somewhat more than a foot so as to dash himself to pieces at the bottom. They were, when compared together, as the interior of a plate compared to that of a tea-caddy. Now a traveller travelling in such realms would easily extricate himself from the plate, but the depths of the tea-caddy would offer him no hope.

Having walked round this mute volcano, we ascended to the side of the one which was now smoking, for the aperture to this was considerably higher than that of the last one mentioned. As we were then situated, the smoke was bearing towards us, and every moment it became more oppressive; but I saw, or thought I saw, that we could skirt round to the back of the crater, so as not to get its full volume upon us; and so I pro-

ceeded, he of the mild voice mildly expostulating, but
always following me.

But when we had ascended to the level of the hole the
wind suddenly shifted, and the column of smoke dis-
persing enveloped us altogether. Had it come upon us
in all its thickest mass I doubt whether it would not have
first stupefied and then choked us. As it was, we ran
for it, and succeeded in running out of it. It affected
me, I think, more powerfully than it did my companion,
for he was the first to regain his speech. 'Sir William,
at any rate, saw nothing like that,' said he, coughing
triumphantly.

I hope that I may never feel or smell anything like it
again. This smoke is emitted from the earth at the
bottom of a deep hole very similar to that above described. The sides of it all round are so steep that it is
impossible to make even an attempt to descend it. By
holding each other's hands we could look over into it one
at a time, and see the very jaws in the rock from which
the stream of sulphur ascends. It comes out quite yellow,
almost a dark yellow, but gradually blanches as it expands
in its course. These jaws in the rock are not in the centre
of the bottom of the pit, but in a sharp angle, as it were,
so that the smoke comes up against one side or wall, and
that side is perfectly encrusted with the sulphur. It was
at the end of the orifice, exactly opposite to this, that we
knelt down and looked over.

The smoke when it struck upon us, immediately above
this wall, was hot and thick and full of brimstone. The
stench for a moment was very bad; but the effect went
off at once, as soon as we were out of it.

The mild voice grasped my hand very tightly as he
crept to the edge and looked over. 'Ah!' he said,
rejoicing greatly, 'Sir William never saw that, nor any
of his party; I am so glad I came again with you. I

wonder whether anybody ever was here before.' Hundreds doubtless have been, and thousands will be. Nine out of every ten men in London, between the ages of fifteen and fifty, would think little of the trouble and less of the danger of getting there; but I could not interfere with the triumph of my friend, so I merely remarked that it certainly was a very singular place.

And then we had to reascend. It was now past eleven o'clock, and as yet we had had no breakfast, for I cannot call that cup of coffee which we took at starting a breakfast, even though the German architect handed to each of us from out of his bed a hunch of beef and a crust of bread. Luckily the air was clear for a while, so that we could see what we were about, and we began to climb up on the side opposite to that by which we had descended.

And here I happened to mention that Miss Ouseley had commissioned me to get two bits of lava, one smooth and the other rough—unfortunately, for at once the mild voice declared that he had found two morsels which would exactly suit the lady's taste. I looked round, and, lo! there was my small friend with two huge stones, each weighing about twenty pounds, which, on the side of the mountain, he was endeavouring to pack under his arms. Now, the mountain here was very steep and very friable; the burnt shingle slipped from under our feet at every step; and, to make matters worse, we were climbing in a slanting direction.

'My dear fellow, it would kill you to carry those lumps to the top,' I said; 'do not think of it.'

But he persevered. 'There were no lumps of lava such as those,' he said, 'to be found at the top. They were just what Miss Ouseley wanted. He thought he would be able to manage with them. They were not so very heavy, if only the ground did not slip so much.' I

said what I could, but it was of no avail, and he followed
me slowly with his sore burden.

I never knew the weather change with such rapidity.
At this moment the sun was bright and very hot, and I
could hardly bear my coat on my shoulders as I crept up
that hill. How my little friend followed with his shawl
and the lava rocks I cannot conceive. But, to own the
truth, going down hill suits me better than going up.
Years and obesity tell upon the wind sooner than they
do on the legs—so, at least, it is with me. Now my mild
friend hardly weighed fifteen ounces, while I——!

And then, when we were again on the ridge, it began
to rain most gloriously. Hitherto we had had mist, but
this was a regular down-pour of rain—such moisture as
the Secretary of Legation had been praying for ever since
we started. Again and again the mild voice offered me
the shawl, which, when I refused it, he wrapped round
the lumps of lava, scorning to be drier than his companion.
From the summit to the ledge we had come down fast
enough, but the ascent was very different. I, at any
rate, was very tired, and my friend was by no means as
fresh as he had been. We were both in want of food, and
our clothes were heavy with wet. He also still carried his
lumps of lava.

At last, all raining as it was, I sat down. How far
we might still be from the top I could not see; but be
it far or be it near, nature required rest. I threw myself
on the ground, and the mild voice not unwillingly crouched
down close to me. 'Now we can both have the shawl,'
said he, and he put it over our joint shoulders; that is, he
put the shawl on mine while the fringe hung over his
own. In half a minute we were both asleep, almost in
each other's arms.

Men when they sleep thus on a mountain-side in the
rain do not usually sleep long. Forty winks is generally

acknowledged. Our nap may have amounted to eighty each, but I doubt whether it was more. We started together, rubbed our eyes, jumped to our feet, and prepared ourselves for work. But, alas! where was the lava?

My impression is that in my sleep I must have kicked the stones and sent them rolling. At any rate, they were gone. Dark and wet as it was, we both went down a yard or two, but it was in vain; nothing could be seen of them. The mild voice handed me the shawl, preparing to descend in their search; but this was too much. 'You will only lose yourself,' said I, laying hold of him, 'and I shall have to look for your bones. Besides, I want my breakfast! We will get other specimens above.'

'And perhaps they will be just as good,' said he, cheerfully, when he found that he would not be allowed to have his way.

'Every bit,' said I. And so we trudged on, and at last reached our mules. From this point men see, or think that they see, the two oceans—the Atlantic and the Pacific—and this sight to many is one of the main objects of the ascent. We saw neither the one ocean nor the other.

We got back to the potrero about three, and found our German friends just sitting down to dinner. The architect was seated on his bed on one side of the table arranging the viands, while the doctor on the other scooped out the brains of a strange bird with a penknife. The latter operation he performed with a view of stuffing, not himself, but the animal. They pressed us to dine with them before we started, and we did so, though I must confess that the doctor's occupation rather set me against my food. 'If it be not done at once,' said he, apologizing, 'it can't be done well;' and he scraped, and scraped, and wiped his knife against the edge of the little table on which the dishes were placed. What had become of the doctor's wife I do not know, but she was not at the potrero when we dined there.

It was evening when we got into Cartago, and very tired we were. My mind, however, was made up to go on to San José that night, and ultimately I did so ; but before starting, I was bound to repeat my visit to the English lady with whom my mild friend lived. Mrs. X—— was, and I suppose is, the only Englishwoman living in Cartago, and with that sudden intimacy which springs up with more than tropical celerity in such places, she told me the singular history of her married life.

The reader would not care that I should repeat it at length, for it would make this chapter too long. Her husband had been engaged in mining operations, and she had come out to Guatemala with him in search of gold. From thence, after a period of partial success, he was enticed away into Costa Rica. Some speculation there, in which he or his partners were concerned, promised better than that other one in Guatemala, and he went, leaving his young wife and children behind him. Of course he was to return very soon, and of course he did not return at all. Mrs. X—— was left with her children, searching for gold herself. ' Every evening,' she said, ' I saw the earth washed myself, and took up with me to the house the gold that was found.' What an occupation for a young Englishwoman, the mother of three children ! At this time she spoke no Spanish, and had no one with her who spoke English.

And then tidings came from her husband that he could not come to her, and she made up her mind to go to him. She had no money, the gold-washing having failed ; her children were without shoes to their feet ; she had no female companion ; she had no attendant but one native man ; and yet, starting from the middle of Guatemala, she made her way to the coast, and thence by ship to Costa Rica.

After that her husband became engaged in what, in those countries, is called 'transit.' Now 'transit' means the privilege of making money by transporting Americans of the United States over the isthmus to and from California, and in most hands has led to fraud, filibustering, ruin, and destruction. Mr. X——, like many others, was taken in, and according to his widow's account, the matter ended in a deputation being sent, from New York I think, to murder him. He was struck with a life-preserver in the streets of San José, never fully recovered from the blow, and then died.

He had become possessed of a small estate in the neighbourhood of Cartago, on the proceeds of which the widow was now living. 'And will you not return home?' I said. 'Yes; when I have got my rights. Look here—' and she brought down a ledger, showing me that she had all manner of claims to all manner of shares in all manner of mines. 'Aurum irrepertum et sic melius situm!' As regards her, it certainly would have been so.

For a coined sovereign, or five-dollar piece, I have the most profound respect. It is about the most faithful servant that a man can have in his employment, and should be held as by no means subject to those scurrilous attacks which a pharisaically moral world so often levels at its head. But of all objects of a man's ambition uncoined gold, gold to be collected in sand, or picked up in nuggets, or washed out of earth, is, to my thinking, the most delusive and most dangerous! Who knows, or has known, or ever seen, any man that has returned happy from the diggings, and now sits contented under his own fig-tree?

My friend Mrs. X—— was still hankering after the flesh-pots of Egypt, the hidden gold of the Central American mountains. She slapped her hands loudly together, for she was a woman of much energy, and declared that she would have her rights. When she had gotten her rights she would go home. Alas! alas! poor lady!

'And you,' said I, to the mild voice, 'will not you return?'

'I suppose so,' said he, 'when Mrs. X—— goes;' and he looked up to the widow as though confessing that he was bound to her service, and would not leave her; not that I think they had the slightest idea of joining their lots together as men and women do. He was too mild for that.

I did ride back to San José that night, and a most frightful journey I had of it. I resumed, of course, my speechless, useless, dolt of a guide—the man whom the Secretary of Legation had selected for me before I started. Again I put my spur on his foot, and endeavoured to spirit him up to ride before me, so that I might know my way in the dark; but it was in vain; nothing would move him out of a walk, and I was obliged to leave him.

And then it became frightfully dark—pitch dark as men say—dark so that I could not see my mule's ears. I had nothing for it but to trust to her; and soon found, by being taken down into the deep bed of a river and through deep water, that we had left the road by which I had before travelled. The beast did not live in San José I knew, and I looked to be carried to some country rancho at which she would be at home. But in a time sufficiently short, I found myself in San José. The creature had known a shorter cut than that usually taken.

CHAPTER XX.

CENTRAL AMERICA—SAN JOSÉ TO GREYTOWN.

MY purpose was to go right across Central America, from ocean to ocean, and to accomplish this it was necessary that I should now make my way down to the mouth of the San Juan river—to San Juan del Norte as it was formerly called, or Greytown as it is now named by the English. This road, I was informed by all of whom I inquired, was very bad,—so bad as to be all but impracticable to English travellers.

And then, just at that moment, an event occurred which added greatly to the ill name of this route. A few days before I reached San José a gentleman resident there had started for England with his wife, and they had decided upon going by the San Juan. It seems that the lady had reached San José, as all people do reach it, by Panamá and Punta-arenas, and had suffered on the route. At any rate, she had taken a dislike to it, and had resolved on returning by the San Juan and the Serapiqui rivers, a route which is called the Serapiqui road.

To do this it is necessary for the traveller to ride on mules for four, five, or six days, according to his or her capability. The Serapiqui river is then reached, and from that point the further journey is made in canoes down the Serapiqui river till it falls into the San Juan, and then down that river to Greytown.

This gentleman with his wife reached the Serapiqui in safety; though it seems that she suffered greatly on the road. But when once there, as she herself said, all her troubles were over. That weary work of supporting herself on her mule, through mud and thorns and thick bushes, of scrambling over precipices and through rivers, was done. She had been very despondent, even from before the time of her starting; but now, she said, she believed that she should live to see her mother again. She was seated in the narrow canoe, among cloaks and cushions, with her husband close to her, and the boat was pushed into the stream. Almost in a moment, within two minutes of starting, not a hundred yards from the place where she had last trod, the canoe struck against a snag or upturned fragment of a tree and was overset. The lady was borne by the stream among the entangled branches of timber which clogged the river, and when her body was found life had been long extinct.

This had happened on the very day that I reached San José, and the news arrived two or three days afterwards. The wretched husband, too, made his way back to the town, finding himself unable to go on upon his journey alone, with such a burden on his back. What could he have said to his young wife's mother when she came to meet him at Southamptom, expecting to throw her arms round her daughter?

I was again lucky in having a companion for my journey. A young lieutenant of the Navy, Fitzm—— by name, whose vessel was lying at Greytown, had made his way up to San José on a visit to the Ouseleys, and was to return at the same time that I went down. He had indeed travelled up with the bereaved man who had lost his wife, having read the funeral service over the poor woman's grave on the lonely shores of the Serapiqui. The road, he acknowledged, was bad, too bad, he thought, for any female; but not more than sufficiently so to make proper excitement for a man. He, at any rate, had come over it safely; but then he was twenty-four, and I forty-four; and so we started together from San José, a crowd of friends accompanying us for the first mile or two. There was that Secretary of Legation prophesying that we should be smothered in the mud; there was the Consul and the Consul's brother; nor was female beauty wanting to wish us well on our road, and maybe to fling an old shoe after us for luck as we went upon our journey.

We took four mules, that was one each for ourselves, and two for our baggage; we had two guides or muleteers, according to bargain, both of whom travelled on foot. The understanding was, that one mule lightly laden with provisions and a pair of slippers and a toothbrush should accompany us, one man also going with us; but that the heavy-laden mule should come along after us at its own pace. Things, however, did not so turn out: on the first day both the men and both the mules lagged behind, and on one occasion we were obliged to wait above an hour for them; but after that we all kept in a string together, having picked up a third muleteer somewhere on the road. We had also with us a distressed British subject, who was intrusted to my tender mercies by the Consul at San José. He was not a good sample of a Britisher; he had been a gold-finder in California, then a filibuster, after that a teacher of the piano in the country part of Costa Rica, and lastly an omnibus driver. He was to act as interpreter for us, which, however, he did not do with much honesty or zeal.

Our road at first lay through the towns of Aredia and Barba, the former of which is a pleasant-looking little village, where, however, we found great difficulty in getting anything to drink. Up to this, and for a few leagues further, the road was very fair, and the land on each side of us was cultivated. We had started at eight A.M., and at about three in the afternoon there seemed to be great doubt as to where we should stop. The leading muleteer wished to take us to a house of a friend of his own, whereas the lieutenant and I resolved that the day's work had not been long enough. I take it that on the whole we were right, and the man gave in with sufficient good humour; but it ended in our passing the night in a miserable rancho. That at the potrero, on the road to the volcanic mountain, had been a palace to it.

And here we got into the forest; we had hitherto been ascending the whole way from San José, and had by degrees lost all appearance of tillage. Still, however, there had been open spaces here and there cleared for cattle, and we had not as yet found ourselves absolutely enveloped by woods. This rancho was called Buena-vista; and certainly the view from it was very pretty. It was pretty and extensive, as I have seen views in Baden and parts of Bavaria; but again there was nothing about which I could rave.

I shall not readily forget the night in that rancho. We were, I presume, between seven and eight thousand feet above the sea-level; and at night, or rather early in the morning, the cold was very severe. Fitzm—— and I shared the same bed; that is, we lay on the same boards, and did what we could to cover ourselves with the same blankets. In that country men commonly ride upon blankets, having them strapped over the saddles as pillions, and we had come so provided; but before the morning was over I heartily wished for a double allowance.

We had brought with us a wallet of provisions, certainly not too well arranged by Sir William Ouseley's most reprehensible butler. Travellers should never trust to but-

lers. Our pièce de résistance was a ham, and lo! it
turned out to a be bad one. When the truth of this fact first
dawned upon us it was in both our minds to go back and
slay that butler : but there was still a piece of beef and
some chickens, and there had been a few dozen of hard-
boiled eggs. But Fitzm—— would amuse himself with
eating these all along the road : I always found when the
ordinary feeding time came that they had not the slightest
effect upon his appetite.

On the next morning we again ascended for about a
couple of leagues, and as long as we did so the road was
still good ; the surface was hard, and the track was broad,
and a horseman could wish nothing better. And then we
reached the summit of the ridge over which we were
passing; this we did at a place called Desenganos, and
from thence we looked down into vast valleys all running
towards the Atlantic. Hitherto the fall of water had been
into the Pacific.

At this place we found a huge shed, with numberless
bins and troughs lying under it in great confusion. The
facts, as far as I could learn, were thus : Up to this point
the government, that is Don Juan Mora, or perhaps his
predecessor, had succeeded in making a road fit for the
transit of mule carts. This shed had also been built to
afford shelter for the postmen and accommodation for the
muleteers. But here Don Juan's efforts had been stopped ;
money probably had failed ; and the great remainder of the
undertaking will, I fear, be left undone for many a long
year.

And yet this, or some other road from the valley of
San José to the Atlantic, would be the natural outlet
of the country. At present the coffee grown in the
central high lands is carried down to Punta-arenas on
the Pacific, although it must cross the Atlantic to reach
its market ; consequently, it is either taken round the

Horn, and its sale thus delayed for months, or it is transported across the isthmus by railway, at an enormous cost. They say there is a point at which the Atlantic may be reached more easily than by the present route of the Serapiqui river; nothing, however, has as yet been done in the matter. To make a road fit even for mule carts, by the course of the present track, would certainly be a work of enormous difficulty.

And now our vexations commenced. We found that the path very soon narrowed, so much so that it was with difficulty we could keep our hats on our heads; and then the surface of the path became softer and softer, till our beasts were up to their knees in mud. All motion quicker than that of a walk became impossible; and even at this pace the struggles in the mud were both frequent and uncomfortable. Hitherto we had talked fluently enough, but now we became very silent; we went on following, each at the other's tail, floundering in the mud, silent, filthy, and down in the mouth.

'I tell you what it is,' said Fitzm—— at last, stopping on the road, for he had led the van, ' I can't go any further without breakfast.' We referred the matter to the guide, and found that Careblanco, the place appointed for our next stage, was still two hours distant.

'Two hours! Why, half an hour since you said it was only a league!' But what is the use of expostulating with a man who can't speak a word of English?

So we got off our mules, and dragged out our wallet among the bushes. Our hard-boiled eggs were all gone, and it seemed as though the travelling did not add fresh delights to the cold beef; so we devoured another fowl, and washed it down with brandy and water.

As we were so engaged three men passed us with heavy burdens on their backs. They were tall, thin, muscular fellows, with bare legs, and linen clothes,—one of them

apparently of nearly pure Indian blood. It was clear that
the loads they carried were very weighty. They were
borne high up on the back, and suspended by a band from
the forehead, so that a great portion of the weight must
have fallen on the muscles of the neck. This was the
post; and as they had left San José some eight hours after
us, and had come by a longer route, so as to take in another
town, they must have travelled at a very fast pace. It
was our object to go down the Serapiqui river in the same
boat with the post. We had some doubt whether we
should be able to get any other, seeing that the owner of
one such canoe had been drowned, I believe in an endeavour to save the unfortunate lady of whom I have spoken;
and any boat taken separately would be much more expensive.

So, as quick as might be, we tied up our fragments and
proceeded. It was after this that I really learned how all-
powerful is the force of mud. We came at last to a track
that was divided crossways by ridges, somewhat like the
ridges of ploughed ground. Each ridge was perhaps a
foot and a half broad, and the mules invariably stepped
between them, not on them. Stepping on them they could
not have held their feet. Stepping between them they
came at each step with their belly to the ground, so that
the rider's feet and legs were trailing in the mud. The
struggles of the poor brutes were dreadful. It seemed to
me frequently impossible that my beast should extricate
himself, laden as he was. But still he went on patiently,
slowly, and continuously; splash, splash; slosh, slosh!
Every muscle of his body was working; and every muscle
of my body was working also.

For it is not very easy to sit upon a mule under such
circumstances. The bushes were so close upon me that
one hand was required to guard my face from the thorns;
my knees were constantly in contact with the stumps of

trees, and when my knees were free from such difficulties, my shins were sure to be in the wars. Then the poor animal rolled so from side to side in his incredible struggles with the mud that it was frequently necessary to hold myself on by the pommel of the saddle. Added to this, it was essentially necessary to keep some sort of guide upon the creature's steps, or one's legs would be absolutely broken. For the mule cares for himself only, and not for his rider. It is nothing to him if a man's knees be put out of joint against the stump of a tree.

Splash, splash, slosh, slosh! on we went in this way for hours, almost without speaking. On such occasions one is apt to become mentally cross, to feel that the world is too hard for one, that one's own especial troubles are much worse than those of one's neighbours, and that those neighbours are unfairly favoured. I could not help think-ing it very unjust that I should be fifteen stone, while Fitzm—— was only eight. And as for that distressed Britisher, he weighed nothing at all.

Splash, splash, slosh, slosh! we were at it all day. At Careblanco— the place of the *white-faced* pigs I understood it to mean;—they say that there is a race of wild hogs with white faces which inhabit the woods hereabouts— we overtook the post, and kept close to them afterwards. This was a pasture farm in the very middle of the forest, a bit of cleared land on which some adventurer had settled himself and dared to live. The adventurer himself was not there, but he had a very pretty wife, with whom my friend the lieutenant seemed to have contracted an inti-mate acquaintance on his previous journey up to San José.

But at Careblanco we only stopped two minutes, during which, however, it became necessary that the lieutenant should go into the rancho on the matter of some article of clothes which had been left behind on his previous journey; and then, again, on we went, slosh, slosh, splash, splash! My shins by this time were black and blue, and I held myself on to my mule chiefly by my spurs. Our way was still through dense forest, and was always either up or down hill. And here we came across the grandest scenery that I met with in the western world; scenery which would admit of raving, if it were given to me to rave on such a subject.

We were travelling for the most part along the side of a volcanic mountain, and every now and then the declivity would become so steep as to give us a full view down into the ravine below, with the prospect of the grand, steep, wooded hill on the other side, one huge forest stretching up the mountain for miles. At the bottom of the ravine one's eye would just catch a river, looking like a moving thread of silver wire. And yet, though the descent was so great, there would be no interruption to it. Looking down over the thick forest trees which grew almost from the side of a precipice, the eye would reach the river some thousand feet below, and then ascend on the other side over a like unbroken expanse of foliage.

Of course we both declared that we had never seen anything to equal it. In moments of ecstacy one always does so declare. But there was a monotony about it, and a want of grouping which forbids me to place it on an equality with scenery really of the highest kind, with the mountains, for instance, round Colico, with the head of the Lake of the Four Cantons, or even with the views of the upper waters of Killarney.

And then, to speak the truth, we were too much engulfed in mud, too thoughtful as to the troubles of the road, to enjoy it thoroughly. 'Wonderful that; isn't it?' 'Yes, very wonderful; fine break; for heaven's sake do get on.' That is the tone which men are apt to adopt under such circumstances. Five or six pounds of thick

mud clinging round one's boots and inside one's trousers
do not add to one's enjoyment of scenery.

Mud, mud; mud, mud! At about five o'clock we
splashed into another pasture farm in the middle of the
forest, a place called San Miguel, and there we rested for
that night. Here we found that our beef also must be
thrown away, and that our bread was all gone. We had
picked up some more hard-boiled eggs at ranchos on the
road, but hard-boiled eggs to my companion were no more
than grains of gravel to a barn-door fowl; they merely
enabled him to enjoy his regular diet. At this place,
however, we were able to purchase fowls—skinny old
hens which were shot for us at a moment's warning;
the price being, here and elsewhere along the road, a
dollar a head. Tea and candles a ministering angel had
given to me at the moment of my departure from San
José. But for them we should have indeed been comfortless, thirsty, and in utter darkness. Towards evening
a man gets tired of brandy and water, when he has been
drinking it since six in the morning.

Our washing was done under great difficulties, as in
these districts neither nature nor art seems to have provided for such emergencies. In this place I got my head
into a tin pot, and could hardly extricate it. But even
inside the houses and ranchos everything seemed to turn
into mud. The floor beneath one's feet became mud with
the splashing of the water. The boards were begrimed
with mud. We were offered coffee that was mud to the
taste and touch. I felt that the blood in my veins was
becoming muddy.

And then we had another day exactly like the former,
except that the ground was less steep, and the vistas of
scenery less grand. The weather also was warmer, seeing
that we were now on lower ground. Monkeys chattered
on the trees around us, and the little congo ape roared

like a lion. Macaws flew about, generally in pairs; and
we saw white turkeys on the trees. Up on the higher
forests we had seen none of these animals.

There are wild hogs also in these woods, and ounces.
The ounce here is, I believe, properly styled the puma,
though the people always call them lions. They grow
to about the size of a Newfoundland dog. The wild cat
also is common here, the people styling them tigers. The
xagua is, I take it, their proper name. None of these
animals will, I believe, attack a man unless provoked or
pressed in pursuit; and not even then if a way of escape
be open to him.

We again breakfasted at a forest clearing, paying a
dollar each for tough old hens, and in the evening we
came to a cacao plantation in the middle of the forest
which had been laid out and settled by an American of
the United States residing in Central America. This
place is not far from the Serapiqui river, and is called
Padregal. It was here that the young lieutenant had
read the funeral service over the body cf that unfortunate
lady.

I went with him to visit the grave. It was a spot in
the middle of a grass enclosure, fenced off rudely so as
to guard it from beasts of prey. The funeral had taken
place after dusk. It had been attended by some twelve
or fourteen Costa Rican soldiers who are kept in a fort
a little below, on the banks of the Serapiqui. Each of
these men had held a torch. The husband was there,
and another Englishman who was travelling with him;
as was also, I believe, the proprietor of the place. So
attended, the body of the Englishwoman was committed
to its strange grave in a strange country.

Here we picked up another man, an American, who
also had been looking for gold, and perhaps doing a turn
as a filibuster. Him too the world had used badly, and

he was about to return with all his golden dreams unaccomplished.

We had one more stage down to the spot at which we were to embark in the canoe—the spot at which the lady had been drowned—and this one we accomplished early in the morning. This place is called the Muelle, and here there is a fort with a commandant and a small company of soldiers. The business of the commandant is to let no one up or down the river without a passport; and as a passport cannot be procured anywhere nearer than San José, here may arise a great difficulty to travellers. We were duly provided, but our recently-picked-up American friend was not; and he was simply told that he would not be allowed to get into a boat on the river.

'I never seed such a d—d country in my life,' said the American. 'They would not let me leave San José till I paid every shilling I owed; and now that I have paid, I ain't no better off. I wish I hadn't paid a d—d cent.'

I advised him to try what some further operation in the way of payment would do, and with this view he retired with the commandant. In a minute or two they both returned, and the commandant said he would look at his instructions again. He did so, and declared that he now found it was compatible with his public duty to allow the American to pass. 'But I shall not have a cent left to take me home,' said the American to me. He was not a smart man, though he talked smart; for when the moment of departure came all the places in the boat were taken, and we left him standing on the shore. 'Well, I'm darned!' he said; and we neither heard nor saw more of him.

That passage down the Serapiqui was not without interest, though it was somewhat monotonous. Here, for the first time in my life, I found my bulk and size to be of advantage to me. In the after part of the canoe sat the master boatman, the captain of the expedition, steering with a paddle. Then came the mails and our luggage, and next to them I sat, having a seat to myself, being too weighty to share a bench with a neighbour. I therefore could lean back among the luggage; and with a cigar in my mouth and a little wooden bicker of weak brandy and water beside me I found that the position had its charms.

On the next thwart sat, cheek by jowl, the lieutenant and the distressed Britisher. Unfortunately they had nothing on which to lean, and I sincerely pitied my friend, who, I fear, did not enjoy his position. But what could I do? Any change in our arrangements would have upset the canoe. And then close in the bow of the boat sat the two natives paddling; and they did paddle without cessation all that day, and all the next till we reached Greytown.

The Serapiqui is a fine river; very rapid, but not so much so as to make it dangerous, if care be taken to avoid the snags. There is not a house or hut on either side of it; but the forest comes down to the very brink. Up in the huge trees the monkeys hung jabbering, shaking their ugly heads at the boat as it went down, or screaming in anger at this invasion of their territories. The macaws flew high over head, making their own music, and then there was the constant little splash of the paddle in the water. The boatmen spoke no word, but worked on always, pausing now and again for a moment to drink out of the hollow of their hands. And the sun became hotter and hotter as we neared the sea; and the musquitoes began to bite; and cigars were lit with greater frequency. 'Tis thus that one goes down the waters of the Serapiqui.

About three we got into the San Juan. This is the

river by which the great lake of Nicaragua empties itself into the sea; which has been the channel used by the transit companies who have passed from ocean to ocean through Nicaragua; which has been so violently interfered with by filibusters, till all such transit has been banished from its waters; and which has now been selected by M. Belly as the course for his impossible canal. It has seen dreadful scenes of cruelty, wrong, and bloodshed. Now it runs along peaceably enough, in its broad, shallow, swift course, bearing on its margin here and there the rancho and provision-ground of some wild settler who has sought to overcome

> 'The whips and scorns of time—
> The oppressor's wrong, the proud man's contumely,'

by looking for bread and shelter on those sad, sunburnt, and solitary banks.

We landed at one such place to dine, and at another to sleep, selecting in each place some better class of habitation. At neither place did we find the owner there, but persons left in charge of the place. At the first the man was a German; a singularly handsome and dirty individual, who never shaved or washed himself, and lived there, ever alone, on bananas and musk-melons. He gave us fruit to take into the boat with us, and when we parted we shook hands with him. Out here every one always does shake hands with every one. But as I did so I tendered him a dollar. He had waited upon us, bringing water and plates: he had gathered fruit for us; and he was, after all, no more than the servant of the river squatter. But he let the dollar fall to the ground, and that with some anger in his face. The sum was made up of the small silver change of the country, and I felt rather little as I stooped under the hot sun to pick it up from out the mud of the garden. Better that

than seem to leave it there in anger. It is often hard
for a traveller to know when he is wished to pay, and
when he is wished not to pay. A poorer-looking individual in raiment and position than that German I have
seldom seen; but he despised my dollar as though it had
been dirt.

We slept at the house of a Greytown merchant, who
had maintained an establishment up the river, originally
with the view of supplying the wants of the American
travellers passing in transit across the isthmus. The
flat-bottom steamers which did some five or six years
since ply upon the river used to take in wood here and
stop for the night. And the passengers were wont to
come on shore, and call for rum and brandy; and in
this way much money was made. Till after a time filibusters came instead of passengers; men who took all
the wood that they could find there—hundreds of dollars'
worth of sawn wood, and brandy also—took it away with
them, saying that they would give compensation when
they were established in the country, but made no present
payment. And then it became tolerably clear that the
time for making money in that locality had passed away.

They came in great numbers on one such occasion,
and stripped away everything they could find. Sawn
wood for their steam-boilers was especially desirable, and
they took all that had been prepared for the usual wants
of the river. Having helped themselves to this, and
such other chattels as were at the moment needed and
at hand, they went on their way, grimly rejoicing. On
the following day most of them returned; some without
arms, some without legs, some even without heads; a
wretched, wounded, mutilated, sore-struck body of filibusters. The boiler of their large steamer had burst,
scattering destruction far and near. It was current
among the filibusters that the logs of wood had been

laden with gunpowder in order to effect this damage. It is more probable, that being filibusters, rough and ready as the phrase goes, they had not duly looked to their engineering properties. At any rate, they all returned. On the whole, these filibusters have suffered dire punishment for their sins.

At any rate, the merchant under whose roof we slept received no payment for his wood. Here we found two men living, not in such squalid misery as that independent German, but nevertheless sufficiently isolated from the world. One was an old Swedish sailor, who seemed to speak every language under the sun, and to have been in every portion of the globe, whether under the sun or otherwise. At any rate we could not induce him to own to not having been in any place. Timbuctoo; yes, indeed, he had unfortunately been a captive there for three years. At Mecca he had passed as an Arab among the Arabs, having made the great pilgrimage in company with many children of Mahomet, wearing the green turban as a veritable child of Mahomet himself. Portsmouth he knew well, having had many a row about the Hard. We could not catch him tripping, though we put him through his facings to the best of our joint geographical knowledge. At present he was a poor gardener on the San Juan river, having begun life as a lieutenant in the Swedish navy. *He* had seen too much of the world to refuse the dollar which was offered to him.

On the next morning we reached Greytown, following the San Juan river down to that pleasant place. There is another passage out to the sea by the Colerado, a branch river which, striking out from the San Juan, runs into the ocean by a shorter channel. This also has been thought of as a course for the projected canal, preferable to that of the San Juan. I believe them to be equally impracticable. The San Juan river itself is so shallow that we were frequently on the ground even in our light canoe.

And what shall I say of Greytown? We have a Consul-General there, or at least had one when these pages were written; a Consul-General whose duty it is, or was, to have under his special care the King of Mosquitia—as some people are pleased to call this coast—of the Mosquito coast as it is generally styled. Bluefields, further along the coast, is the chosen residence of this sable tyrant; but Greytown is the capital of his dominions. Now it is believed that, in deference to the feelings of the United States, and to the American reading of the Clayton-Bulwer treaty, and in deference, I may add, to a very sensible consideration that the matter is of no possible moment to ourselves, the protectorate of the Mosquito coast is to be abandoned. What the king will do I cannot imagine; but it will be a happy day I should think for our Consul when he is removed from Greytown.

Of all the places in which I have ever put my foot I think that this is the most wretched. It is a small town, perhaps of two thousand inhabitants, though this on my part is a mere guess, at the mouth of the San Juan, and surrounded on every side either by water or impassable forests. A walk of a mile in any direction would be impossible, unless along the beach of the sea; but this is of less importance, as the continual heat would prevent any one from thinking of such exercise. Sundry Americans live here, worshipping the almighty dollar as Americans do, keeping liquor shops and warehouses; and with the Americans, sundry Englishmen and sundry Germans. Of the female population I saw nothing except some negro women, and one white, or rather red-faced owner of a rum shop. The native population are the Mosquito Indians; but it seems that they are hardly allowed to live in Greytown. They are to be seen paddling about in their canoes, selling a few eggs and chickens, catching turtle, and not rarely getting drunk. They would seem from their colour and physiognomy to be a cross between the negro and the Indian; and such I imagine to be the case. They have a language of their own, but those on the coast almost always speak English also.

My gallant young friend, Fitzm——, was in command of a small schooner inside the harbour of Greytown. As the accommodation of the city itself was not inviting, I gladly took up my quarters under his flag until the English packet, which was then hourly expected, should be ready to carry me to Colon and St. Thomas. I can only say that if I was commander of that schooner I would lie outside the harbour, so as to be beyond the ill-usage of those frightful musquitoes. The country has been well named Mosquitia.

There was an American man-of-war and also an English man-of-war—sloops-of-war both I believe technically—lying off Greytown; and we dined on board them both, on two consecutive days. Of the American I will say, speaking in their praise, that I never ate such bacon and peas. It may be that the old hens up the Serapiqui river had rendered me peculiarly susceptible to such delights; but nevertheless, I shall always think that there was something peculiar about the bacon and peas on board the American sloop-of-war 'St. Louis.'

And on the second day the steamer came in; the 'Trent,' Captain Moir; we then dined on board of her, and on the same night she sailed for Colon. And when shall I see that gallant young lieutenant again? Putting aside his unjust, and I must say miraculous, consumption of hard-boiled eggs, I could hardly wish for a better travelling companion.

CHAPTER XXI.

CENTRAL AMERICA—RAILWAYS, CANALS, AND TRANSIT.

How best to get about this world which God has given us is certainly one of the most interesting subjects which men have to consider, and one of the most interesting works on which men can employ themselves.

The child when born is first suckled, then fed with a spoon; in his next stage his food is cut up for him, and he begins to help himself; for some years after that it is still carved under parental authority; and then at last he sits down to the full enjoyment of his own leg of mutton under his own auspices.

Our development in travelling has been much of the same sort, and we are now perhaps beginning to use our own knife and fork, though we hardly yet understand the science of carving; or at any rate, can hardly bring our hands to the duly dexterous use of the necessary tools.

We have at least got so far as this, that we perceive that the leg of mutton is to be cooked and carved. We are not to eat hunks of raw sheep cut off here and there. The meat to suit our palates should be put on a plate in the guise of a cleanly slice, cut to a certain thickness, and not exceeding a certain size.

And we have also got so far as this, that we know that
the world must be traversed by certain routes, prepared
for us originally not by ourselves, but by the hand of
God. We were great heroes when we first got round
the Cape of Good Hope, when we first crossed the
Atlantic, when we first doubled Cape Horn. We were
then learning to pick up our crumbs with our earliest
knives and forks, and there was considerable peril in the
attempt. We have got beyond that now, and have perceived that we may traverse the world without going
round it. The road from Europe to Asia is by Egypt
and the Isthmus of Suez, not by the Cape of Good Hope.
So also is the road from Europe to the West of America,
and from the East of America to Asia by the isthmus of
Central America, and not by Cape Horn.

We have found out this, and have, I presume, found
out also that this was all laid out for us by the hands of
the Creator,—prepared exactly as the sheep have been
prepared. It has been only necessary that we should
learn to use the good things given us.

That there are reasons why the way should not have
been made absolutely open we may well suppose, though
we cannot perhaps at present well understand. How
currents of the sea might have run so as to have impeded
rather than have assisted navigation, had the two Americas
been disjoined; how pernicious winds might have blown,
and injurious waters have flowed, had the Red Sea opened
into the Mediterranean, we may imagine, though we cannot know. That the world's surface, as formed by God,
is best for God's purposes, and therefore certainly best for
man's purposes, that most of us must believe.

But it is for us to carve the good things which are put
before us, and to find out the best way in which they
may be carved. We may, perhaps, fairly think that we
have done much towards acquiring this knowledge, but

we certainly know that there is more yet to be done.
We have lines of railways from London to Manchester;
from Calais across France and all the Germanies to
Eastern Europe; from the coast of Maine, through the
Canadas, to the central territories of the United States;
but there are no lines yet from New York to California,
nor from the coast of the Levant to Bombay and Calcutta.

But perhaps the two greatest points which are at this
moment being mooted with reference to the carriage
about the world of mankind and man's goods, concern
the mode in which we may most advantageously pass
across the isthmuses of Suez and Panama. These are
the two land obstacles in the way of navigation, of direct
water carriage round the earth's belt—obstacles as they
appear to us, though in truth so probably locks formed by
the Almighty for the assistance of our navigation.

For many years, it is impossible to say how many, but
for some few centuries as regards Panama, and for many
centuries as regards Suez, this necessity has been felt, and
the minds of men in those elder days inclined naturally to
canals. In the days of the old kings of Egypt, antecedent
to Cleopatra, attempts were made to cut through the sands
and shallow lakes from the eastern margin of the Nile's
delta to the Red Sea; and the idea of piercing Central
America in some point occurred to the Spaniards immediately on their discovering the relative position of the
two oceans. But in those days men were infants, not as
yet trusted with the carving-knife.

The work which unsuccessfully filled the brains of so
many thoughtful men for so many years has now been
done—at any rate to a degree. Railways have been
completed from Alexandria on the Mediterranean to Suez
on the Red Sea, and from Panama on the Pacific, to
Aspinwall or Colon on the Caribbean Sea. These railways are now at work, and passengers are carried across

with sufficient rapidity. The Isthmus of Suez, over which the line of railway runs for something over two hundred miles, creates a total delay to our Indian mails and passengers of twenty-four hours only, and the lesser distance of the American isthmus is traversed in three hours. Were rapidity here as necessary as it is in the other case—and it will doubtless become so—the conveyance from one sea to the other need not create a delay of above twelve hours.

But not the less are many men—good and scientific men too—keenly impressed with the idea that the two isthmuses should be pierced with canals, although these railways are at work. All mankind has heard much of M. Lesseps and his Suez canal. On that matter I do not mean to say much here. I have a very strong opinion that such canal will not and cannot be made ; that all the strength of the arguments adduced in the matter are hostile to it; and that steam navigation by land will and ought to be the means of transit through Egypt. But that matter is a long way distant from our present subject. It is with reference to the transit over the other isthmus that I propose to say a few words.

It is singular, or perhaps, if rightly considered, not singular, that both the railways have been constructed mainly by Anglo-Saxon science and energy, and under the pressure of Anglo-Saxon influence ; while both the canal schemes most prevalent at the present day owe their repute to French eloquence and French enthusiasm. M. Lesseps is the patron of the Suez canal, and M. Belly of that which is, or is not to be, constructed from San Juan del Norte, or Greytown, to the shores of the Pacific.

There are three proposed methods of crossing the isthmus, that by railway, that by canal, and a third by the ordinary use of such ordinary means of conveyance as the land and the waters of the country afford.

As regards railway passage, one line being now open and at work, has those nine points in its favour which possession gives. It does convey men and goods across with great rapidity, and is a reality, doing that which it pretends to do. Its charges, however, are very high; and it would doubtless be well if competition, or fear of competition, could be made to lower them. Five pounds is charged for conveying a passenger less than fifty miles; no class of passengers can cross at a cheaper fare; and the rates charged for goods are as high in comparison. On the other side, it may be said that the project was one of great risk, that the line was from its circumstances very costly, having been made at an expense of about thirty-two thousand pounds a mile—I believe, however, that a considerable portion of the London and Birmingham line was equally expensive—and that trains by which money can be made cannot run often, perhaps only six or seven times a month each way.

It is, however, very desirous that the fares should be lowered, and the great profits accruing to the railway prove that this may be done. Eventually they doubtless will be lowered.

The only other line of railway which now seems to be spoken of as practicable for the passage of the isthmus is one the construction of which has been proposed across the republic of Honduras, from a spot called Port Cortez, in the Bay of Honduras, on the northern or Atlantic side, to some harbour to be chosen in the Bay of Fonseca, on the southern or Pacific side. Mr. Squier, who was Chargé d'Affaires from the United States to Central America, and whose work on the republics of Central America is well known, strongly advocates this line, showing in the first place that from its position it would suit the traffic of the United States much better than that of Panama; as undoubtedly it would, seeing that the transit from New York to California, viâ Panama, must go down south as far as latitude 7° north; whereas, by the proposed route through Honduras it need not descend below lat. 13° north, thus saving double that distance in the total run each way.* Mr. Squier then goes on to prove that the country of Honduras is in every way suited for the purposes of a railway; but here I am not sure that he carries me with him. The road would have to ascend nearly three thousand feet above the sea-level; and though it may be true that the grades themselves would not be more severe than many that are now to be found on railways in full work in other countries, nevertheless it must be felt that the overcoming such an altitude in such a country, and the working over it when overcome, would necessarily add greatly to the original cost of the line, and the subsequent cost of running. The Panama line goes through a country comparatively level. Then the distance across Honduras is one hundred and fifty miles, and it is computed that the line would be two hundred miles: the length of the Panama line is forty-seven or forty-eight miles.

The enormous cost of the Panama line arose from the difficulty of obtaining the necessary sort of labour. The natives would not work as they were wanted, and Europeans

* Not that we may take all that Mr. Squier says on this subject as proved. His proposed route for the traffic of the United States is from the western coast of Florida to the chosen port, Port Cortez, in Honduras; and he attempts to show that this is pretty nearly the only possible passage in those seas free from huricanes and danger. But this passage is right across the Gulf of Mexico, and vessels would have to stem the full force of the gulf-stream on their passage down from Florida.

In all such matters where a man becomes warm on a scheme, he feels himself compelled to prove that the gods themselves have pointed out his plan as the only one fit for adoption—as the only one free from all evil—and blessed with every advantage. We are always over-proving our points.

Y

died there ; so that, at last, labour was imported from the coast of New Granada. At the high level named as the summit of the Honduras route, the climate would no doubt be comparatively mild, and labour easy to be borne ; but near the coast of the Bays, both of Honduras and Fonseca, the heat would be as great as at Aspinwall and Panama, and the effects probably the same.

As regards our British traffic, the route by the Isthmus of Panama is the better situated of the two. Looking at a map of the world—and it is necessary to take in the whole world, in order that the courses of British trade may be seen—it does not seem to be of much consequence, as regards distance, whether a bale of goods from London to Sydney should pass the isthmus by Honduras or Panama ; but in fact, even for this route, the former would labour under great disadvantages. A ship in making its way from Honduras up to Jamaica has to fight against the trade winds. On this account our mail steamer from Belize to Jamaica is timed only at four miles an hour, though the mail to Honduras is timed at eight miles an hour. This would be the direct route from the terminus of the Honduras line to Europe, and matters would be made only worse if any other line were taken. But the track from Panama to Jamaica is subject to what sailors call a soldier's wind ; even working to St. Thomas, and thereby getting a stronger slant of the trade winds against them, our mail steamers can make eight or nine miles an hour.

As regards our trade to Chili and Peru, it is clear that Honduras is altogether out of our way ; and as regards our coming trade to Frazer River and Vancouver's Island, though the absolute distance, viâ Honduras, would be something shorter, that benefit would be neutralized by the disadvantageous position of the Bay of Honduras as above explained.

But the great advantage which the Panama line enjoys

is the fact of its being already made. *It has the nine points which possession gives it.* Its forty-eight miles cost one million six hundred thousand pounds. It cannot be presumed that two hundred miles through Honduras could be made for double that sum ; and seeing that the Honduras line would be in opposition to the other, and only be used if running at fares lower than those of its rival, I cannot see how it would pay, or where the money is to be procured. I am not aware that the absolute cost of the proposed line through Honduras has been accurately computed.

As regards the public interest, two lines would no doubt be better than one. Competition is always beneficial to the consumer ; but in this case, I do not expect to see the second line made in our days. That there will in future days be a dozen ways of commodiously crossing the isthmus—when we have thoroughly learned how best to carve our leg of mutton—I do not at all doubt.

It may be as well to state here that England is bound by a treaty with Honduras, made in 1836, to assist in furthering the execution of this work by our countenance, aid, and protection, on condition that when made, we Britishers are to have the full use of it; as much so, at least, as any other people or nation. And that, as I take it, is the sole and only meaning of all those treaties made on our behalf with Central America, or in respect to Central America—Clayton-Bulwer Treaty, new Ouseley Treaty, and others ; namely, that we, who are desirous of excluding no person from the benefits of this public world-road, are not ourselves to be excluded on any consideration whatever. And may we not boast that this is the only object looked for in all our treaties and diplomatic doings ? Is it not for that reason that we hold Gibraltar, are jealous about Egypt, and resolved to have Perim in our power ? Is it not true that we would fain make all ways open to all

men? that we would have them open to ourselves, certainly, but not closed against any human being? If that,
and such like, be not what our diplomatists are doing, then
I, for one, misunderstand their trade.

So much for the two railways, and now as to the proposed canals. Here no happy undertaking can boast of
the joys of possession. No canal is as yet open, carrying
men and goods with, shall we say, twenty-five per cent.
profit on the outlay. Ah! that is an elysium which does
not readily repeat itself. O thou thrice happy Colonel
Totten, who hast constructed a railway resulting in such
celestial beatitude!

The name of canals projected across the isthmus has
been legion, and the merits of them all have in their time
been hotly pressed by their special advocates. That most
to the north, which was the passage selected by Cortes and
pressed by him on the Spanish government, would pass
through Mexico. The line would be from the Gulf of
Campechay, up the river Coatzacoalcoz, to Tehuantepec
on the Pacific. This was advocated as lately as 1845, but
has now, I believe, been abandoned as impracticable.
Going south down the map, the next proposition of which
I can find mention is for a canal from the head of the Lake
of Dulce through the state of Guatemala; the Lake or
Gulf of Dulce being at the head of the Gulf of Honduras.
This also seems to have been abandoned. Then we come
to the proposed Honduras railway of which mention has
been made.

Next below this we reach a cluster of canals, all going
through the great inland lake of Nicaragua. This scheme,
or one of these schemes, has also been in existence since
the times of the early Spaniards; and has been adhered to
with more or less pertinacity ever since. This Lake of
Nicaragua was to be reached either direct by the river
San Juan, or by entering the river San Juan from the

ocean by the river Colorado, which is in effect a branch of the San Juan; the projected canal would thus ascend to the lake. From thence to the Pacific various passages for egress have been suggested; at first it was intended, naturally, to get out at the nearest practicable point, that being probably at San Juan del Sur. They have San Juans and San Josés quite at pleasure about these countries.

Then came the grand plan of the present French emperor, bearing at least his name, and first published, I think, in 1846. This was a very grand plan, of course. The route of 'transit' was to be right up the Lake of Nicaragua to its northern point; there the canal was to enter the River Tipitapa, and come out again in the northern Lake of Managua; from thence it was to be taken out to the Pacific at the port of Realejo. This project included the building of an enormous city, which was to contain the wealth of the new world, and to be, as it were, a new Constantinople between the two lakes; but the scheme has been abandoned as being too costly, too imperial.

And now we have M. Belly's scheme; his scheme and pamphlet of which I will say a few words just now, and therefore I pass on to the others.

The line of the River Chargres, and from thence to the town of Panama—being very nearly the line of the present railway—was long contemplated with favour, but has now been abandoned as impracticable; as has also the line over the Isthmus of Darien, which was for a while thought to be the most feasible, as being the shortest. The lie of the land, however, and the nature of the obstacles to be overcome, have put this scheme altogether out of the question.

Next and last is the course of the River Atrato, which runs into the Gulf of Darien, but which is, in fact, the first of the great rivers of South America; first, that is, counting them as commencing from the isthmus. It runs down from the Andes parallel to the coast of the Pacific, and is navigable for many miles. The necessary surveys, however, for connecting this river with the Pacific have never yet been made ; and even if this plan were practicable, the extremely low latitude at which the Pacific ocean would be reached would make such a line bad for our trade, and quite out of the question for the chief portion of the American 'transit.'

It appears, therefore, that there are insuperable objections to all these canal routes, unless it be to some route passing through the Lake of Nicaragua. By reference to a map of Central America it will be seen that the waters of this lake, joined to those of the San Juan river, comprise the breadth of nearly the whole isthmus, leaving a distance not exceeding twenty miles to be conquered by a canal. At first sight this appears to be very enticing, and M. Belly has been enticed. He has been enticed, or at any rate writes as though this were the case. Anything worded more eloquently, energetically, and grandiloquently, than his pamphlet in favour of this route I have not met, even among French pamphlets.

M. Felix Belly describes himself as a 'publiciste,' and chevalier of the order of Saint Maurice and Lazarus, and of the order of Medjidie. As such he has made a convention with Don Thomas Martinez, President of the republic of Nicaragua, and with Don Juan Rafael Mora, President of the republic of Costa Rica, in accordance with which he, Chevalier Belly, is to cut a canal or water route for ships through the territories of those potentates, obtaining thereby certain vast privileges, including the possession of no small portion of those territories, and the right of levying all manner of tolls on the world's commerce which is to pass through his canal. And the potentates above named are in return to receive from M. Belly very considerable subsidies out of these tolls. They bind themselves, moreover, to permit no other traffic or transit through their

country, securing to M. Belly for ninety-nine years the
monopoly of the job : and granting to him the great diplomatic privilege of constituting his canal, let it be here or
there, the boundary of the realms of these two potentates.

What strikes me with the greatest wonder on reading
—not the pamphlet, for that is perhaps more wonderful
in other respects—but the articles of the convention, is, that
these three persons, the potentates aforesaid and the chevalier, should have among them the power of doing all this ;
or that they should even have had the power of agreeing
to do all this ; for really up to this period one seems hardly
to have heard in England much about any one of them.

That there should be presidents of these two republics
is supposed, as there are also, doubtless, of San Salvador
and Venezuela, and all the other western republics ; but
it is to be presumed that as presidents of republics they
can have themselves no more power to give away a
ninety-nine years' possession of their lands and waters
than can any other citizen. Mr. Buchanan could hardly
sell to any Englishman, however enterprising, the right
of making a railway from New York to San Francisco.
The convention does certainly bear two other signatures,
which purport to be those of the ministers of foreign
affairs attached to those two republics; but even this
hardly seems to give us a sufficient guarantee of power.
What if we should put our money into the canal, and
future presidents should refuse to be bound by the agreement?

But M. Belly's name stands on his side alone. No
foreign minister or aide-de-camp is necessary to back his
signature. The two potentates having agreed to give
the country, he will agree to make the canal—he,
M. Belly, Publiciste and Chevalier. It is to cost altogether,
according to his account, 120,000,000 francs—say, four
million eight hundred thousand pounds sterling. Of a

company, chairman, and directors we hear nothing. We cannot find that the shares are in the market. Probably they may be too valuable. On our own Stock Exchange the matter does not seem to be much known, nor do we perceive that it is quoted among French prices. Nevertheless, M. Belly has the four million eight hundred thousand pounds already in his breeches pocket, and he will make the canal. I wonder whether he would drain London for us if we were to ask him.

But wonderful as is the fact that these three gentlemen should be about to accomplish this magnificent undertaking for the world, the eloquence of the language in which the undertaking is described is perhaps more wonderful still.

' On the first of May, 1858, at Rivas, in Nicaragua, in the midst of a concourse of circumstances full of grandeur, a convention was signed which opens to civilization a new view and unlimited horizons. The hour has come for commencing with resolution this enterprise of cutting the Isthmus of Panama. . . . . The solution of the problem must be no longer retarded. It belongs to an epoch which has given to itself the mission of pulling down barriers and suppressing distances. It must be regarded, not as a private speculation, but as a creation of public interest—not as the work of this people or that party, but as springing from civilization itself.' Then M. Belly goes on to say that this project, emanating from a man sympathetic with the cause and a witness of the heroism of Central America, namely himself, possesses advantages—which of course could not attach to any scheme devised by a less godlike being.

It may be seen that I have no great belief in the scheme of M. Belly; neither have I in many other schemes of the present day emanating from Englishmen, Americans, and others. But it is not that disbelief, but my admiration for French eloquence which urges me to make the above translation. Alas! I feel that I have lost so much of the Gallic fragrance! The Parisian aroma has escaped from the poor English words!

Is not this peculiar eloquence used in propagating all French projects for increased civilization? From the invention of a new constitution to that of a new shirt is it even wanting? We, with our stupid, unimaginative platitudes, know no better than to write up 'Eureka' when we think we have discovered anything. But a Frenchman tells his countrymen that they need no longer be mortals; a new era has come; let them wear his slippers and they will walk as gods walk. How many new eras have there not been? Who is not sick of the grandiloquence of French progress? 'Now—now we have taken the one great step. The dove at length may nestle with the kite, the lamb drink with the wolf. Men may share their goods, certain that others will share with them. Labour and wages, work and its reward, shall be systematized. Now we have done it, and the world shall be happy.' Well; perhaps the French world is happy. It may be that the liberty which they have propagated, the equality which they enjoy, and the fraternity which they practise, is fit for them!

But when has truly mighty work been heralded by magniloquence? Did we have any grand words from old George Stephenson, with his 'vera awkward for the cou'? Was there aught of the eloquent sententiousness of a French marshal about the lines of Torres Vedras? Was Luther apt to speak with great phraseology? If words ever convey to my ears a positive contradiction of the assertion which they affect to make, it is when they are grandly antithetical and magnificently verbose. If, in addition to this, they promise to mankind 'new epochs, new views, and unlimited horizons,' surely no further proof can be needed that they are vain, empty, and untrue.

But the language in which this proposal for a canal is couched is hardly worth so much consideration—would be worth no consideration at all, did it not come before us now as an emblem of that which at this present time is the most pernicious point in the French character—a false boasting of truth and honesty, with little or no relish for true truth and true honesty.

The present question is, whether M. Belly's canal scheme be feasible ; and, if feasible, whether he has, or can attain, the means of carrying it out?

In the first place it has already come to pass that the convention signed with such unlimited horizons has proved to be powerless. It is an undoubted fact that it was agreed to by the two presidents ; and as far as one of them is concerned, it is, I fear, a fact also that for the present he has sufficient power in his own territory to bind his countrymen, at any rate for a time, by his unsupported signature. Don Juan Rafael Mora, in Costa Rica, need care for no congress. If he were called dictator instead of president the change would only be in the word. But this is not exactly so in Nicaragua. There, it seems, the congress has refused to ratify the treaty as originally made. But they have, I believe, ratified another, in which M. Belly's undertaking to make the canal is the same as before, but from which the enormous grant of land, and the stipulations as to the boundary line of the territories are excluded.

In M. Belly's pamphlet he publishes a letter which he has received from Lord Malmesbury, as Secretary of State for Foreign Affairs—or rather a French translation of such a letter. It is this letter which appears to have given in Central America the strongest guarantee that something is truly intended by M. Belly's project.

Both in the pamphlet, and in the convention itself, repeated reference is made to the French government; but no document is given, nor even is any positive assertion made, that the government of the emperor in any way recognizes the scheme. But if this letter be true, and truly translated, Lord Malmesbury has done so to a certain extent. 'And I am happy,' says the letter, 'to be able to assure you that the stipulations of the treaty made between Great Britain and the United States, commonly called the Clayton-Bulwer Treaty, are in my opinion applicable to your project, if you put it in execution.'* And then this letter, written to a private gentleman holding no official position, is signed by the Secretary of State himself. M. Belly holds no official position, but he is addressed in his translation of Lord Malmesbury's letter as 'Concessionnaire du Canal de Nicaragua.'

Such a letter from such a quarter has certainly been very useful to M. Belly. In the minds of the presidents of the republics of Central America it must have gone far to prove that England at any rate regards M. Belly as no adventurer. There are many of the clauses of the convention to which I should have imagined that the English Secretary of State for Foreign Affairs would not have given an assent, although he might not be called on to express dissent. In the 26th Article it is stipulated that during the making of the canal—which if it were to be made at all would be protracted over many years— two French ships-of-war should lie in the Lake of Nicaragua, it having been stipulated by Art. 24 that no other ships-of-war should be admitted; thus giving to France a military occupation of the country. And by Art. 28 it is agreed that any political squabble re-

* See note to page 29, 12th edition. I have not happened to meet with any earlier edition of the work.

lative to this convention should be referred to a tribunal of
seven; two to be named by the company, and one each
by France, England, the United States, Nicaragua, and
Costa Rica. It is, I imagine, hardly probable that the
English government would send one member to such a
tribunal, in which France would have three voices to her
one, two of which voices would be wholly irresponsible.

Of course the letter does not bind Lord Malmesbury
or any secretary for foreign affairs to the different articles
of the convention; but if it be a genuine letter, I cannot
but think it to have been imprudent.*

The assistance of Lord Malmesbury has been obtained
by the easy progress of addressing a letter to him. But
to seduce the presidents of Central America a greater
effort has been made. They are told that they are the
wisest of the earth's potentates. 'Carrera, of Guatemala,
though an Indian and uneducated, is a man of natural
genius, and has governed for fifteen years with a wisdom
which has attracted to him the unanimous adherence of
his colleagues.' 'Don Juan Mora, of Costa Rica, the
hero of Rivas, has not had to spill a drop of blood in
maintaining in his cities an order much more perfect than
any to be found in Europe. He is a man, " hors de
ligne," altogether out of the common; and although he
counts scarcely forty years, but few political examples of
old Europe can be compared to him.' And as for General
Martinez, President of Nicaragua, 'since he has arrived
at the direction of affairs there, he would have healed all

---

* M. Belly speaks of his convention as having been adopted by
France, England, and the United States. 'Adopted, as it already
is, by the United States, by England, and by France, and as it soon
will be by the contracting Powers of the Treaty of Paris, it will
become '——the saviour of the world, &c. &c. What basis there
is for this statement, as regards France and the United States, I do
not know. As regards England, I presume Lord Malmesbury's
letter affords that basis.

the wounds of the country—had not the fatal influence of North American spirit paralyzed all his efforts.' What wonder that Presidents so spoken of should sign away their lands and waters?

But presuming all political obstacles to be removed, and that as regards the possession of the land, and the right of making a canal through it, everything had been conceded, there remain two considerable difficulties. In the first place, the nature of the waters and land, which seems to prohibit the cutting of a canal, except at an expense much more enormous than any that has been ever named; and, secondly, the amount of money to be collected, even if M. Belly's figures be correct. He states that he can complete the work for four million eight hundred thousand pounds. From whence is that sum to be procured?

As regards the first difficulty, I, from my own knowledge, can say nothing, not being an engineer, and having seen only a small portion of the projected route. I must therefore refer to M. Belly's engineer, and those who hold views differing from M. Belly. M. Belly's engineer-in-chief is M. Thomé de Gamond, who, in the pamphlet above alluded to, puts forward his calculations, and sends in his demand for the work at four million eight hundred thousand pounds. The route is by the river San Juan, a portion of which is so shallow that canoes in their course are frequently grounded when the waters are low, and other part of which consist of rapids. It then goes through the lake, a channel through which must be dredged or cleared with gunpowder before it can carry deep-sea ships, and then out to the Pacific by a canal which must be cut through the mountains. There is nothing in the mere sound of all this to make a man who is ignorant on the subject, as I and most men are, feel that the work could not be done for the sum named.

But before investing cash in the plan, one would like to be sure of the engineer, and to know that he has made his surveys very accurately.

Now it appears that M. Thomé de Gamond has never set foot in Central America; or, if he has done so now—and I do not know whether he has or has not—that he never had done so when he drew out his project. Nor, as it would appear, has he even done this work, trusting to the eyes and hands of others. As far as one can learn, no surveys whatsoever have been taken for this gigantic scheme.

The engineer tells us that he has used marine charts and hydrographical drawings made by officers of various nations, which enable him to regard his own knowledge as sufficiently exact as far as shores and levels of the rivers, &c., are concerned; and that with reference to the track of his canal, he has taken into his service— 'utilisé'—the works of various surveying engineers, among them Colonel Child, the American. They, to be sure, do leave him at a loss as to the interior plateau of the Mosquito country, and some regions to the east and south of the lake—the canal must enter the lake by the southeast;—but this is a matter of no moment, seeing that all these countries are covered by virgin forests, and can therefore easily be arranged! Gentlemen capitalists, will you on this showing take shares in the concern?

The best real survey executed with reference to any kindred project was that made by Colonel Child, an officer of engineers belonging to the United States. I believe I may say this without hesitation; and it is to Colonel Child's survey that M. Belly most frequently refers. But the facts, as stated by Colonel Child, prove the absolute absurdity of M. Belly's plan. He was employed in 1851 by an American company, which, as it went to the considerable expense of having such work absolutely done, was no doubt in earnest in its intentions with reference to a canal. Colonel Child did not actually report against the canal. He explained what could be done for a certain sum of money, leaving it to others to decide whether, in effecting so much, that sum of money would be well laid out. He showed that a canal seventeen feet deep might be made—taking the course of the San Juan and that of the lake, as suggested by M. Belly—for a sum of thirty-one millions of dollars, or six million two hundred thousand pounds.

But when the matter came to be considered by men versed in such concerns, it was seen that a canal with a depth of only seventeen feet of water would not admit of such vessels as those by which alone such a canal could be beneficially used. Passengers, treasure, and light goods can easily be transhipped and carried across by railway. The canal, if made at all, must be made for the passage of large vessels built for heavy goods. For such vessels a canal must hold not less than twenty-five feet of water. It was calculated that a cutting of such depth would cost much more than double the sum needed for that intended to contain seventeen feet—more, that is, than twelve million four hundred thousand pounds. The matter was then abandoned, on the conviction that no ship canal made at such a cost could by any probability become remunerative. In point of time it could never compete with the railway. Colonel Child had calculated that a delay of two days would take place in the locks; and even as regards heavy goods, no extreme freight could be levied, as saving of expense with them would be of much greater object than saving of time.

That this decision was reached on good grounds, and that the project, then, at any rate, was made bonâ fide there can, I believe, be no doubt. In opposition to such a decision, made on such grounds, and with no encourage-

ment but that given by the calculations of an engineer who
has himself made no surveys, I cannot think it likely that
this new plan will ever be carried out. The eloquence
even of M. Belly, backed by such arguments, will hardly
collect four million eight hundred thousand pounds ; and
even if it did, the prudence of M. Belly would hardly
throw such an amount of treasure into the San Juan
river.

As I have before said, there appears to have been ˙no
company formed. M. Belly is the director, and he has
a bureau of direction in the Rue de Provence. But
though deficient as regards chairmen, directors, and shareholders, he is magnificently provided with high-sounding
officials. Then again there comes a blank. Though the
corps of officers was complete when I was in Costa Rica,
at any rate as regards their names, the workmen had not
arrived ; not even the skilled labourers who were to come
in detachments of forty-five by each mail packet. The
mail packets came but not the skilled labourers.

Shortly before my arrival at San José there appeared
in the journal published in that town a list of officers to
be employed by M. Felix Belly, the Director-General
' De la Compañie Del Canal Atlantico-Pacifico.' The
first of these is Don Andres Le Vasseur, Minister Pleni-
potentiary, Veteran Officer of the Guard Imperial, Commander of the Legion of Honour, and Knight of the Order
of St. Gregory. He is Secretary-General of the Direction.
Then there are other secretaries. In the first place,
Prince Polignac, Veteran Officer of the Cavalry of the
Cazadores in Africa, &c. He at any rate is a fact ! for did
I not meet him and the O'Gorman Mahon—Nicodemus
and Polyphemus—not ' standing naked in the open air,'
but drinking brandy and water at the little inn at Esparza ?
' Arcades ambo !' The next secretary is Don Henrique
Le Vasseur. He is Dibujador fotografo, which I take to

mean photographical artist ; and then Don Andres L'Heritier ; he is the private secretary.

We next come to the engineers. With reference to geology and mineralogy, M. Belly has employed Don José Durocher, whose titles, taken from the faculty of science at Rennes, the Legion of Honour, &c., are too long to quote. Don Eugénio Ponsard, who also is not without his titles, is the working engineer on these subjects. And then joined to them as adjutant-engineer is Don Henrique Peudifer, whose name is also honoured with various adjuncts.

The engineers who are to be intrusted with the surveys and works of the canals are named next. There are four such, to whom are joined five conductors of the works and eight special masters of the men.

All these composed an expedition which left Southampton on the 17th of February, 1859,—or which should so have left it, had they acted up to M. Belly's promises.

Then by the packet of the 2nd of March, 1859, there came—or at least there should have come, for we are told that they sailed—another expedition. I cannot afford to give all the names, but they are full-sounding and very honourable. Among them there was a maker of bricks, who in his own country had been a chief of the works in the imperial manufactory of porcelain at Sèvres. Having enticed him from so high a position, it is to be hoped that M. Belly will treat him well in Central America. There are, or were, hydrographical engineers and agricultural engineers, master carpenters, and masters of various other specialties.

I fear all these gentlemen came to grief on the road, for I think I may say that no such learned troops came through with the mail packets which left Southampton on the days indicated.

Then by the following steamers there would, it is stated,

be despatched in succession an inspector of telegraphs, an engineer for making gas, an engineer to be charged with the fabrication of the iron way, an agriculturist-in-chief, a scientific commission for geology, mineralogy, meteorology, and natural history in general. And attached to all the engineers will come—or now long since should have come —the conductors of works and special masters of men, who are joined with them in their operations. These are to consist principally of veteran soldiers of the Engineers and the Artillery.

These gentlemen also must, I fear, have been cast away between Southampton and ,St. Thomas, if they left the former port by either of the two mail steamers following those two specially indicated. I think I may say positively that no such parties were forwarded from St. Thomas.

The general inspection of the works will be intrusted ultimately to a French and to an English engineer. The Frenchman will of course be M. Thomé de Gamond. The Englishman to be 'Mr. Locke, Member of Parliament.' If, indeed, this latter assertion were true ! But I think I may take upon myself to say that it is untrue.

All the above certainly sounds very grand, especially when given at full length in the Spanish language. Out there, in Central America, the list is effective. Here, in England, we should like to see the list of the directors as well, and to have some idea how much money has been subscribed. Mankind perhaps can trust M. Belly for much, but not for everything.

In the month of May, Don Juan Rafael Mora, the President of Costa Rica, left his dominions and proceeded to Rivas, in Nicaragua, to assist at the inauguration of the opening of the works of the canal. When I and my companion met him at Esparza, accompanied by Nicodemus and Polyphemus, he was making this journey. M. Belly has already described in eloquent

language how on a previous occasion this potentate con-
descended to leave his own kingdom and visit that of
a neighbour; thus sacrificing individual rank for the
benefit of humanity and civilization. He was willing to
do this even once again. Having borrowed a French man-
of-war to carry him from Punta-arenas, in his own territories, to St. Juan del Sur, in the territory of Nicaragua,
he started with his suite, of whom the Prince and the
O'Gorman were such distinguished members. But, lo!
when he arrived at Rivas, a few miles up from San Juan
del Sur—at Rivas, where with gala holiday triumph the
canal was to be inaugurated—the canal from whence
were to come new views and unlimited horizons—lo!
when he there arrived, no brother-president was there to
meet him, no M. Belly, attended by engineers-in-chief
and brickmakers from Sèvres, to do him honour. There
was not even one French pupil from the Polytechnic
School to turn a sod with a silver spade. In lieu of this
some custom-house officer of Nicaragua called upon poor
Don Juan to pay the usual duty on bringing his portmanteau into Rivas. Other new views and other unlimited horizons had, it seems, been drawing on M. Belly.

One of the first words of which a man has to learn
the meaning on reaching these countries is 'transit.'
Central America can only be great in the world—as
Egypt can be only great—by being a passage between
other parts of the world which are in themselves great.
We Englishmen all know Crewe; Crewe has become a
town of considerable importance, as being a great railway junction. Men must reach Crewe and leave Crewe
continually, and the concourse there has rendered labour
necessary; labourers of all sorts must live in houses, and
require bakers and grocers to supply them. So Crewe
has grown up and become important; and so will Central
America become important. Aspinwall—Colon as we

call it—has become a town in this way within the last ten years.

'Transit,' in these parts means the trade of carrying people across Central America; and a deal of 'transit' has been done and money made by carrying people across Nicaragua by way of the great lake. This has hitherto been effected by shallow-bottomed boats. I will say one word or so on the subject when I have done, as I very soon shall have done, with M. Belly.

Now it is very generally thought that M. Belly, when he speaks of this canal, means 'transit.' There can be no question but that a great carrying trade might be opened, much to the advantage of Nicaragua, and to the advantage of Costa Rica also though not to the same extent. If all this canal grandiloquence would pave the way to 'transit,' might it not be well? What if another agreement could be made, giving to M. Belly and his company the sole right of 'transit' through Nicaragua, till the grand canal should be completed? a very long lease—might not something be done in this way? But Don Juan Mora there, Don Juan of Costa Rica, that man altogether 'hors de ligne,' grand as he is, need know nothing about this. Let him, left quite in darkness as to this new view, these altered unlimited horizons, go to Rivas if he will, and pay his custom dues.

It may be that I have written at too great length, and with an energy disproportionate to the subject, on this matter of the Nicaraguan canal scheme. I do not know that the English public generally, or at any rate that portion of it which may perhaps read my book, is very deeply interested in the subject. We hear now and then something of the Clayton-Bulwer Treaty, and a word or two is said about the Panama route to Australia, but the subject is not generally interesting to us, as is that of the passage through Egypt. We can reach Australia by another and a shorter route; and as for Vancouver's Island and Frazer River, they as yet are very young.

But the matter will become of importance. And to a man in Central America, let his visit to that country be ever so short, it becomes at once important. To me it was grievous to find a work so necessary to the world as this of opening a way over the isthmus, tampered with, and to a degree hindered by a scheme which I cannot but regard as unreal. But unreal as it may be, this project has reached dimensions which make it in some way worthy of notice. A French ship-of-war was sent to take the President Mora and his suite on their unfortunate journey to Rivas; and an English-ship-of war was sent to bring them back. The extension of such courtesies to the president of a republic in Central America may be very well; but men, seeing on what business this president was travelling, not unnaturally regarded the courtesy as an acknowledgment of the importance of M. Belly's work.

I do not wish to use hard names, but I cannot think that the project of which I have been speaking covers any true intention of making a canal. And such schemes, if not real, if not true in the outward bearings which they show to the world, go far to hinder others which might be real. And now I will say nothing further about M. Belly.

As I have before stated, there was some few years since a considerable passenger traffic through Central America by the route of the Lake of Nicaragua. This of course was in the hands of the Americans, and the passengers were chiefly those going and coming between the Eastern States and California. They came down to Greytown, at the mouth of the San Juan river, in steamers, from New York, and I believe from various American ports, went up the San Juan river in other steamers with flat bottoms prepared for those waters, across the lake in the same way, and then by a good road over the intervening neck of land between the lake and the Pacific.

Of course the Panama railway has done much to interfere with this. In the first place, a rival route has thus been opened; though I doubt whether it would be a quicker route from New York to California if the way by the Lake were well organized. And then the company possessing the line of steamers running to Aspinwall from New York has been able to buy off the line which would otherwise run to Greytown.

But this rivalship has not been the main cause of the total stoppage of the Nicaraguan route. The filibusters came into that land and destroyed everything. They dropped down from California on Realejo, Leon, Manaqua, Granada, and all the western coast of Nicaragua. Then others came from the South-Eastern States, from Mobile and New Orleans, and swarmed up the San Juan river, devouring everything before them. There can be no doubt that Walker's idea, in his attempt to possess himself of this country, was that he could thus become master of the passage across the isthmus. He saw, as so many others have seen, the importance of the locality in this point of view; and he probably felt that if he could make himself lord of the soil by his own exertions, and on his own bottom, his mother country, the United States, would not be slow to recognize him. ' I,' he would have said, ' have procured for you the ownership of the road which is so desirable for you. Pay me, by making me your lieutenant here, and protecting me in that position.'

The idea was not badly planned, but it was of course radically unjust. It was a contemplated filching of the road. And Walker found, as all men do find, that he could not easily get good tools to do bad work. He tried the job with a very rough lot of tools; and now, though he has done much harm to others, he has done very little good to himself. I do not think that we shall hear much more of him.

And among the worst of the injuries which he has done is this disturbance of the Lake traffic. This route has been altogether abandoned. There, in the San Juan river, is to be seen one old steamer with its bottom upwards, a relic of the filibusters and their destruction. All along the banks tales are told of their injustice and sufferings. How recklessly they robbed on their journey up the country, and how they returned back to Greytown—those who did return, whose bones are not whitening the Lake shores—wounded, maimed, and miserable.

Along the route traders were beginning to establish themselves, men prepared to provide the travellers with food and drink, and the boats with fuel for their steam. An end for the present has been put to all this. The weak governments of the country have been able to afford no protection to these men, and placed as they were, beyond the protection of England or the United States, they have been completely open to attack. The filibusters for a while have destroyed the transit through Nicaragua; and it is hardly matter of surprise that the presidents of that and the neighbouring republics should catch at any scheme which proposes to give them back this advantage, especially when promise is made of the additional advantage of effectual protection.

It is much to be desired, on all accounts, that this route should be again opened. Here, I think, is to be found the best chance of establishing an immediate competition with the Panama railway. For although such a route will not offer the comfort of the Panama line, or, till it be well organized, the same rapidity, it would nevertheless draw to it a great portion of the traffic, and men and women going in numbers would be carried at cheaper rates; and these cheaper rates in Nicaragua would probably at once lessen the fares now charged by the Panama railway. Competition would certainly be advantageous, and for the present I see no other opening for a competitive route.

A railway along the banks of the San Juan would, I fear, be too expensive. The distance is above one hundred and fifty miles, and the line would be very costly. But a line of rails from the Lake to the Pacific might be made comparatively at a small outlay, and would greatly add to the comfort and rapidity of the passage.

To us Englishmen it is a matter of indifference in whose hands the transit may be, so long as it is free, and open to all the world; so long as a difference of nationality creates no difference in the fares charged or in the facilities afforded. For our own purposes, I have no doubt the Panama line is the best, and will be the route we shall use. But we should be delighted to see a second line opened. If Mr. Squier can accomplish his line through Honduras, we will give him great honour, and acknowledge that he has done the world a service. In the mean time, we shall be very happy to see the Lake transit re-established.

CHAPTER XXII.

THE BERMUDAS.

IN May I returned from Greytown and the waters of the San Juan to St. Thomas, spending a few days at Aspinwall and Panama on my journey, as I have before explained; and on this occasion, that of my fourth visit to St. Thomas, I was happy enough to escape without any long stay there. My course now lay to the Bermudas, to which islands a steamer runs once a month from that disagreeable little depôt of steam navigation. But as this boat is fitted to certain arrivals and despatches, not at St. Thomas, but at Halifax, and as we reached St. Thomas late on the night of the day on which she should have sailed, and as my missing that vessel would have entailed on me another month's sojourn, and that a summer month, among those islands, it may be imagined that I was rather lively on entering the harbour;—keenly lively to ascertain whether the ' Delta,' such is the name of the Bermuda boat, was or was not gone on her mission.

' I see her red funnel right across the harbour,' said the chief officer, looking through infinite darkness. I disbelieved him and accused him of hoaxing me. ' Look yourself,' said he, handing me his glass. But all the glasses in the world won't turn darkness into light. I know not by what educational process the eyes of sailors become like those of cats. In this instance the chief officer had seen aright, and then, after a visit to the 'Delta,' made at 2 A.M., I went to bed a happy man.

We started the next day at 2 P.M., or rather I should say the same day, and I did no more than breakfast on shore. I then left that favoured island, I trust for the last time,—an island which I believe may be called the white man's grave with quite as much truth as any place on the coast of Africa. We steamed out, and I stood on the stern taking a last look at the three hills of the panorama. It is certainly a very pretty place seen from a moderate and safe distance, and seen as a picture. But it should be seen in that way and in no other.

We started, and I at any rate, with joy. But my joy was not of long duration, for the 'Delta' rolled hideously. Screw boats—propellers as the Americans call them with their wonted genteel propriety—always do roll, and have been invented with the view of making sea-passages more disagreeable than they were. Did any one of my readers ever have a berth allotted to him just over the screw? If so, he knows exactly the feeling of being brayed in a mortar.

In four days we reached Bermuda, and made our way into St. George's harbour. Looking back at my fortnight's sojourn there, it seems to me that there can be no place in the world as to which there can be less to be said than there is about this island,—sayings at least of the sort in which it is my nature to express itself. Its geological formation is, I have no doubt, mysterious. It seems to be made of white soft stone, composed mostly of little shells ; so soft, indeed, that you might cut Bermuda up with a handsaw. And people are cutting Bermuda up with hand-saws. One little island, that on which the convicts are established, has been altogether so cut up already. When I visited it, two fat convicts were working away slowly at the last fragment.

But I am no geologist, and can give no opinion favourable or otherwise as to that doctrine that these islands are the crater of an extinct volcano; only, if so, the seas in those days must have held a distance much more respectful than at present. Every one of course knows that there are three hundred and sixty-five of these islands, all lying within twenty miles in length and three in breadth. They are surrounded too by reefs, or rocks hidden by water, which stretch out into the sea in some places for eight or ten miles, making the navigation very difficult; and, as it seemed to me, very perilous.

Nor am I prepared to say whether or no the Bermudas was the scene of Ariel's tricksy doings. They were first discovered in 1522, by Bermudez, a Spaniard; and Shakespere may have heard of them some indistinct surmises, sufficient to enable him to speak of the 'still vexed Bermoothes.' If these be the veritable scenes of Prospero's incantations, I will at any rate say this—that there are now to be found stronger traces of the breed of Caliban than that of Ariel. Strong, however, of neither; for though Caliban did not relish working for his master more keenly than a Bermudian of the present day, there was nevertheless about him a sort of energy which is altogether wanting in the existing islanders.

A gentleman has lately written a book—I am told a very good book—called 'Bermuda as a Colony, a Fortress, and a Prison.' This book, I am sure, gives accurately all the information which research could collect as to these islands under the headings named. I made no research, and pretend only to state the results of cursory observation.

As a fortress, no doubt it is very strong. I have no doubt on the matter, seeing that I am a patriotic Englishman, and as such believe all English fortifications to be strong. It is, however, a matter on which the opinion of no civilian can be of weight, unless he have deeply studied the subject, in which case he so far ceases to be a civilian. Everything looked very clean and apple-pie; a great many flags were flying on Sundays and the Queen's birthday; and all seemed to be ship-shape. Of the importance to us of the position there can be no question. If it should ever come to pass that we should be driven to use an armed fleet in the Western waters, Bermuda will be as serviceable to us there as Malta is in the Mediterranean. So much for the fortress.

As to the prison, I will say a word or two just now, seeing that it is in that light that the place was chiefly interesting to me. But first for the colony.

Snow is not prevalent in Bermuda, at least not in the months of May and June; but the first look of the houses in each of its two small towns, and indeed all over the island, gives one the idea of a snow storm. Every house is white, up from the ground to the very point of the roof. Nothing is in so great demand as whitewash. They whitewash their houses incessantly, and always include the roofs. This becomes a nuisance, from the glare it occasions; and is at last painful to the eyes. They say there that it is cleanly and cheap, and no one can deny that cleanliness and economy are important domestic virtues.

There are two towns, situated on different islands, called St. George and Hamilton. The former is the head-quarters of the military; the latter of the governor. In speaking of the place as a fortress, I should have said that it is the summer head-quarters of the admiral in command of the Halifax station. The dockyard, which is con-nected with the convict establishment, is at an island called Ireland; but the residence of the admiral is not far from Hamilton, on that which the Bermudians call the 'Continent.'

I spent a week in each of these towns, and I can hardly

say which I found the most triste. The island, or islands, as one must always say—using the plural number—have many gifts of nature to recommend them. They are extremely fertile. The land, with a very moderate amount of cultivation, will give two crops of ordinary potatoes, and one crop of sweet potatoes in the year. Most fruits will grow here, both those of the tropics and of the more northern latitudes. Oranges and lemons, peaches and strawberries, bananas and mulberries thrive,—or would thrive equally well, if they were even slightly encouraged to do so.

No climate in the world probably is better adapted for beetroot, potatoes, onions, and tomatoes. The place is so circumstanced geographically that it should be the early market-garden for New York—as to a certain small extent it is. New York cannot get her early potatoes—potatoes in May and June—from her own soil; but Bermuda can give them to her in any quantity.

Arrowroot also grows here to perfection. The Bermudians claim to say that their arrowroot is the best in the world; and I believe that none bears a higher price. Then the land produces barley, oats, and Indian corn; and not only produces them, but produces two, sometimes three crops a year. Let the English farmer with his fallow field think of that.

But with all their advantages Bermuda is very poor. Perhaps, I should add, that on the whole, she is contented with her poverty. And if so, why disturb such contentment?

But, nevertheless, one cannot teach oneself not to be desirous of progress. One cannot but feel it sad to see people neglecting the good things which are under their feet. Lemons and oranges there are now none in Bermuda. The trees suffered a blight some year or two since, and no effort has been made to restore them. I saw no fruit of any description, though I am told I was there in the proper season, and heard much of the fruit that there used to be in former days. I saw no vegetables but potatoes and onions, and was told that as a rule the people are satisfied with them. I did not once encounter a piece of meat fit to be eaten, excepting when I dined on rations supplied by the Convict establishment. The poultry was somewhat better than the meat, but yet of a very poor description. Both bread and butter are bad; the latter quite uneatable. English people whom I met declared that they were unable to get anything to eat. The people, both white and black, seemed to be only half awake. The land is only half cultivated; and hardly half is tilled of that which might be tilled.

The reason of this neglect, for I maintain that it is neglect, should however be explained. Nearly all the islands are covered with small stunted bushy cedar-trees. Not cedars such as those of Lebanon, not the cedar-trees of Central America, nor those to which we are accustomed in our gardens at home. In Bermuda they are, as I have said, low bushy trees, much resembling stunted firs. But the wood, when it can be found large enough, is, they say, good for ship-building; and as ship-building has for years been a trade in these islands, the old owners of the property do not like to clear their land.

This was all very well as long as the land had no special virtue—as long as a market, such as that afforded by New York, was wanting. But now that the market has been opened, there can be no doubt—indeed, nobody does doubt —that if the land were cleared, its money value would be greatly more than it now is. Every one to whom I spoke admitted this, and complained of the backwardness of the island in improvements. But no one tries to remedy this now.

They had a Governor there some years ago who did much to cure this state of things, who did show them that money was to be made by producing potatoes and sending them out of the island. This was Sir W. Reid, the man of storms. He seems to have had some tolerably efficient idea of what a Governor's duty should be in such a place as Bermuda. To be helped first at every table, and to be called ' Your Excellency,' and then to receive some thousands a year for undergoing these duties is all very well; is very nice for a military gentleman in the decline of years. It is very well that England can so provide for a few of her old military gentlemen. But when the military gentlemen selected can do something else besides, it does make such a difference! Sir W. Reid did do much else; and if there could be found another Sir W. Reid or two to take their turns in Bermuda for six years each, the scrubby bushes would give way, and the earth would bring forth her increase.

The sleepiness of the people appeared to me the most prevailing characteristic of the place. There seemed to be no energy among the natives, no idea of going a-head, none of that principle of constant motion which is found so strongly developed among their great neighbours in the United States. To say that they live for eating and drinking would be to wrong them. They want the energy for the gratification of such vicious tastes. To live and die would seem to be enough for them. To live and die as their fathers and mothers did before them, in the same houses, using the same furniture, nurtured on the same food, and enjoying the same immunity from the dangers of excitement.

I must confess that during the short period of my sojourn there, I myself was completely overtaken by the same sort of lassitude. I could not walk a mile without fatigue. I was always anxious to be supine, lying down whenever I could find a sofa; ever anxious for a rocking-chair, and solicitous for a quick arrival of the hour of bed, which used to be about half-past nine o'clock. Indeed this feeling became so strong with me that I feared I was ill, and began to speculate as to the effects and pleasures of a low fever and a Bermuda doctor. I was comforted, however, by an assurance that everybody was suffering in the same way. 'When the south wind blows it is always so.'—'The south wind must be very prevalent then,' I suggested. I was told that it was very prevalent. During the period of my visit it was all south wind.

The weather was not hot—not hot at least to me who had just come up from Panama, and the fiery furnace of Aspinwall. But the air was damp and muggy and disagreeable. To me it was the most trying climate that I had encountered. They have had yellow fever there twice within the last eight years, and on both occasions it was very fatal. Singularly enough on its latter coming the natives suffered much more than strangers. This is altogether opposed to the usual habits of the yellow fever, which is imagined to be ever cautious in sparing those who are indigenous to the land it visits.

The working population are almost all negroes. I should say that this is quite as much a rule here as in any of the West Indies. Of course there are coloured people—men and women of mixed breed; but they are not numerous as in Jamaica; or, if so, they are so nearly akin to the negro as not to be observed. There are, I think, none of those all but white ladies and gentlemen whose position in life is so distressing.

The negroes are well off; as a rule they can earn 2s. 6d. a day, from that to 3s. For exceptional jobs, men cannot be had under a dollar, or 4s. 2d. On these wages they can live well by working three days a week, and such appears to be their habit. It seems to me that no enfranchised negro entertains an idea of daily work. Work to them is an exceptional circumstance, as to us may be a spell of fifteen or sixteen hours in the same day. We do such a thing occasionally for certain objects, and for certain objects they are willing to work occasionally.

The population is about eleven thousand. That of the negroes and coloured people does not much exceed that of the whites. That of the females greatly exceeds that of the males, both among the white and coloured people. Among the negroes I noticed this, that if not more active than their brethren in the West Indies, they are at least more civil and less sullen in their manner. But then again, they are without the singular mixture of fun and vanity which makes the Jamaica negro so amusing for a while.

These islands are certainly very pretty; or I should perhaps say that the sea, which forms itself into bays and creeks by running in among them, is very pretty. The water is clear and transparent, there being little or no sand on those sides on which the ocean makes its entrance; and clear water is in itself so beautiful. Then the singular way in which the land is broken up into narrow necks, islands, and promontories, running here and there in a capricious, half-mysterious manner, creating a desire for amphibiosity, necessarily creates beauty. But it is mostly the beauty of the sea, and not of the land. The islands are flat, or at any rate there is no considerable elevation in them. They are covered throughout with those scrubby little trees; and, although the trees are green, and therefore when seen from the sea give a freshness to the landscape, they are uninteresting and monotonous on shore.

I must not forget the oleanders, which at the time of

2 A

my visit were in full flower;—which, for aught I know, may be in full flower during the whole year. They are so general through all the islands, and the trees themselves are so covered with the large, straggling, but bright blossoms, as to give quite a character to the scenery. The Bermudas might also be called the oleander isles.

The government consists of a Governor, Council, and House of Assembly ;—King, Lords, and Commons again. Twenty years ago I should thoroughly have approved of this; but now I am hardly sure whether a population of ten or twelve thousand individuals, of whom much more than half are women, and more than half the remainder are negroes, require so composite a constitution. Would not a strict Governor, with due reference to Downing Street, do almost as well? But then to make the change; —that would be difficulty.

'We have them pretty well in hand,' a gentleman whispered to me who was in some shape connected with the governing powers. He was alluding, I imagine, to the House of Assembly. Well, that is a comfort. A good majority in the Lower House is a comfort to all men —except the minority.

There are nine parishes, each returning four members to this House of Assembly. But though every parish requires four members, I observe that half a clergyman is enough for most of them. But then the clergymen must be paid. The council here consists chiefly of gentlemen holding government offices, or who are in some way connected with the government; so that the Crown can probably contrive to manage its little affairs. If I remember rightly Gibraltar and Malta have no Lords or Commons. They are fortresses, and as such under military rule; and so is Bermuda a fortress. Independently of her purely military importance, her size and population is by no means equal to that of Malta. The population of

Malta is chiefly native, and foreign to us;—and the population of Bermuda is chiefly black.

But then Malta is a conquered colony, whereas Bermuda was 'settled' by Britons, as the word goes. That makes all the difference. That such a little spot as Bermuda would in real fact be better without a constitution of its own, if the change could only be managed, that I imagine will be the opinion of most men who have thought about the matter.

And now for the convict establishment. I received great kindness and hospitality from the controller of it; but this, luckily, does not prevent my speaking freely on the matter. He had only just then newly arrived from England, had but now assumed his new duties, and was therefore neither responsible for anything that was amiss, or entitled to credit for what had been permanently established there on a good footing. My own impression is that of the latter there was very little.

In these days our penal establishments and gaol arrangements generally, are, certainly, matters of very vital importance to us. In olden times, and I include the last century and some part of this among olden times, we certainly did not manage these matters well. Our main object then was to get rid of our ruffians;—to punish them also, certainly; but, as a chief matter, to get rid of them. The idea of making use of them, present or future use, had hardly occurred to us; nor had we begun to reflect whether the roguery of coming years might not be somewhat lessened by curing the rogues—by making them not rogues. Now-a-days we are reflecting a good deal on this question.

Our position lately has been all altered. Circumstances have done much to alter it; we can no longer get rid of the worst class of criminals by sending them to Botany Bay. Botany Bay has assumed a will of its own, and

2 A 2

will not have them at any price. But philanthropy has done
more even than circumstances, very much more. We have
the will, the determination as well as the wish, to do well
by our rogues, even if we have not as yet found the way ;
and this is much. In this, as in everything else, the way
will follow the will, sooner or later.

But in the mean time we have been trying various experi-
ments, with more or less success ; forgiving men half their
terms of punishment on good behaviour; giving them
tickets of leave ; crank-turning ; solitary confinement ;
pietising—what may be called a system of gaol sanctity,
perhaps the worst of all schemes, as being a direct
advertisement for hypocrisy ; work without result, the
most distressing punishment going, one may say, next to
that of no work at all; enforced idleness, which is horrible
for human nature to contemplate ; work with result, work
which shall pay ; good living, pound of beef, pound of
bread, pound of potatoes, ounce of tea, glass of grog, pipe
of tobacco, resulting in much fat, excellent if our prisoners
were stalled oxen to be eaten ; poor living, bread and
water, which has its recommendations also, though it be
so much opposed to the material humanity of the age ;
going to school, so that life if possible may be made
to recommence ; very good also, if life would recommence ;
corporal punishment, flogging of the body, horrible to
think of, impossible to be looked at; spirit punishment,
flogging of the soul, best of all if one could get at the soul
so as to do it effectually.

All these schemes are being tried ; and as I believe
that they are tried with an honest intent to arrive at that
which is best, so also do I believe that we shall in
time achieve that which is, if not heavenly best, at
any rate terrestrially good ;—shall at least get rid certainly of all that is hellishly bad. At present, however,
we are still groping somewhat uncertainly. Let us

try for a moment to see what the Bermuda groping has done.

I do not in the least doubt that the intention here also has been good : the intention, that is, of those who have been responsible for the management of the establishment. But I do not think that the results have been happy.

At Bermuda there are in round numbers fifteen hundred convicts. As this establishment is one of penal servitude, of course it is to be presumed that those sent there are either hardened thieves, whose lives have been used to crime, or those who have committed heavy offences under the impulse of strong temptation. In dealing with such men I think we have three things to do. Firstly, to rid ourselves of them from amongst us, as we do of other nuisances. This we should do were we to hang them ; this we did do when we sent them to Botany Bay ; this we certainly do when we send them to Bermuda. But this, I would say, is the lightest of the three duties. The second is with reference to the men themselves ; to divest them, if by any means it may be possible, of their roguery ; to divest them even of a little of their roguery, if so much as that can be done ; to teach them that trite lesson of honesty being the best policy,—so hard for men to learn when honesty has been, as it were, for many years past out of their sight, and even beyond their understanding. This is very important, but even this is not the most important. The third and most important object is the punishment of these men ; their punishment, sharp, hard to bear, heavy to body and mind, disagreeable in all ways, to be avoided on account of its odiousness by all prudent men ; their condign punishment, so that the world at large may know and see, and clearly acknowledge,—even the uneducated world,—that honesty *is* the best policy.

That the first object is achieved, I have said. It is achieved as regards those fifteen hundred, and, as far as I know, at a moderate cost. Useful work for such men is to be found at Bermuda. We have dockyards there, and fortifications which cannot be made too strong and weather-tight. At such a place works may be done by convict labour which could not be done otherwise. Whether the labour be economically used is another question; but at any rate the fifteen hundred rogues are disposed of, well out of the way of our pockets and shop windows.

As to the second object, that of divesting these rogues of their roguery, the best way of doing that is the question as to which there is at the present moment so much doubt. As to what may be the best way I do not presume to give an opinion; but I do presume to doubt whether the best way has as yet been found at Bermuda. The proofs at any rate were not there. Shortly before my arrival a prisoner had been killed in a row. After that an attempt had been made to murder a warder. And during my stay there one prisoner was deliberately murdered by two others after a faction fight between a lot of Irish and English, in which the warders were for some minutes quite unable to interfere. Twenty-four men were carried to the hospital dangerously wounded, as to the life of some of whom the doctor almost despaired. This occurred on a day intervening between two visits which I made to the establishment. Within a month of the same time three men had escaped, of whom two only were retaken; one had got clear away, probably to America. This tells little for the discipline, and very little for the moral training of the men.

There is no wall round the prison. I must explain that the convicts are kept on two islands, those called Boaz and Ireland. At Boaz is the parent establishment, at which live the controller, chaplains, doctors, and head officers. But here is the lesser number of prisoners, about six hundred. They live in ordinary prisons. The other nine hundred are kept in two hulks, old men-of-war moored by the breakwaters, at the dockyard establishment in Ireland. It was in one of these that the murder was committed. The labour of these nine hundred men is devoted to the dockyard works. There is a bridge between the two islands over which runs a public road, and from this road there are ways equally public, as far as the eye goes, to all parts of the prison. A man has only to say that he is going to the chaplain's house, and he may pass all through the prison, —with spirits in his pocket if it so please him. That the prisoners should not be about without warders is no doubt a prison rule; but where everything is done by the prisoners, from the building of stores to the picking of weeds and lighting of lamps, how can any moderate number of warders see everything, even if they were inclined? There is nothing to prevent spirits being smuggled in after dark through the prison windows. And the men do get rum, and drunkenness is a common offence. Prisoners may work outside prison walls; but I remember no other prison that is not within walls—that looks from open windows on to open roads, as is here the case.

'And who shaves them?' I happened to ask one of the officers. 'Oh, every man has his own razor; and they have knives too, though it is not allowed.' So these gentlemen who are always ready for faction fights, whose minds are as constantly engaged on the family question of Irish *versus* English, which means Protestant against Catholic, as were those of Father Tom Maguire and Mr. Pope, are as well armed for their encounters as were those reverend gentlemen.

The two murderers will I presume be tried, and if found guilty probably hanged; but the usual punishment for outbreaks of this kind seems to be, or to have been, flogging. A man would get some seventy lashes; the Governor of the island would go down and see it done; and then the lacerated wretch would be locked up in idleness till his back would again admit of his bearing a shirt. 'But they'll venture their skin,' said the officer; 'they don't mind that till it comes.' 'But do they mind being locked up alone?' I asked. He admitted this, but said that they had only six—I think six—cells, of which two or three were occupied by madmen; they had no other place for lunatics. Solitary confinement is what these men do mind, what they do fear; but here there is not the power of inflicting that punishment.

What a piece of work for a man to step down upon —the amendment of the discipline of such a prison as this! Think what the feeling among them will be when knives and razors are again taken from them, when their grog is first stopped, their liberty first controlled. They sleep together, a hundred or more within talking distance, in hammocks slung at arm's length from each other, so that one may excite ten, and ten fifty. Is it fair to put warders among such men, so well able to act, so ill able to control their actions?

'It is a sore task,' said the controller who had fallen down new upon this bit of work; 'it is dreadful to have to add misery to those who are already miserable.' It is a very sore task; but at the moment I hardly sympathized with his humanity.

So much for the Bermuda practice of divesting these rogues of their roguery. And now a word as to the third question; the one question most important, as I regard it, of their punishment. Are these men so punished as to deter others by the fear of similar treatment? I presume it may be taken for granted that the treatment, such as it is, does become known and the nature of it understood among those at home who are, or might be, on the path towards it.

Among the lower classes, from which these convicts do doubtless mostly come, the goods of life are chiefly reckoned as being food, clothing, warm shelter, and hours of idleness. It may seem harsh to say so thus plainly; but will any philanthropical lover of these lower classes deny the fact? I regard myself as a philanthropical lover of those classes, and as such I assert the fact; nay, I might go further and say that it is almost the same of some other classes. That many have knowledge of other good things, wife-love and children-love—heart-goods, if I may so call them; knowledge of mind-goods, and soul-goods also, I do not deny. That such knowledge is greatly on the increase I verily believe; but with most among us back and belly, or rather belly and back, are still supreme. On belly and back must punishment fall when sinners such as these are to be punished.

But with us—very often I fear elsewhere, but certainly at that establishment of which we are now speaking—there is no such punishment at all. In scale of dietary among subjects of our Queen, I should say that honest Irish labourers stand the lowest; they eat meat twice a year, potatoes and milk for six months, potatoes without milk for six, and fish occasionally if near the shore. Then come honest English labourers; they generally have cheese, sometimes bacon. Next above them we may probably rank the inhabitants of our workhouses; they have fresh meat perhaps three times a week. Whom shall we name next? Without being anxious to include every shade of English mankind, we may say soldiers, and above them sailors; then, perhaps, ordinary mechanics. There must be many another ascending step before we come to the Bermuda convict, but it would be long to name them.

But now let us see what the Bermuda convict eats and drinks every day.

He has a pound of meat; he has good meat too, lucky dog, while those wretched Bermudians are tugging out their teeth against tough carcasses! He has a pound and three ounces of bread; the amount may be of questionable advantage, as he cannot eat it all; but he probably sells it for drink. He has a pound of fresh vegetables; he has tea and sugar; he has a glass of grog—exactly the same amount that a sailor has; and he has an allowance of tobacco-money, with permission to smoke at midday and evening, as he sits at his table or takes his noontide pleasant saunter. So much for belly.

Then as to back, under which I include a man's sinews. The convict begins the day by going to chapel at a quarter-past seven; his prayers do not take him long, for the chaplain on the occasion of my visit read small bits out of the Prayer-book here and there, without any reference to church rule or convict-establishment reason. At half-past seven he goes to his work,—if it does not happen to rain, in which case he sits till it ceases. He then works till five, with an hour and a half interval for his dinner, grog, and tobacco. He then has the evening for his supper and amusements. He thus works for eight hours, barring the rain, whereas in England a day labourer's average is about ten. As to the comparative hardness of their labour there will of course be no doubt. The man who must work for his wages will not get any wages unless he works hard. The convict will at any rate get his wages, and of course spares his sinews.

As to clothes, they have, and should have exactly what is best suited to health. Shoes when worn out are replaced. The straw hat is always decent, and just what one would wish to wear oneself in that climate. The jacket and trousers have the word 'Boaz' printed over them in rather ugly type; but one would get used to that. The flannel shirts, &c., are all that could be desired.

Their beds are hammocks like those of sailors, only not subject to be swung about by the winds, and not hung quite so closely as those of some sailors. Did any of my readers ever see the beds of an Irish cotter's establishment in county Cork? Ah! or of some English cotter's establishments in Dorsetshire, Wiltshire, and Somersetshire?

The hospital arrangements and attendance are excellent as regards the men's comfort; though the ill arrangement of the buildings is conspicuous, and must be conspicuous to all who see them.

And then these men, when they take their departure, have the wages of their labour given to them,—so much as they have not spent either licitly in tobacco, or illicitly in extra grog. They will take home with them sixteen pounds, eighteen pounds, or twenty pounds. Such is convict life in Bermuda,—unless a man chance to get murdered in a faction fight.

As to many of the comforts above enumerated it will of course be seen that they are right. The clothes, the hospital arrangements, and sanitary provision are, and should be, better in a prison than they can, unfortunately, be at present among the poor who are not prisoners. But still they must be reckoned among the advantages which convicted crime enjoys.

It seems to be a cruel task, that of lessening the comforts of men who are, at any rate, in truth not to be envied—are to be pitied rather, with such deep, deep pity! But the thing to look to, the one great object, is to diminish the number of those who must be sent to such places. Will such back and belly arrangements as those I have described deter men from sin by the fear of its consequences?

Why should not those felons—for such they all are, I presume, till the term of their punishment be over—why should they sleep after five? why should their diet be more than strong health requires? why should their hours of work be light? Why that drinking of spirits and smoking of tobacco among men whose term of life in that prison should be a term of suffering? Why those long twelve hours of bed and rest, spent in each other's company, with noise, and singing, and jollity? Let them eat together, work together, walk together if you will; but surely at night they should be separated! Faction fights cannot take place unless the fighters have time and opportunity to arrange them.

I cannot but think that there should be great changes in this establishment, and that the punishment, which undoubtedly is intended, should be made to fall on the prisoners. 'Look at the prisoners' rations!' the soldiers say in Bermuda when they complain of their own; and who can answer them?

I cannot understand why the island governor should have authority in the prison. He from his profession can know little or nothing about prisons, and even for his own work,—or no work—is generally selected either from personal favour or from military motives, whereas the prison governor is selected, probably with much care, for his specialities in that line. And it must be as easy and as quick for the prison governor to correspond with the Home Office as for the island governor to correspond with the Colonial Office. There has undoubtedly been mischief done by the antagonism of different authorities. It would seem reasonable that all such establishments should be exclusively under the Home Office.

(365)

CHAPTER XXIII.

CONCLUSION.

From Bermuda I took a sailing vessel to New York, in company with a rather large assortment of potatoes and onions. I had declared during my unlucky voyage from Kingston to Cuba that no consideration should again tempt me to try a sailing vessel, but such declarations always go for nothing. A man in his misery thinks much of his misery; but as soon as he is out of it it is forgotten, or becomes matter for mirth. Of even a voyage in a sailing vessel one may say that at some future time it will perhaps be pleasant to remember that also. And so I embarked myself along with the potatoes and onions on board the good ship 'Henrietta.'

Indeed, there is no other way of getting from Bermuda to New York; or of going anywhere from Bermuda—except to Halifax and St. Thomas, to which places a steamer runs once a month. In going to Cuba I had been becalmed, starved, shipwrecked, and very nearly quaranteened. In going to New York I encountered only the last misery. The doctor who boarded us stated that a vessel had come from Bermuda with a sick man, and that we must remain where we were till he had learnt what was the sick man's ailment. Our skipper, who knew the vessel in question, said that one of their crew had been drunk in

Bermuda for two or three days, and had not yet worked it off. But the doctor called again in the course of the day, and informed us that it was intermittent fever. So we were allowed to pass. It does seem strange that sailing vessels should be subjected to such annoyances. I hardly think that one of the mail steamers going into New York would be delayed because there was a case of intermittent fever on board another vessel from Liverpool.

It is not my purpose to give an Englishman's ideas of the United States, or even of New York, at the fag end of a volume treating about the West Indies. On the United States I should like to write a volume, seeing that the government and social life of the people there—of that people who are our children—afford the most interesting phenomena which we find as to the new world ;—the best means of prophesying, if I may say so, what the world will next be, and what men will next do. There, at any rate, a new republic has become politically great and commercially active : whereas all other new republics have failed in those points, as in all others. But this cannot be attempted now.

From New York I went by the Hudson river to Albany, and on by the New York Central Railway to Niagara ; and though I do not mean to make any endeavour to describe that latter place as such descriptions should be—and doubtless are and have been—written, I will say one or two words which may be of use to any one going thither.

The route which I took from New York would be, I should think, the most probable route for Englishmen. And as travellers will naturally go up the Hudson river by day, and then on from Albany by night train,* seeing that there is nothing to be seen at Albany, and that these

---

* It would be well, however, to visit Trenton Falls by the way, which I did not do. They are but a short distance from Utica, a town on this line of railway.

trains have excellent sleeping accommodation—a lady, or indeed a gentleman, should always take a double sleeping-berth, a single one costs half a dollar, and a double one a dollar,—this outlay has nothing to do with the travelling ticket;—it will follow that* he, she, or they will reach Niagara at about 4 A.M.

In that case let them not go on to what is called the Niagara Falls station, but pass over at a station called the Suspension Bridge—very well known on the road—to the other or Canada side of the water, and thence go to the Clifton Hotel. There can be no doubt as to this being the site at which tourists should stop. It is one of those cases in which to see is to be sure. But if the traveller be carried on to Niagara Falls station, he has a long and expensive journey to make back; and the United States side of the water will be antagonistic to him in doing so. The ticket from Albany to Niagara cost me six dollars; the carriage from Niagara to the Clifton Hotel cost me five. It was better to pay the five than to remain where I was; but it would have been better still to have saved them. I mention this as passengers to the Falls have no sort of intimation that they should get out at the Suspension Bridge; though they are all duly shaken out of their berths, and inquired of whether or not they be going west.

Nothing ever disappointed me less than the Falls of Niagara—but my raptures did not truly commence for the first half-day. Their charms grow upon one like the conversation of a brilliant man. Their depth and breadth and altitude, their music, colour, and brilliancy are not fully acknowledged at the first moment. It may be that my eye is slow; but I can never take in to its full enjoyment any view or any picture at the first glance. I found this to be especially the case at Niagara. It was only by long gazing and long listening that I was able to appreciate the magnitude of that waste of waters.

My book is now complete, and I am not going to 'do the Falls,' but I must bid such of my readers as may go there to place themselves between the rocks and the waters of the Horse-shoe Fall after sunset—well after sunset; and there remain—say for half an hour. And let every man do this alone ; or if fortune have kindly given him such a companion, with one who may leave him as good as alone. But such companions are rare.

The spot to which I allude will easily make itself known to him, nor will he have any need of a guide. He will find it, of course, before the sun shall set. And, indeed, as to guides, let him eschew them, giving a twenty-five cent piece here and there, so that these men be not ruined for want of custom. Into this spot I made my way, and stood there for an hour, dry enough. The spray did reach my coat, and the drops settled on my hair ; but nevertheless, as a man not over delicate, I was dry enough. Then I went up, and when there was enticed to put myself into a filthy oil-skin dress, hat, coat, and trousers, in order that I might be conducted under the Falls. Under the Falls ! Why ; I had been under the Falls ; but still, wishing to see everything, I allowed myself to be caparisoned.

A sable conductor took me exactly to the spot where I had been before. But he took me also ten yards further, during which little extra journey I became soaking wet through, in spite of the dirty oil-cloth. The ducking cost me sixty cents, or half a crown.

But I must be allowed one word as to that visit after sunset ; one word as to that which an obedient tourist will then see. In the spot to which I allude the visitor stands on a broad safe path, made of shingles, between the rock over which the water rushes and the rushing water. He will go in so far that the spray rising back from the bed of the torrent does not incommode him. With this exception, the further he can go the better; but here also circumstances will clearly show him the spot. Unless the water be driven in by a very strong wind, five yards make the difference between a comparatively dry coat and an absolutely wet one.

And then let him stand with his back to the entrance, thus hiding the last glimmer of the expiring day. So standing he will look up among the falling waters, or down into the deep misty pit, from which they reascend in almost as palpable a bulk. The rock will be at his right hand, high and hard, and dark and straight, like the wall of some huge cavern, such as children enter in their dreams. For the first five minutes he will be looking but at the waters of a cataract,—at the waters, indeed, of such a cataract as we know no other, and at their interior curves, which elsewhere we cannot see. But by-and-by all this will change. He will no longer be on a shingly path beneath a waterfall; but that feeling of a cavern wall will grow upon him, of a cavern deep, deep below roaring seas, in which the waves are there, though they do not enter in upon him; or rather not the waves, but the very bowels of the deep ocean. He will feel as though the floods surrounded him, coming and going with their wild sounds, and he will hardly recognize that though among them he is not in them. And they, as they fall with a continual roar, not hurting the ear, but musical withal, will seem to move as the vast ocean waters may perhaps move in their internal currents. He will lose the sense of one continued descent, and think that they are passing round him in their appointed courses. The broken spray that rises from the depth below, rises so strongly, so palpably, so rapidly, that the motion in every direction will seem equal. And then, as he looks on, strange colours will show themselves through the mist; the shades of gray will become green and blue, with ever and anon a

2 B

flash of white; and then, when some gust of wind blows in with greater violence, the sea-girt cavern will become all dark and black. Oh, my friend, let there be no one there to speak to thee then; no, not even a heart's brother. As you stand there speak only to the waters.

So much for Niagara. From thence, I went along Lake Ontario, and by the St. Lawrence to Montreal, being desirous of seeing the new tubular railway bridge which is being erected there over the St. Lawrence close to that town. Lake Ontario is uninteresting, being altogether too large for scenery, and too foggy for sight-seeing if there were anything to see. The travelling accommodation, however, is excellent. The points of interest in the St. Lawrence are the thousand islands, among which the steamer glides as soon as it enters the river; and the rapids, of which the most singularly rapid is the one the vessel descends as it nears Montreal. Both of these are very well, but they do not require to be raved about. The Canadian towns at which one touches are interesting as being clean and large, and apparently prosperous;—also as being English, for we hardly reach the French part of Canada till we get down to Montreal.

This tubular bridge over the St. Lawrence, which will complete the whole trunk line of railway from Portland on the coast of Maine, through the two Canadas, to the States of Michigan and Wisconsin, will certainly be one of the most wonderful works of scientific art in the world. It is to consist of different tubes, resting on piers placed in the river bed at intervals sufficient to provide for the free navigation of the water. Some of these, including the centre and largest one, are already erected. This bridge will be over a mile and a half in length, and will cost the enormous sum of one million four hundred thousand pounds, being but two hundred thousand pounds short of the whole cost of the Panama railway.

I only wish that the shareholders may have as good a dividend.

From Montreal I went down Lake Champlain to Saratoga Springs, the great resort of New Yorkers when the weather in the city becomes too hot for endurance. I was there late in June, but was very glad at that time to sit with my toes over a fire. The country about Saratoga is by no means pretty. The waters, I do not doubt, are very healthy, and the hotels very good. It must, I should think, be a very dull place for persons who are not invalids.

From Saratoga I returned to New York, and from New York sailed for Liverpool in the exceedingly good ship 'Africa,' Captain Shannon. I have sailed in many vessels, but never in one that was more comfortable or better found.

And on board this most comfortable of vessels I have now finished my book, as I began it on board that one, of all the most uncomfortable, which carried me from Kingston in Jamaica to Cien Fuegos in the island of Cuba.

THE END.

LONDON: PRINTED BY WILLIAM CLOWES AND SONS, STAMFORD STREET.